Excel 5.0
A progressive course for new users

2nd Edition

Jim Muir

Senior Lecturer in Business Computing at
Bournemouth University. He has had a wide
experience of teaching IT skills at a variety of levels.

Letts Educational
Aldine Place
London W12 8AW

1997

2nd Edition 1996
Reprinted 1996
Reprinted 1997

A CIP record for this book is available from the British Library.

ISBN 1 85805 191 6

Typeset by KAI, Nottingham, UK

Printed in Great Britain by Ashford Colour Press, Gosport.

contents

introduction

This book is intended for any new user of Excel 5 who needs to acquire a good working knowledge of the package in order to process numeric data of any kind, for example sales figures, profit and loss calculations, budgets, stock movements, expenditure, etc. It is equally suitable to be used by students in the classroom or open-learning workshop, or by the general user for home study. The book assumes no prior experience of other spreadsheet packages.

structure

Excel features are introduced in the context of practical business activities and problems to be solved, with the opportunity for further practice and consolidation.

The material has been organised into 24 units, each taking approximately 1 hour to complete. Every unit has the following features:

i)   introductory material plus a list of the skills covered in the unit and the prior skills required to tackle it successfully;

ii) activities for acquiring and practising the techniques, in the context of practical business problems;

iii) solutions to activities (where appropriate);

iv) screen dumps to help you check your learning;

v)   summaries of commands and functions.

The units are designed to be worked through in sequence, as activities build on the skills acquired in earlier units, and may use spreadsheets/charts created in previous activities.

Solutions are given in the appendix, where appropriate. A summary of commands and functions is given at the end of each unit.

what's new in the second edition

Readers of the second edition should benefit from the restructuring of the material into 24 shorter and more manageable units, (6 in the first edition), each taking approximately one hour to complete.

a note to lecturers and students

This learning material requires little, if any, input by lecturers, and can therefore be used in programmes based on independent learning. The same material is also available as a photocopiable resource pack (call 0181 740 2266 for details of the cost and terms of an institutional site licence). A disk containing the work achieved at the end of each unit is available free of charge to lecturers using the book as a course text. These solutions can be given to students to enable them to check their own work.

Jim Muir
May 1996

what are spreadsheets?

Since the personal computer's initial impact on business in the 80's, three types of business software have emerged as industry standards – the word processor, the database management system and the spreadsheet.

This is hardly surprising as they fulfil three key business needs.

All businesses need to cope with the volumes of text that they create – letters, memos, reports etc. – hence the word processor.

They need to store and retrieve records of all types – stock, personnel, customer etc. – hence the need for database management systems.

Their third major need is the handling of numeric data – sales, profits, financial forecasts, stock movements and mathematical models of all kinds. The spreadsheet meets this need.

For many years businesses have used manual spreadsheets – large sheets of squared paper divided into columns and rows. Managers have used these sheets of paper 'spread out' on their desks to analyse various types of business information.

For example, it has been estimated that up to a third of a manager's time is typically spent preparing budgets. This involves such operations as manipulating, calculating and analysing numeric information, using formulae, inserting text and drawing graphs.

When the data changes, lengthy and tedious recalculation becomes necessary.

A computer spreadsheet is simply the equivalent of this sheet of squared paper, with in-built calculating facilities.

A simple example of an Excel spreadsheet is shown on the opposite page, calculating a student's personal finances. The columns represent the months, and the rows various categories of income and expenditure. The balance at month end is carried forward to the next month.

You could use this data in a variety of ways:

❐   as a record of your past finances

❐   to budget for future expenditure

❐   to compare expenditure patterns month by month

❐   to model possible increases in income or expenditure – what if rent rises by 10% in Week 5?

❐   to draw graphs illustrating any of the above.

	A	B	C	D	E	F
			PERSONAL FINANCES - TERM 1			
	INCOME	Week 1	Week 2	Week 3	Week 4	Week 5
	Opening Bals.	£0.00	£1,015.00	£885.00	£755.00	£625.00
	Grant	£500.00				
	Bank Loan	£400.00				
	Parents	£300.00				
	Total Income	£1,200.00	£1,015.00	£885.00	£755.00	£625.00
	EXPENDITURE					
	Accommodation	£60.00	£60.00	£60.00	£60.00	£60.00
	Food and Travel	£30.00	£35.00	£35.00	£35.00	£35.00
	Books	£75.00	£15.00	£15.00	£15.00	£15.00
	Other	£20.00	£20.00	£20.00	£20.00	£20.00
	Total Expenditure	£185.00	£130.00	£130.00	£130.00	£130.00
	CLOSING BALS.	£1,015.00	£885.00	£755.00	£625.00	£495.00

spreadsheet terminology

A spreadsheet is a grid of vertical *columns* and horizontal *rows*.

Where column and row intersect is a box or *cell*.

The cell *reference* or address consists of two coordinates – the column letter followed by the row number (as in a street map).

Cell can contain *text* (labels) or *numbers* (values).

Certain cells can contain *formulae* which tell the spreadsheet to perform calculations, e.g. add a column or work out a percentage. These formulae ensure that totals are automatically recalculated when the values in the spreadsheet are changed.

Excel use the term 'worksheet' for their computer spreadsheet – I shall use it too from Unit 1 onwards.

advantages of spreadsheets

It is much easier to use a computerised spreadsheet, such as Excel, than to perform manual calculations. A spreadsheet is a general-purpose tool that can be used to solve a wide variety of problems – any information that can be represented as columns and rows.

The advantages of spreadsheets should now be obvious:

❏ Reducing the drudgery of calculations

❏ Reducing errors

❏ Freeing user time to concentrate on problem solving

❏ Allowing users to examine alternative solutions

❏ Producing quicker results

In the units that follow you will realise these advantages for yourself and gain an important business skill.

Creating and using a worksheet

Skills to be learned	Activity
Cell data – clearing	3.6
Cell data – editing	3.4 – 3.6
Cell data – entering	3.1 – 3.2
Cell selection	2.13
Columns – widening	3.7
Dialogue Boxes – using	2.16
Exiting Excel	2.22
Help – using	2.18 – 2.21
Keyboard commands	2.12, 2.17
Loading Excel	1
Menus – using	2.15
Mouse operation	2.10
Rows – enlarging	3.8
Scrolling	2.11
Shortcut keys	2.17
Window size – changing	1.5 – 1.9

Previous skills needed to tackle this unit

None

Introduction

In this unit you'll learn such essential preliminaries as starting up the Excel package, using the mouse, and finding your way around the worksheet screen. Then you'll create your first worksheet and find out how to input and alter data. With a little practice, you will find them straightforward. Make sure that you read and follow the instructions in these activities carefully. You are bound to make a few mistakes at first – these are part of learning – but you will learn how to put them right for yourself.

Activity 1   Loading and running Excel

Excel is a Windows application. This means that Excel will not run unless the Microsoft Windows software package is already loaded – up and running.

How this is done will depend on how your computer has been set up. The following instructions will cover most situations:

1   First turn on your computer (and the screen too if necessary)

     If a screen appears that resembles Figure 1 below then Windows has automatically loaded. Proceed to section 3 now.

2   If Windows has *not* loaded then try the following in turn:

   a. Some PC's, especially those in colleges, display a main menu system when first turned on. Is there a menu option for Windows or Excel? If so take it, ie type the number or letter of the option followed by the **Enter** or Return key. This large L-shaped key on the right of the keyboard is marked with a curled arrow.

   b. Perhaps all that displays is the prompt C:\> or similar.

       This is the MS-DOS or operating system prompt. Type **WIN** and press the **Enter** key.

       If this doesn't work try the following:

   c. Type the command **DIR/W** and press the **Enter** Key.

       A list of names appear in square brackets; these are names of directories.

       Identify one named **[WINDOWS]** or similar.

       Type the command **CD \WINDOWS** and press the Enter key.

       You are now in the directory (part of the hard disk) that contains the Windows programs.

       Type the command **WIN** and press the Enter key.

       Windows should now load – see Figure 1 opposite.

3   Look at Figure 1 carefully. (Your Windows startup screen may look different, depending on what programs you have on your PC and how Windows was installed) The Program Manager window should open when Windows starts; perhaps overlaid by another window or so.

     In the window are various icons (small pictures of applications) that can be run from Windows. If you can already see one entitled 'Microsoft Excel' , 'Excel 5.0', 'Microsoft Office' or similar then skip to section 6.

4   If you can't find Excel yet don't give up! You will probably need to open another window to find it.

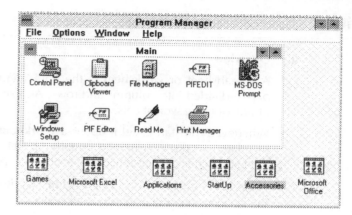

Figure 1

Look for an icon labelled 'Applications', 'Windows Applications' or 'Microsoft Office'. (Ignore any icons labelled 'Main', 'Accessories' or 'Games')

Use your desktop mouse to move the arrow-shaped pointer around the screen; this is the screen pointer or cursor. It will change shape, depending on the operation that you are carrying out.

Move it on top of the icon.

Now click the mouse button *twice* in quick succession – if there is more than one button on your mouse then use the leftmost button.

5 A further window will open. Again, the number of icons in this window will depend on how your PC has been set up.

6 Identify the Microsoft Excel icon – see Figure 2, move the screen pointer on top of it, and 'double click' as before.

Microsoft
Excel

Figure 2

If a further window opens, revealing another Excel icon, then double click this too. Excel will begin to load from the PC's hard disk (confirmed by an hour-glass symbol) and after a few seconds a blank workbook screen appears.

Activity 2   Understanding the worksheet screen

1   Overview

A spreadsheet or **worksheet** is the equivalent of a large sheet of paper, divided into columns and rows. An Excel workbook consists of one or more worksheets.

Whenever you start Excel it opens a **Workbook Window** – a group of related worksheets named initially Sheet1, Sheet2 etc. Look at the Excel screen; it actually consists of two windows:

Around the outside is the **Application Window** that carries out all the Excel commands – menus, tool bars etc.

Within the Application window is the **Document Window.** This consists of the worksheet itself, divided into columns and rows, plus other features such as scroll bars and sheet numbers.

2   Before we start using the keyboard or mouse let's identify the main components of the Excel screen. Keep referring to the labelled diagram below, *but don't use the keyboard or mouse yet;* don't worry if your screen is slightly different, we're just identifying the main features at the moment.

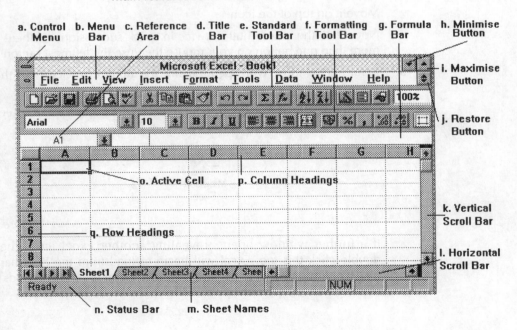

Figure 3

3   a.   The Control Menu Box. We won't be using this feature very much; it offers commands (eg changing the window size) that can be better performed by other means.

b. **The Menu Bar.** The Menu Bar at the top of the screen show a list of menu options – File, Edit, View etc.

    The Excel commands are grouped under these menus.

c. **The Reference Area.** Shows the row and column number of the active cell – see o below.

d. **The Title Bar.** Whenever a new workbook is opened Excel gives it a temporary or default name, Book1, Book2 etc. This name will change when you save the workbook.

e. & f. **The Tool Bars.** There are two tool bars immediately below the menu bar; each consists of a row of buttons that you 'click' to carry out Excel tasks. Often a button is a shortcut alternative to a menu command, sometimes there is no menu alternative to using a button.

    The Standard Toolbar offers options such as opening and closing files, cutting and pasting, printing etc.

    The Formatting Toolbar allows you to alter the appearance and alignment of data in your workbook.

    In these units we concentrate mainly on the menu versions of commands, rather than using buttons. A key to the tool bars is included at the end of this unit.

g. **The Formula Bar.** Shows whatever is in entered in the active cell – see o. This is a new workbook so all the cells are blank.

    At the top right of the screen are various buttons marked with arrow heads; these control the size of the workbook screen:

h. **The Minimise Button.** Reduces the size of the screen to a small icon.

i. **The Maximise Button.** Increases the window to full-screen size. Sometimes there are two – one for the whole application window and one for the inner cell area – the document window.

j. **The Restore Button.** Restores the window to its original size.

k. & l. **The Vertical and Horizontal Scroll Bars.** Allow you to move around a worksheet. The present worksheet window can only show a small fraction of the total worksheet size; potentially each sheet in a workbook can be 256 columns across and 16,384 rows down!

m. **Sheet Names.** A new workbook consists of a number of blank worksheets, having the default names Sheet1, Sheet2 etc. Collectively these form a workbook. Each sheet is marked with a name **tab** – the name in bold indicates which sheet is currently selected or 'active'.

    Sheet1 should be selected at the moment.

    Click on each name tab in turn to open a new sheet – they are all blank at the moment. You may have to re-size the document window if the sheet names are not in view – see section 8.

On the left of the sheet names are a number of arrow buttons to move quickly through a group of worksheets. Try these out, returning to Sheet1.

n. **The Status Bar.** Displays information about the current command; no command has been issued yet so it reads 'Ready'.

o. **The Active Cell.** At the moment the top left cell A1 is the active cell – the one currently selected and shown by a heavy border. As we will see later, you cannot enter information into a cell unless it has first been selected and made 'active'.

p. **Column Headings** and q, **The Row headings.** These contain the column references (letters) and the row references (numbers). Jointly they give the cell *reference,* eg A1, D5.

4   Now that we've identified the basic screen components let's try some of them out; keep referring to Figure 3.

First we will experiment with the screen size; this often causes problems when you're starting out.

5   **Minimising the Window Size.**

As explained in Section 1 above there are two windows in the Excel screen; each of these can be re-sized independently of the other window.

Move the screen pointer onto the topmost **Minimise** button at the top right of the screen.

Click the mouse button once. The whole workbook disappears, and you return to Windows.

At the bottom left of the screen is an Excel icon; this represents the minimised worksheet – The Excel application is still running, but cannot be used until it is restored to normal size.

Move the screen pointer onto this icon and 'double click', i.e. click the mouse button twice in quick succession.

Workbook1 reappears – try again if it doesn't.

6   **Troubleshooting:** If you can't locate the Excel icon it is probably behind another open window. Hold down the Alt key then press the Tab key – this key is on the left of the keyboard and marked with two opposite-facing arrows. Continue to keep Alt pressed down and press the Tab key – Windows runs through all your open applications until it finds Excel – see Figure 4.

Microsoft Excel - Book1

Figure 4

Release the **Tab** then the **Alt** key and you are returned to Excel.

7   **Maximising and Restoring the Window Size.**

First of all check whether there are two sets of Maximise/Minimise buttons. Sometimes two sets are visible – the top set for the Application Window and a set below for the Document Window – see section 1. If so click the topmost Maximise button – the Excel window fills the whole screen.

If not click the **Restore** button and the window reverts to its previous size.

If there is a Restore button below the Maximise and Minimise buttons on your workbook click it. This restores the size of the document window and makes two other changes:

The document window gets its own Title Bar – 'Book1'.

The document window gets it own Maximise and Minimise buttons.

Click the **Minimise** button *for the document window,* ie the lower of the two sets of buttons. The outer Application Window is not affected, but the inner Document window is shrunk to an icon entitled 'Book1'.

Double click this icon to restore it.

8   **Adjusting Window Size.**

It is also possible to alter the size of the workbook window by 'dragging' the sides. Move the screen pointer to the bottom right-hand corner of the document window – the screen pointer changes to a double-headed arrow when correctly located.

Now press down the mouse button and keep it pressed down.

Drag the edge of the worksheet diagonally towards the top left of the screen until you have reached cell **D8.** Then let go.

Your document window should now look like Figure 5.

Similarly drag the bottom right-hand corner of the **application** window so that it fits closely around the document window – see Figure 6. If you can't see the sides then you may need to click the Restore button first.

Restore the both windows to a workable size by reversing this dragging process.

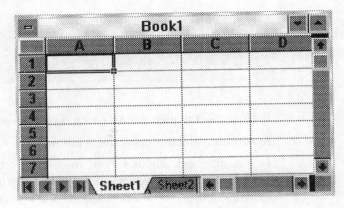

Figure 5

Notice that the side of a window can also be dragged in order to adjust the window size.

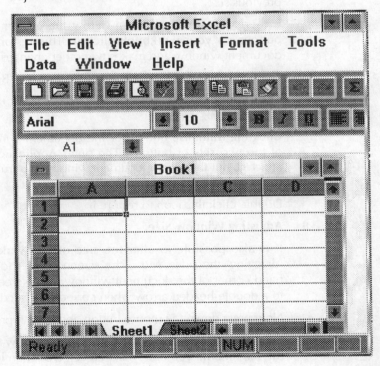

Figure 6

9   Moving a Window.

Move the pointer onto the Title Bar at the top of the screen.

Press down the mouse button then drag the mouse – the whole window can be moved. This is useful if part of the window is off-screen.

If the document window is currently displaying its own title bar – see Section 7 – then try moving this too.

10 Mouse Control.

You have now learnt the 3 basic mouse actions:

clicking	locate screen pointer, press mouse button once
double clicking	locate screen pointer and press mouse button twice in quick succession
dragging	locate screen pointer, hold down button while moving mouse, release button.

From now on I shall be using these names to refer to these actions.

11 Scrolling Around the Screen.

There are several ways to change the part of the worksheet window currently being displayed on screen. Try these:

a. Move your pointer to the **vertical scroll bar** and locate it on the **down arrow** button. Click once and the worksheet scrolls up a few rows – notice the row numbers change – row 1 is no longer the top row

b. Hold the mouse button on the down arrow button down and the rows scroll continuously.

    Now use the up arrow button to reverse the scrolling.

    Row 1 will eventually move to the top of the window again.

c. Now move the pointer halfway down the vertical scroll bar and click.

    The rows scroll down, a screenful at a time.

    Now identify the square **scroll box** on the vertical scroll bar.

    Try dragging this box – it will scroll the worksheet more quickly.

    Repeat these operations for the **horizontal** scroll bar which controls the columns.

12 Keyboard Commands.

Let's try out some keyboard commands which also change the screen position:

a. Hold down the **Ctrl** key and press the **Home** key – you are returned to the top of the worksheet – cell A1 is the active cell.

b. Hold down the **Ctrl** key and press the **down arrow** key on the keyboard – you are taken to the last row of the worksheet. (if the worksheet is not empty you are moved to the last row containing an entry)

    Now hold down the **Ctrl** key and press the **right arrow** key.

    You are taken to the last column of the worksheet.

c. Now try out the key combinations,

    Ctrl – left arrow

    Ctrl – up arrow

    You will return to the top of the worksheet again.

The Page Up and Page down keys can also be used)

Hint: These keys are vital – not only in moving to cells, but also in finding your way back to the correct part of the worksheet – you can avoid that lost panicky feeling when all your data seems to have disappeared. Usually it is out of view in another part of the worksheet!

13 Selecting Individual Cells.

Return to the top of the worksheet and click cell **A2.** You have just selected a cell, the reference box shows that it has become the active cell.

Now move the screen pointer to cell **C3,** using either the mouse or the arrow keys on the keyboard. This becomes the active cell.

Experiment a few more times and select cells **H12, F18** and **E14.**

Now using the screen controls, select cells **M84, HJ127** and **E216** in turn.

14 Selecting groups of Cells.

One can also select groups or ranges of cells and whole columns or rows.

Move to cell **A1** and drag the screen pointer down and across to cell **D6.** Release the mouse button and 24 cells should be selected in all – see Figure 7.

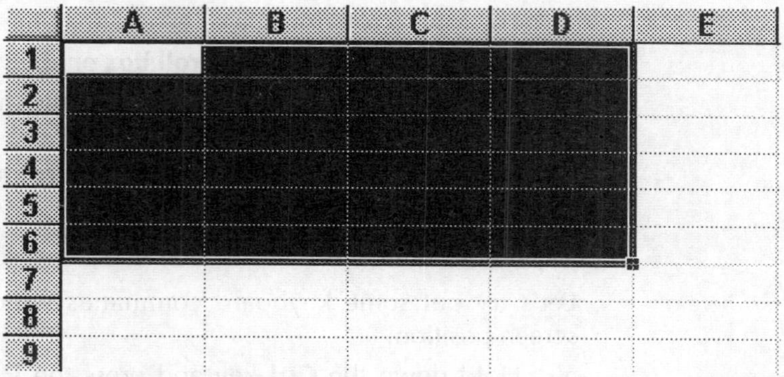

Figure 7

Notice that A1, the first cell selected, remains white while the others go dark.

A1 remains the **active** cell in the range.

The cell **range** A1 to D6 is now selected.

Deselect this cell range by clicking the worksheet outside the selected range of cells.

Hint. Selecting or 'highlighting' cells is an essential first step in many operations; it requires a little practice to select ranges of cells.

15 Menus.

Now let's try selecting some commands from the Menu Bar. Menus are your major means of issuing commands.

Choosing a command involves two steps:

a. opening the menu, and,

b. selecting an option.

Move the screen pointer onto the **Menu Bar** and click the word **Edit.**

This opens the **Edit** menu and displays a pull-down menu of commands – see Figure 8. Edit is a typical menu – it contains a number of options, each of which executes a command.

Edit		Menu
Undo Entry	Ctrl+Z	
Can't Repeat	F4	
Cu_t	Ctrl+X	
Copy	Ctrl+C	
Paste	Ctrl+V	Menu Options
Paste Special...		
Fill	▶	
Clear	▶	
Delete...		
Delete Sheet		
Move or Copy Sheet...		
Find...	Ctrl+F	
Replace...	Ctrl+H	
Go To...	F5	
Links...		

Figure 8

Click elsewhere on the worksheet and close the **Edit** menu.

Now open the **Edit** menu again; this time click the **Go To** option.

A *dialog box* appears – see Figure 9.

16 Dialog Boxes are used when you need to enter some further information about the option that you have chosen. Sometimes this information is entered by clicking a button, sometimes by entering information from the keyboard. Standard dialog box buttons are:

Cancel   Cancel Command

OK   Execute Command

Help   Seek help on command

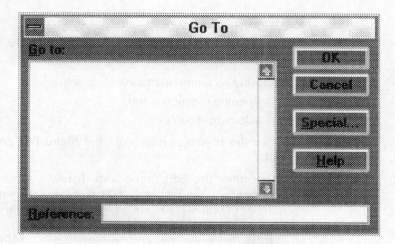

Figure 9

Enter the cell reference **C4** in the Reference box – you may need to click it first to locate the cursor there.

Click the **OK** button.

The **Go To** option goes to the named cell (C4) and activates it.

17 **Shortcut Keys.**

Some Excel users (usually proficient typists) may prefer to issue commands from the keyboard, rather than using the mouse and pull-down menus. You will notice that each menu title on the Menu Bar has one of its letters underlined – File, Edit, View etc.

If you hold down the **Alt** key then type the appropriate letter the menu selection will be displayed – try this.

Press the Alt or the **F10** key to close the menu.

There are similar shortcuts for the menu selections themselves, and many other Excel features. In these units we shall use the mouse rather than the keyboard to issue commands.

18 **Calling Up Help.**

Excel provides a comprehensive online help and tutorial facility. You can call Help either by:

a.   pressing the **F1** key,

b.   Clicking the **Help Button** on the Standard Toolbar,

c.   Using the **Help** menu.

Often Excel Help is *context sensitive* – you can click a Help button and get specific guidance on what you are doing currently,.

Move the screen pointer onto the Menu Bar and click the **Help** menu.

Select the **Index** option.

The Help screen opens. Let's look for help on cell addresses.

Click the **C** button and an alphabetic list appears – use the Scroll Bar or the

Page Down Key to reach the topic **Cell Addresses**

Click on this option and the help text for this topic is displayed.

19 Moving Around in Help.

There are several ways of using Help which we will briefly examine:

Click the **Back** button at the top of the Help text. You are returned to the Help screen.

Now use the index buttons to locate help on the **Maximise** button

When you have read it click the **Back** button to return to the Help screen again.

Now click on the **History** button at the top of the screen – the history window opens showing you a list of the help screens you have used.

Return to the ADDRESS topic listed.

Now click the **Search** button at the top of the help text window.

The Search dialog box appears, it allows you to type in the help topic directly

Type the topic **Minimize** – as you type a number of alternatives are offered in the scroll box below – see Figure 10.

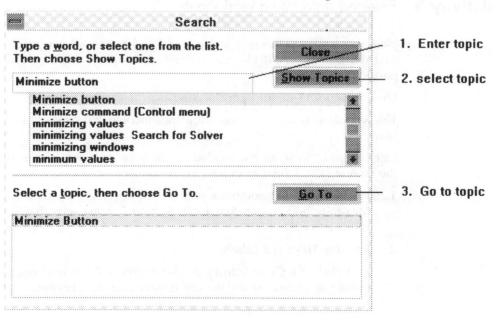

Figure 10

Click the topic **Minimize button** then click the **Show Topics** button.

Finally click the **Goto** button and the relevant help text is displayed

20 **Exiting Help.**

Open the **File** menu on the help screen (not on the Excel workbook)and select the **Exit** option. You are returned to the workbook.

21 **Using The Help Button.**

Look at the Standard Tool Bar at the top of the screen. The Help button is marked with a question mark and arrow – see the key to the Tool Bar at the end of this unit. If it is not in view then you may need to maximise the Application Window

Click the Help button once; the screen pointer changes to a question mark.

Open the **Edit** menu and select the **Goto** option. Excel offers you help on this option.

Exit from Help as before.

22 **Exiting from Excel.**

Click the File option on the Menu Bar.

The File menu opens. Click the **Exit** option at the bottom of the menu and you leave Excel. As you have entered no data in the worksheet you should not be prompted to save it. If you are offered this option click the **No** button.

Activity 3 Entering data into a worksheet

Now that we know our way around the Excel screen we can create our first worksheet. We'll choose a simple example – managing one's personal finances.

Look at Figure 11 on the opposite page.

The worksheet is based around a student's income and expenditure for a term.

Later on you can adapt it if you like to suit your own circumstances; for the moment enter the data exactly as shown here.

1 First enlarge the workbook windows if necessary by clicking the Maximise button. (see Activity 2, Section 7) Make sure that **Sheet1** is the active sheet.

2 **Entering Titles and Labels.**

First click cell **C1** to activate it. The reference C1 is now displayed in the reference area and the cell is outlined with a border.

	A	B	C	D	E	F
1			PERSONAL FINANCES - WEEK 1			
2	INCOME					
3	Opening Bals.		0			
4	Grant		500			
5	Loan		400			
6	Parents		300			
7	Total Income					
8						
9	EXPENDITURE					
10	Accomodation		60			
11	Food		30			
12	Books		75			
13	Other		20			
14	Total Expenditure					

Figure 11

Now enter the title shown in Figure 11 – PERSONAL FINANCES – TERM 1 – use capital letters.

Notice that the title displays in the Formula Bar as you type it.

Press **Enter** and the title appears, displayed across several cells; this is as it should be.

We are now ready to enter the cell labels in column A. (a *label* is anything like a column or row heading that labels or identifies cells)

Activate cell **A2** (i.e. click it) and enter the first label INCOME.

Hints: Whenever you enter or change a cell's contents you need to complete the entry. There are several ways to do this:

❐ press Enter

❐ click the next cell

❐ press one of the arrow keys

❐ click the 'tick' box that appears next to the Formula Bar

Text is automatically aligned to the left of the cell.

Forgetting to complete the entry causes a number of problems, e.g. menu options being dimmed and unavailable. Always check this if your next command fails to execute.

Carry on and complete all the labels in column 1, including the wrong spelling of 'Accomodation'! Don't worry if some labels overlap into the next column.

Enter the column heading 'Week 1' in cell **C2**.

Errors: Use the Backspace key to correct any errors that you notice while completing an entry. Don't worry about errors that you notice at a later stage – we will correct them in later sections.

3 **Checking Spelling.**

First click cell A1; now move the screen pointer onto the Spell Check button on the Standard toolbar; it is marked with a tick and 'ABC' – a small label appears to identify it – see Figure 12

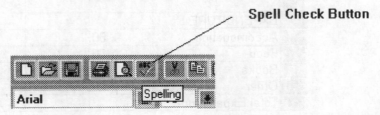

Spell Check Button

Figure 12

Double click the button. Excel compares all the text in the selected cells with its dictionary

A dialog box opens, telling you that the abbreviation 'Bals'. is not in the dictionary – click the **Ignore** button.

Next the label 'Accomodation' is selected; it has been misspelt with only one 'm' Excel suggests the correct spelling. Click the **Change** button.

Continue until all the text is checked.

Note: Spell Checkers will not recognise most abbreviations and proper names, unless you add them to the dictionary. An Add button is provided to do this.

4 **Editing Cell Contents Using the Formula Bar.**

Let's Alter the text in cell A5 from 'Loan' to 'Bank Loan'

First click cell **A5** to activate it. The text appears in the Formula Bar at the top of the screen.

Now move the screen pointer in front of the first letter of 'Loan' in the *Formula Bar*

– the pointer changes to a vertical bar.

Click to place a flashing cursor there – this marks the *insertion point*.

Type the word 'Bank' and press **Enter**

The cell is amended.

5 **In-Cell Editing.**

You can also edit cell contents directly without using the Formula Bar. Let's alter the label 'Food' in cell A11 to 'Food and Travel'.

Move the screen pointer to cell **A11** and double click the space after the word 'Food'

A flashing cursor marking the insertion point should be placed there – if not keep trying!

Amend the label to 'Food and Travel' and press **Enter.**

6   **Information Only – Deleting.**

If you need to delete any character, you must place the insertion point in the same way as above, then:

❑ Use the Delete key to delete to the right of the insertion point

❑ Use the Backspace key to delete to the left of the insertion point.

❑ Relocate the pointer by clicking another cell.

Overtyping: To overtype the contents of a cell, just click the cell to select it and start typing. There is no need to delete the contents first.

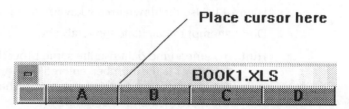

Place cursor here

Figure 13

7   **Widening Columns.**

Some of the labels in Column A are too wide for their cells. Try out these alternative methods:

a.   Locate the screen pointer on the vertical line that separates column heading A from Column heading B – see Figure 13

The pointer changes to a double-headed arrow.

Now press down the mouse button and drag the column to the **right** until its width is **16.00.** The width is given in the Reference Area.

b.   Click the column designator, i.e. the 'A' in the column heading. The whole column is selected.

Open the **Format** menu and select **Column** then **Width.**

A dialog box is displayed.

Enter the new width as 15, and click the **OK** button.

c.   Click the column designator A again to select the column if necessary.

Open the **Format** menu and select **Column** then **Autofit selection.**

The width is automatically adjusted to fit the longest entry

8   Altering the Row Height.

We will now make row 1 higher to emphasise the title.

Locate the screen pointer on the horizontal line that separates row designator 1 from row designator 2.

Drag the row down until the height is 15.00. (you can also select the row then use the **Row** option on the **Format** menu to achieve the same result)

9   Entering Numeric Data.

This is the same procedure as for cell labels.

Activate cell **C3** and type the number 0.

Press Enter and the number is aligned to the right of the cell.

Hint. Make sure that this is the number 0 and not the letter O (a common source of error)

Complete the other income and expenditure items as shown in Figure 11. Use the **down arrow** key to complete each entry.

Don't attempt to calculate the totals yet.

Hint. To amend the data use the same procedures as in sections 2-6 above. If the number entered is too wide for the column Excel alerts you to this by a row of hash signs (####). You must then widen the column.

10   Optional: If you are not proceding to the next unit then Save and Close the workbook. Saving is covered in detail in the next unit. For the moment proceed as follows:

Open the **File** menu (click File on the Menu Bar) and select the **Save** option.

A dialog box appears – see Figure 14.

At the moment the workbook has the default name BOOK1.XLS – see the File Name box, top left.

First make sure that you have a suitable, formatted floppy disk in the diskette drive.

Click the down arrow button on the **Drives** box and select a: from the list offered.

Amend the file name to **TERMS** (the box should already be selected).

If you have made a mistake click the **Cancel** button and start again, otherwise click the **OK** button.

The Summary Information dialog box appears next, click the **Cancel** button.

Default file name

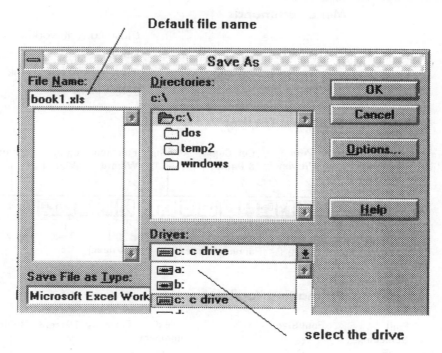

select the drive

Figure 14

The file takes a few seconds to save to A drive – the Status Bar shows the save process and the drive light should come on to confirm this.

When you return to your workbook you will see the name of the workbook, TERMS.XLS, displayed in the title bar.

Summary of commands

Notes

Menu commands show the menu name first, followed by the command to choose from the menu, e.g. Edit-Clear means open the Edit menu and select the Clear command.

Keyboard commands use the dash symbol to indicate keys that should be pressed down at the same time, e.g. Ctrl-Home.

Keyboard commands

Ctrl-Home	Go to cell A1
Ctrl-Down Arrow Key	Go to last row of the worksheet
Ctrl-Right Arrow Key	Go to last column of worksheet
F1	Select Help

Menu commands

File-Close	Close current workbook
File-Exit	Exit Excel
File-Save	Save current workbook
Help	Select Help

Standard Toolbar

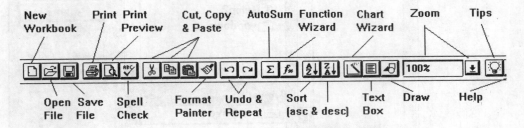

New Workbook · Print · Print Preview · Cut, Copy & Paste · AutoSum · Function Wizard · Chart Wizard · Zoom · Tips

Open File · Save File · Spell Check · Format Painter · Undo & Repeat · Sort (asc & desc) · Text Box · Draw · Help

Formatting Toolbar

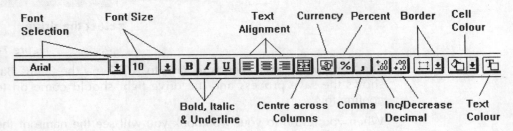

Font Selection · Font Size · Text Alignment · Currency · Percent · Border · Cell Colour

Bold, Italic & Underline · Centre across Columns · Comma · Inc/Decrease Decimal · Text Colour

Further worksheet essentials

Skills to be learned	Activity
Addition	1
Cell data – clearing	1.5
Cell data – copying, pasting	4
Filling Right	7.6
Formulae	1
Retrieving a workbook	3
Saving the workbook	2
Subtraction	1.7
SUM function	1.1

Previous skills needed to tackle this unit

Skill	Covered in Unit
How to open a workbook and enter simple worksheet data	1

Previous work needed

The workbook TERMS created in Unit 1

Introduction

In the first unit we learnt the basic skills of opening a new workbook and entering some simple data into a worksheet. This unit shows you how to use formulae and functions to perform calculations, how to delete, edit and copy data and how to close and open an existing workbook.

Activity 1 Using formulae

Formulae are used as to perform a variety of operations such as calculations.

A formula is placed in a cell in the same way as text or numbers. It can be very simple, such as adding the contents of 2 cells, or complex, containing mathematical or financial functions.

You must always start a formula with an equal (=) sign; it tells Excel that you are about to apply a formula to a cell.

If you are not continuing from the previous unit then you will need to open the workbook **TERMS** created in Unit 1. Make sure that **Sheet1** is the active sheet.

1   Addition.

Now that we have entered the first week's income and expenditure figures we can add them using formulae.

To calculate total income, first activate cell **C7** and type an = sign.

The = sign appears in the formula bar, alongside four buttons, including a 'tick' and a 'cross' button.

Now type the formula **SUM(C3:C6)** next to the = sign.

This is the formula to add or sum the range of four cells C3 to C6.

Click the **tick** button next to the formula. (or press Enter)

The results of the formula are displayed in cell C7 – the income total of 1200.

Hint: If you make a mistake entering the formula or get an error message, you can edit or delete a formula as follows using the Formula Bar:

❐   Use the Delete key to delete to the right of the insertion point

❐   Use the Backspace key to delete to the left of the insertion point.

❐   Relocate the pointer by clicking another cell.

Notes on the Sum Function.

SUM is an Excel **function** and is a lot quicker than typing the full formula C3+C4+C5+C6.

Functions and formulae may be typed in upper or lower case.

SUM is also expandable – if another row is inserted into this range of 4 cells at a later stage, say between rows 4 and 5, the new cell would automatically be included in the range. This is not the case if one types the formula out in full using the + sign.

2   Adding Up Columns – Shortcuts.

We will now use a formula to add up the total expenditure.

Activate cell **C14** and type **=SUM(**

Move the screen pointer to the first expenditure item, cell **C10.**

Hold down the mouse button and drag the pointer down to cell **C13.**

Four cells are enclosed by a dotted box.

Type the final right bracket and the formula bar should read **SUM(C10:C13)**

(If you have made a mistake then click the cross (X) box on the formula bar and start again.)

Click the tick box and the result of the formula – 185 – is displayed.

3   **Amending Formulae – Error Messages.**

Try the following:

Activate cell **C7** and move the pointer onto the Formula Bar; it reads SUM(C3:C6)

Alter the formula to SUM(C3:**C7**) and click the tick box to execute the new formula.

The error message 'Cannot resolve circular references' appears.

Click the **Help** button in the dialog box for help on this error. As C7 is the 'destination' cell – the cell containing the formula – it cannot also be one of the cells to be summed as this is 'circular'.

Exit Help using the **File** menu then click the **OK** button on the dialog box.

Correct the formula to its original SUM(C3:C6) and execute it again.

4   Excel has a range of error messages, we'll look at one more for the moment.

Activate cell **C14** and amend **SUM** to **SIM.**

Execute this formula (use the Enter key or tick box)

The error message #NAME? appears in the cell. Make sure that C14 is still selected but don't correct it just yet.

5   **Clearing Cell Contents.**

Move the screen pointer to the Menu Bar at the top of the screen.

Click the **Edit** menu to select it.

The Edit menu opens – select the **Clear** then the **All** option.

The cell is cleared. (nb you can use the Delete key instead of the Clear command)

6   **Adding Columns – the SUM Button.**

The Sum button offers the quickest way of adding a column of figures.

We need to add the expenditure cells again; activate cell **C14** if necessary.

The **Sum** button is on the Standard tool bar and is marked with the Greek letter Sigma (like a capital M on its side – see key at end of unit)

Click the **Sum** button once and the formula appears in the formula bar. Check that it is correct.

Click the Sum button again and the formula is executed, the total of 185 appears in cell C14.

7   **Subtraction Formulae.**

We now need to subtract total expenditure from total income to find the closing balance for week 1.

Activate cell **C16** and type the formula **=C7-C14**

Execute the formula as before and the closing balance for week 1 (1015) appears in cell C16.

Your worksheet should now be the same as Figure 1.

	A	B	C	D	E	F
1			PERSONAL FINANCES - TERM 1			
2	INCOME		Week 1			
3	Opening Bals.		0			
4	Grant		500			
5	Bank Loan		400			
6	Parents		300			
7	Total Income		1200			
8						
9	EXPENDITURE					
10	Accommodation		60			
11	Food and Travel		30			
12	Books		75			
13	Other		20			
14	Total Expenditure		185			
15						
16	CLOSING BALS.		1015			

Figure 1

Activity 2   Saving your workbook

If you have continued straight on from Unit 1 then at the moment your workbook is only saved in the computer's main memory. It could be lost for ever if your PC crashes or the power goes off. You need to save it permanently as a named file on disk. In these units I make the assumption that you will want to save your work on a diskette (A drive) not on the computer's hard disk (C drive). All future references assume this.

If you have already saved the workbook as TERMS then open the **File** menu and select **Save** to save the present version and continue with the next activity.

1   Open the **File** menu (click File on the Menu Bar) and select the **Save As** option.

A dialog box appears – see Figure 2.

Default file name

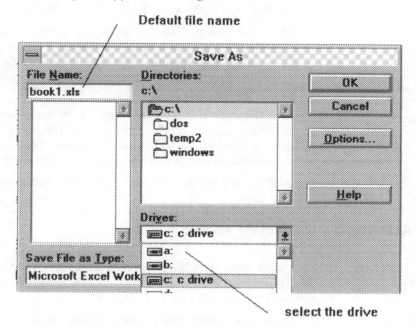

select the drive

Figure 2

2   At the moment the workbook has the default name BOOK1.XLS – see the File Name box, top left. **.XLS** is the *extension* automatically assigned to all Excel workbook files, but we want to save it under a more meaningful name than BOOK1.

Note: A filename can be 1 – 8 characters long, and can consist of any combination of letters, numbers and certain special characters (! ?_ etc) but not blanks or dashes.

First make sure that you have a suitable, formatted floppy disk in the diskette drive.

Click the down arrow button on the **Drives** box and select a: from the list offered.

Amend the file name to **TERMS** (the box should already be selected.)

If you have made a mistake click the **Cancel** button and start again, otherwise click the **OK** button.

The Summary Information dialog box appears next, allowing you to save further information about the workbook; the author's name is already completed.

We won't use this feature yet; click the Cancel button.

The file takes a few seconds to save to A drive – the Status Bar shows the save process and the drive light should come on to confirm this.

3   When you return to your workbook you will see the name of the workbook, TERMS.XLS, displayed in the title bar.

Hint: Get into the habit of saving your document regularly as you work, not just when you exit Excel. Use the **Save** not the **Save As** command to do this, remember that any data keyed in since your last Save command has not yet been saved permanently.

This feature can be useful if you have made some irrecoverable error in your workbook; you can close the workbook without saving the errors, then open it again. The workbook will be retrieved as it was before your last Save command.

4   At this point use the **File** menu and select **Exit** to exit from Excel.

Activity 3   Loading an existing workbook

Your workbook TERMS has been saved to disk on A drive as an Excel file. To work on it again you must use this name to retrieve it from disk and load it into main memory.

1   Start Excel again. A new blank workbook appears with the default name BOOK1. We will close it as we want to work on an existing workbook.

Open the **File** menu and select the **Close** option (not Exit).

The document window goes blank, as no workbook is in use.

2   If you saved your TERMS workbook to a diskette then obviously the first step is to ensure that this disk is in drive A.

Open the **File** menu and select **Open.** A dialog box appears.

It is similar to the Save as dialog box shown in Figure 2 in the last activity.

3   **Retrieving a File by Typing the Name.**

If you are sure of the file name and the drive (as we should be) then simply type them in the File Name box – it is already selected.

Type **A:\TERMS.XLS** and Click the **OK** button.

The file will load from disk and appear on screen.

If not check your spelling and that you are using the correct diskette.

Open the **File** menu and select the **Close** option again.

4   **Retrieving a File From the File List.**

Alternatively you can open a file by choosing it from a list.

Open the **File** menu and select the **Open** option.

This time we may need to select the drive.

Move the screen pointer onto the Drives box and click the Down Arrow button. Select the **a**: drive icon.

The workbook TERMS.XLS appears in the **Files** box to the left of the dialog box.

Click it to select it, then click the **OK** button again.

The file will load from disk and appear on screen.

5   **Independent Activity.**

Close the workbook as before. Open the File menu again and look at the bottom of the menu. You should see the workbook listed near the bottom of the menu. Click it to load the workbook again. Excel remembers the last 4 workbooks that you used in this way.

Activity 4   Copying cells and deleting data

At the moment we only have data for one week. We are going to copy this data into the next column to create week 2, and modify certain cells. We will then experiment with a number of ways to move, copy, and delete cells. They are all useful in certain contexts, so make sure that you try out all these activities.

1   **Copying.**

This involves selecting one or more cells, and then copying them to another part of the worksheet.

First select all the cells containing the Week 1 data; move the screen pointer onto cell **C2,** and drag down to column **C16.**

Note: If you select the wrong cells then merely click anywhere on the worksheet to remove the selection and try again

Open the **Edit** menu and select **Copy** (not Cut)

The selected area is now enclosed by a flowing dotted line called the Marquee.

2   **Pasting.**

Next we must indicate where the cells are to be copied to.

Activate cell **D2** – the cell where you want to start pasting from.

Open the **Edit** menu and select **Paste.**

The cells are copied to a new location, and the Marquee remains around the area that you copied, allowing you to paste it again if you wish.

Remove the Marquee by pressing the **Esc** key.

Notes: Whenever you copy cells, Excel stores them in a temporary memory area called the Clipboard. They stay there until they are replaced by some other Copy or Cut command

If you have made a mistake then open the Edit menu and select the Undo Paste command.

3   Notice that not only the data but also the formulae are copied. Excel automatically adjusts the cell references in the formulae to refer to their new location in Column D. For this reason they are called *relative references.* Click the formulae cells D7, D14 and D16 to check this.

4   **Cutting and Pasting.**

Cutting cells physically removes them from their original location so that they can be pasted to a new one. It is a similar operation to copying.

Select the cells for week 2 as before, i.e. cell range **D2** to **D16.**

Open the **Edit** menu and select the **Cut** option; (not Copy) the cells are surrounded by the marquee as before.

Activate cell **E2,** then open the **Edit** menu and select **Paste.**

This time the column is moved a column to the right, leaving column D blank.

Note: You may use the Cut, Copy and Paste tools on the Tool Bar – see the Toolbar key at the end of this unit instead of menu commands.

5   **Clearing Ranges of Cells.**

Let's now clear the copied column – in the next section we will learn a better way of copying columns using the Fill command.

Select the cells in column E if necessary, then open the **Edit** menu and select **Clear** then **All.**

Click the **OK** button and the cells are cleared – the contents are deleted; no copy is made to the clipboard as with the Cut and Copy commands.

Hint: As before you can use the Edit-Undo command to restore deleted data

6   **Copying Cells Using Fill Right.**

Move the screen pointer onto cell **C2.**

Hold down the mouse button and drag down the column to cell **C16.**

Keeping the mouse button pressed down, drag the screen pointer across to select the same number of cells in the next column. Now let go.

You should now have selected 2 columns – see Figure 3.

You may need to try more than once to get it right. Use Undo or Clear on the Edit menu if you make a mistake.

7   Now open the **Edit** menu and select **Fill** then **Right.**

The contents of column C – data and formulae – are copied to column D.

(If the copying is incorrect then open the Edit menu again and select **Undo Fill Right**)

Select cell **D2** and amend the column label to **'Week 2'.**

	A	B	C	D
1			PERSONAL FINANCE	
2	INCOME		Week 1	
3	Opening Bals.		0	
4	Grant		500	
5	Bank Loan		400	
6	Parents		300	
7	Total Income		1200	
8				
9	EXPENDITURE			
10	Accommodation		60	
11	Food and Travel		30	
12	Books		75	
13	Other		20	
14	Total Expenditure		185	
15				
16	CLOSING BALS.		1015	

Figure 3

8   The values in cells D4 to D6 for Grant, Loan And Parents will need to be deleted; they are 'one-off' income items only applying to week 1.

Drag from **D4** down to **D6** to select these 3 cells.

Open the **Edit** menu and select **Clear** then **All.**

Notice how the totals in column D are automatically re-calculated.

(If you have cleared the wrong cells then open the Edit menu again and select Undo Clear)

Notice that your closing balance for week 2 is now a negative amount, an insolvent -185. However this is because we have not yet carried forward the closing balance of 1015 from week 1 to the opening balance for week 2. Let's do this with a formula.

9 We want the value in cell D3, the opening balance for week 2, to equal C16, the closing balance for week 1.

Activate cell **D3** and type **=C16**

Click the Tick button to execute the formula and the week 2 totals are recalculated – your closing balance for week 2 is now a healthy 830.

10 Now make the following amendments to week **2**:

Food and Travel   35

Books   15

The closing balance is now   885

11 We can now use week 2 as our model for the next 3 weeks.

First select the week 2 values and the 3 adjacent columns, i.e. 4 columns in all, cells **D2 – G16**.

Then use the **Edit-Fill-Right** command as before.

The contents of column D (week 2) are copied into columns E, F and G.

The closing balance at the end of week 5 should be 495 – see Figure 4.

	A	B	C	D	E	F	G
1			PERSONAL FINANCES - TERM 1				
2	INCOME		Week 1	Week 2	Week 3	Week 4	Week 5
3	Opening Bals.		0	1015	885	755	625
4	Grant		500				
5	Bank Loan		400				
6	Parents		300				
7	Total Income		1200	1015	885	755	625
8							
9	EXPENDITURE						
10	Accommodation		60	60	60	60	60
11	Food and Travel		30	35	35	35	35
12	Books		75	15	15	15	15
13	Other		20	20	20	20	20
14	Total Expenditure		185	130	130	130	130
15							
16	CLOSING BALS.		1015	885	755	625	495

Figure 4

Amend the week numbers in row 2.

Hints. Remember to use the Undo command, as before if you make a mistake. Remember to save the changes that you have made – use Save (not Save as) on the File menu.

12 If you are not continuing with the next unit then save and close the workbook.

Summary of commands and functions

Notes

Menu commands show the menu name first, followed by the command to choose from the menu, e.g. Edit-Clear means open the Edit menu and select the Clear command.

Menu commands

Edit-Clear-All	Delete cell contents
Edit-Copy	Copy selected cells
Edit-Cut	Remove selected cells
Edit-Delete	Delete selected rows or columns
Edit-Delete Sheet	Delete selected worksheet
Edit-Fill-Right	Copy selected cells into selected right hand columns
Edit-Goto	Go to a specified cell
Edit-Paste	Insert cut or copied cells at a specified location
Edit-Undo	Undo previous operation
File-Close	Close current workbook
File-Exit	Exit Excel
File-New	Open new, blank workbook
File-Open	Retrieve an existing workbook

Functions

=SUM()	Add a range of cells

Standard toolbar

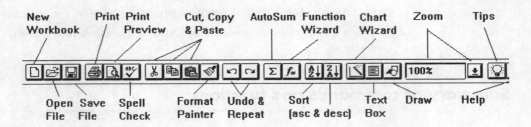

New Workbook | Print | Print Preview | Cut, Copy & Paste | AutoSum | Function Wizard | Chart Wizard | Zoom | Tips

Open File | Save File | Spell Check | Format Painter | Undo & Repeat | Sort (asc & desc) | Text Box | Draw | Help

Formatting toolbar

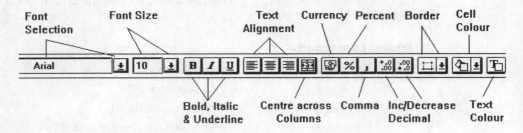

Font Selection | Font Size | Text Alignment | Currency | Percent | Border | Cell Colour

Bold, Italic & Underline | Centre across Columns | Comma | Inc/Decrease Decimal | Text Colour

Formatting, copying and printing your worksheet

Skills to be learned   **Activity**

Skill	Activity
Bold text – adding	1.1
Cell borders – adding	1.7
Cell data – alignment	1.3
Centring Titles	1.6
Character size	1.2
Columns – deleting and Inserting	1.5
Copying a worksheet	11
Fonts – selecting	1.2
Formatting – Manual1	1
Freezing titles and labels	1.10
Gridlines – removing	1.10
Number and Currency formats – selecting	1.4
Page Setup	1
Printing a worksheet	2
Rows – inserting and deleting	1.5
Text – adding blocks	1.12

Previous skills needed to tackle this unit

Skill	Covered in Unit
How to open a workbook and enter simple worksheet data.	1
How to edit and delete data	2

Previous work needed

The workbook TERMS created in Units 1 and 2.

Introduction

You now have a valid working model of the first 5 weeks finances for Term 1. In this unit you will learn how to format your worksheet. Excel allows you to alter the worksheet format in many ways, including the type size and style, and column width and alignment. You will also learn how to use printer and page settings.

Activity 1 Formatting the worksheet

If you are not continuing from the previous unit then you will need to open the workbook **TERMS** created in Unit 1. Make sure that **Sheet1** is the active sheet.

1 **Emboldening.**

First we will put the title and cell labels in bold.

Drag to select the title and the column headings – cells **A1** to **G2**.

Click the **Bold** button on the Formatting Tool Bar – marked with a capital B. (See Figure 1.)

The cells are emboldened. (You may also wish to use the *Italic* or <u>Underline</u> buttons, marked with capital I or U)

Now select the row labels in column A and embolden them – you may need to widen column A now.

Repeat this operation to embolden the closing balances in row **16**.

2 **Character Size and Fonts.**

Select the row labels in column A.

Click the **Font Size button** – see Figure 1.

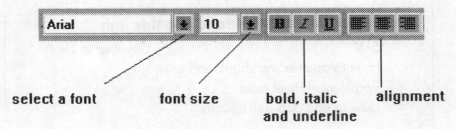

select a font   font size   bold, italic and underline   alignment

Figure 1

At the moment all characters on the worksheet are the default size of **10** point.

Click **8** – you may need to scroll it into view – the cell labels are now in a smaller font.

You may also like to experiment with different fonts or typefaces, using the **Font** button – see Figure 1. The ones that your current printer is capable of printing are shown in black rather than pale grey.

3   **Alignment.**

At the moment the numeric values are aligned to the right of the cells. This is the default for numbers. It can look neater to centre them under the column headings.

Select all the cells containing numeric data , i.e. cells **C3** to **G16.**

On the Formatting Tool Bar are a group of 3 alignment buttons, showing left, centre and right alignment – see Figure 1.

Click the centre button. The values are centred.

4   **Number and Currency Formats.**

Let's alter the way numeric values are displayed. Select all the numeric cells again if necessary (C3 – G16).

Open the **Format** menu and select the **Cells** option; the Format Cells dialog box is displayed.

Click the **Number** tab and the dialog box changes – see Figure 2.

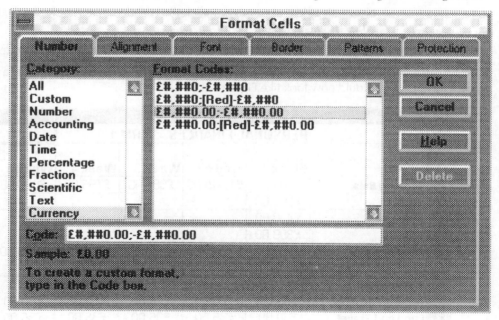

Figure 2

Select the **Currency** option from the **Category** list, then select a suitable format from the **Format Codes** list. The format shown in Figure 2 displays numbers to 2 decimal places, and the £ currency symbol. A sample is shown at the bottom of the dialog box.

Troubleshooting: Check in the Format Codes list if your copy of Excel has been set up to show the pound rather than the dollar currency symbol. If not you can type this format directly into the Code box at the bottom of the screen.

Hint. Always use the Format-Cells option to add currency symbols. *Do not* enter currency symbols directly. If you do this then Excel will regard the values as text, not numbers, and be unable to use them in calculations.

5   **Inserting and Deleting Columns and Rows.**

Click the column designator at the top of column B; this selects the whole column.

Open the **Edit** menu and select **Delete.**

Column B is deleted and subsequent columns are shifted to the left. All the cell references and formulae are automatically adjusted to reflect their new position.

Hint. Removing a blank column should cause no problems, but removing a column containing data and formulae obviously could. You can select Undo from the Edit column if you delete the wrong column or row.

Now let's insert an extra row; click the row designator for Row 2 – the whole row is selected.

Open the **Insert** menu and choose **Rows.** A new blank row is inserted.

The worksheet has a neater and more balanced appearance and should now look like Figure 3.

	A	B	C	D	E	F
1		PERSONAL FINANCES - TERM 1				
2						
3	INCOME	Week 1	Week 2	Week 3	Week 4	Week 5
4	Opening Bals.	£0.00	£1,015.00	£885.00	£755.00	£625.00
5	Grant	£500.00				
6	Bank Loan	£400.00				
7	Parents	£300.00				
8	Total Income	£1,200.00	£1,015.00	£885.00	£755.00	£625.00
9						
10	EXPENDITURE					
11	Accommodation	£60.00	£60.00	£60.00	£60.00	£60.00
12	Food and Travel	£30.00	£35.00	£35.00	£35.00	£35.00
13	Books	£75.00	£15.00	£15.00	£15.00	£15.00
14	Other	£20.00	£20.00	£20.00	£20.00	£20.00
15	Total Expenditure	£185.00	£130.00	£130.00	£130.00	£130.00
16						
17	CLOSING BALS.	£1,015.00	£885.00	£755.00	£625.00	£495.00

Figure 3

6   **Centring the Title.**

It would look neater to centre the title across columns A to F – the area of the worksheet that will eventually be printed.

Select cell range **1A** to **1F**

Click the **Centre Across Columns** Button on the Formatting Toolbar – see key at the end of this unit.

The title is centred across the columns selected. If you decide to widen the worksheet later you will need to re-centre the title.

7   **Adding Borders.**

Borders can be used to mark off various sections of the worksheet and make it easier to read – see Figure 4 below.

First we will put a double border around the worksheet.

Drag to select cells **A1** to **F17.**

Open the **Format** menu and select **Cells.**

A dialog box appears, click the **Border** tab and new options are shown:

Click the Outline option in the **Border** box,

Select the double line button in the **Style** box.

Finally click the **OK** button – you are returned to the worksheet.

Click to remove the highlight from the cells – the worksheet is enclosed in a double box.

8   Now let's draw some single lines to mark off different sections of the worksheet.

Select cells **A9** to **F9.**

Open the **Format** menu and select **Cells.** The dialog box opens again, click the **Border** button again if necessary.

Select the **Bottom** and **Single Line** options.

Click the **OK** button – this places a single line at the bottom of row 9.

Troubleshooting. Removing unwanted borders. Use the same commands, i.e. select the relevant cells, and select Cells from the Format menu.Then click the relevant style button to deselect the unwanted border.

9   **Independent Activity.**

The Formatting Toolbar supplies a Borders button. Identify it and click the down arrow button; use it to:

❏   draw a single line under cells **A16** to **F16.**

❏   give the cells in column **A** a single right hand border.

10 **Gridline Display.**

The gridlines marking the cell boundaries can be turned off to emphasise the borders that we have drawn.

Open the **Tools** menu and choose **Options.** A dialog box opens.

Click the **Gridlines** button – the X disappears as this option is deselected.

Click the **OK** button, and the gridlines disappear.

(this will not prevent the gridlines displaying when the worksheet is printed)

Your worksheet should now look like Figure 4.

	A	B	C	D	E	F
1		**PERSONAL FINANCES - TERM 1**				
2						
3	**INCOME**	**Week 1**	**Week 2**	**Week 3**	**Week 4**	**Week 5**
4	**Opening Bals.**	£0.00	£1,015.00	£885.00	£755.00	£625.00
5	**Grant**	£500.00				
6	**Bank Loan**	£400.00				
7	**Parents**	£300.00				
8	**Total Income**	£1,200.00	£1,015.00	£885.00	£755.00	£625.00
9						
10	**EXPENDITURE**					
11	**Accommodation**	£60.00	£60.00	£60.00	£60.00	£60.00
12	**Food and Travel**	£30.00	£35.00	£35.00	£35.00	£35.00
13	**Books**	£75.00	£15.00	£15.00	£15.00	£15.00
14	**Other**	£20.00	£20.00	£20.00	£20.00	£20.00
15	**Total Expenditure**	£185.00	£130.00	£130.00	£130.00	£130.00
16						
17	**CLOSING BALS.**	**£1,015.00**	**£885.00**	**£755.00**	**£625.00**	**£495.00**

Figure 4

11 **Freezing Titles and Labels.**

We will add a note to the bottom of the worksheet. This means that the worksheet will become too large to view all at once. Before one scrolls to another part of the worksheet it is possible to 'freeze' both the titles and the column and row labels so that they are always in view, and so keep a track of what each row or column represents.

Click cell **B4,** then open the **Windows** menu and select the **Freeze Panes** option.

All cells above and to the left of this cell are frozen.

Try scrolling across and down; the column and row labels stay there as a constant reference.

To Unfreeze Panes. Open the Windows menu and select **Unfreeze Panes**

12   **Entering and Justifying Blocks of Text.**

Although Excel does not offer full word processing facilities, blocks of text, such as brief notes, can be added to worksheets.

Click the **Text Box** tool on the Standard Tool Bar – see key at the end of this unit.

Now move the screen pointer to cell B19.

Drag to draw a text box large enough to hold the text shown in figure 5.

The text is aligned into this text box.

Notes: The text box may be re-sized by dragging it. It can be deleted by clicking it to select it, then pressing the Delete key

Text within the box can be edited, emboldened etc in the usual ways.

	A	B	C	D	E
1				PERSONAL FINANCES - TERM 1	
2					
3	INCOME	Week 1	Week 2	Week 3	Week 4
14	Other	£20.00	£20.00	£20.00	£20.00
15	Total Expenditure	£185.00	£130.00	£130.00	£130.00
16					
17	CLOSING BALS.	£1,015.00	£885.00	£755.00	£625.00
18					
19			Worksheet showing the income		
20			and expenditure for the first 5		
21			weeks of the Autumn Term		
22					
23					
24					

Figure 5

Activity 2   Printing a worksheet

To print a worksheet properly you must give Excel instructions on what and how to print – which cells, number of copies, and so on.

1   **Setting the Print Area.**

First select the entire worksheet area that you want to print – cells A1 to F22.

Open the **File** menu and select **Print** – the Print dialog box appears.

Click the **Selection** button – the selected cells only will be printed, not any blank areas outside it. This is important when the worksheet becomes larger.

Before you print click the **Page Setup** button.

2   **Page Setup.** The Page Setup dialog box appears – make sure that the Sheet option is displayed – see Figure 6.

Notice also that the cells in the **Print Area** are confirmed – ignore the $ signs inserted.

Make sure that two boxes **'Row and Column Headings'** and **'Gridlines'** are both unchecked, i.e. there is no 'X' in either of them. (it is usual to print a worksheet without the row and column headings and gridlines, if it is not too large or detailed)

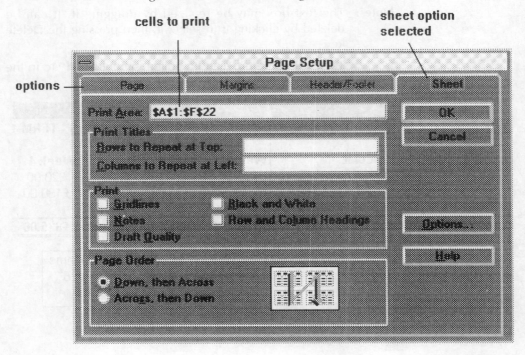

Figure 6

3   **Other Page Settings.**

Next click the **Page** tab on the Page Setup dialog box; a new set of options are displayed. Your printer may offer the following settings, if so they will appear in black rather than pale grey. Check the following:

❑ **Orientation:** Normally worksheets are printed in *portrait,* i.e. vertically down the page. Wide worksheets can be printed in *landscape* – horizontally across the page.

❑ **Paper:** The current paper size is displayed, normally A4

❏ **Scaling:** You can adjust the size of the printed area to fit the paper size.

❏ **Fit to:** will adjust the size of the the printed area to fit on one or more pages.

4 **Margins and Alignment.**

Now click the Margin tab – a new set of options are displayed.

Click the **'Center Horizontally'** and **'Center Vertically'** boxes. This will centre the printout on the page.

Now click the **OK** button – you are returned to the **Print** dialog box

5 **The Printer.**

Make sure that the printer is :

❏ Switched on

❏ Set online – check switch and warning light,

❏ Connected via cable to your computer,

❏ has paper in it.

Check these in turn if the next section does not produce a printout.

6 **Print Preview.**

Click the **Print Preview** button.

The Print Preview screen appears, showing how the worksheet will appear on the printed page

There are various option along the top of the screen; *Do not use any of these options for now:*

❏ **Next** and **Previous** are for multi-page worksheets.

❏ **Margins** displays the current margin settings.

❏ **Print** and **Setup** allow us to either proceed with printing or go back to the Page Setup menus.

Now move the screen pointer over the printed area – it changes to a magnifying glass shape. Click, and the area under the pointer is enlarged.

You can scroll around to look at other parts of the worksheet.

The **Zoom** button will return you to full page mode.

Now finally if you are happy with the print preview, click the **Print** button at the top of the screen.

(If you are not happy then the **Close** button will cancel printing)

The worksheet should start printing now.

7 **Troubleshooting.** If your worksheet won't print check the previous stages again.

Finally check that the correct printer is selected as follows:

Open the **File** menu and select the **Print** option again.

Click the Printer Setup button and check in the **Printer Setup** dialog box that the correct printer is selected.

8   Save and close the workbook.

Activity 3   Consolidation – check your progress

We are going to extend the worksheet to cover a 10-week term.

I shall keep the instructions to a minimum, as you have already practised the operations involved.

1   Retrieve the TERMS workbook.

Make sure that Sheet1 is selected

First select the week 5 column, i.e. cells **F1-F17** and keep the mouse button pressed down.

Drag across the worksheet to select the next 5 columns G–K.

These will hold the data for weeks 6-10.

2   Now use the Edit-Fill-Right command to copy the data across.

Remember that you can always use the Undo command if you make a mistake.

3   Some minor amendments need to be made next:

a.   amend the week numbers for weeks 6–10.

b.   amend the note at the bottom of the worksheet

c.   you may also find that columns F to J have a double right hand border – copied from the format for the week 5 column.

Use the **Format-Cells** menu to remove or change unwanted cell borders.

Weeks 6-10 are reproduced as Appendix 1 – check it with your version.

4   You will see that by the end of week 10 you are £155 in debt. Activity 5 will show you how to try and solve this!

Activity 4   Copying a worksheet

We are going to copy the worksheet Sheet1 and then modify the copy.

1   Make sure that the **Sheet1** tab is selected.

Hold down the **Ctrl** key, place the cursor on the **Sheet1** tab and drag with the mouse.

The cursor changes to represent a copy of the worksheet, marked with a '+' sign.

2   Drag the cursor onto the Sheet2 tab.

Release the *mouse button* then the *Ctrl* key. Excel copies Sheet1, renaming it Sheet1 (2).

3   Click the tab for Sheet1 (2). It opens, becoming the active worksheet; it is a replica of Sheet1.

Troubleshooting. If you forgot to hold down the Ctrl key, or released it too soon, then you may have merely moved Sheet1 to a new position rather than copied it.

In this case merely use the mouse to drag it back to its original position and try again.

Activity 5   Testing assumptions. What if?

A major advantage of worksheets is the ability to test out various assumptions by altering the values and noting the results – the so-called 'what if' factor .

In our example we will find out what would happen if we cut down on the term's expenditure so that we can end the term in the black.

1   Make the following two changes to Sheet1 (2) for weeks **6-10:** The easiest way is to amend the relevant value for week 6, then Fill-Right.

☐   Reduce the amount spent on books to zero.

☐   Spend £5 less on food and travel per week.

However you still end the term with a £55 overdraft!

Save the worksheet at this point.

2   Let's assume that you find a part time job at £20 a week from week 7 onwards. This involves inserting an extra row to hold this new income category.

First select the row designator for row 7.

Open the **Insert** menu and select **Rows.**

A new row is inserted, label it 'Part Time Job'.

Now insert 20 for 7–10 weeks.

If entered correctly, this extra income means that you end the term with £25.

This is obviously only a simple example of building alternative models, based on different assumptions. In later units we will use more sophisticated analysis tools.

3   If you are not continuing with the next unit then save and close the workbook.

Summary of commands

Notes

Menu commands show the menu name first, followed by the command to choose from the menu, e.g. Edit-Clear means open the Edit menu and select the Clear command.

Menu commands

Edit-Clear-All	Delete cell contents
Edit-Delete	Delete selected rows or columns
Edit-Undo	Undo previous operation
File-Close	Close current workbook
File-Exit	Exit Excel
File-New	Open new, blank workbook
File-Open	Retrieve an existing workbook
File-Page Setup	Amend page settings for printing
File-Print	Print worksheet
File-Save	Save current workbook
Format-AutoFormat	Apply Excel built-in format
Format-Cells-Border	Add cell borders
Format-Column-Width	Adjust column width
Format-Cells-Font	Embolden, Italics, character size and style
Format-Cells-Alignment	Align text blocks
Format-Cells-Number	Format numbers, percentages etc.
Format-Row-Height	Adjust row height
Insert-Column	Insert a blank column
Insert-Rows	Insert a blank row
Tools-Options-View	Do/do not display gridlines etc.
Window-Freeze Panes	Freeze row and column headings.
Window-Unfreeze Panes	Unfreeze row and column headings.

Standard toolbar

New Workbook   Print   Print Preview   Cut, Copy & Paste   AutoSum   Function Wizard   Chart Wizard   Zoom   Tips

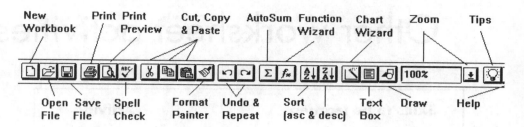

Open File   Save File   Spell Check   Format Painter   Undo & Repeat   Sort (asc & desc)   Text Box   Draw   Help

Formatting toolbar

Font Selection   Font Size   Text Alignment   Currency   Percent   Border   Cell Colour

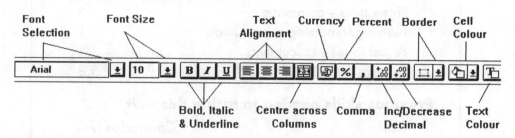

Bold, Italic & Underline   Centre across Columns   Comma   Inc/Decrease Decimal   Text Colour

Other worksheet activities

Skills to be learned	Activity
Absolute addressing	5.8
Averages – calculating	5
Deleting a worksheet	3
Formatting – automatic	6
Naming/renaming a workbook	1
Percentages – calculating	5
Relative addressing	5.8

Previous skills needed to tackle this unit

Skill	Covered in Unit
How to open a workbook and enter simple worksheet data.	1
How to edit and delete data	2
Copying a Worksheet	3
Using the SUM Function	2

Previous work needed

The workbook TERMS created in units 1–3

Introduction

In this unit you will be rounding off your basic worksheet skills and learning how to name and delete worksheets. You will also be using the Excel automatic formatting features and learning some more simple functions. You will be given the chance to check your progress with some independent work.

Activity 1   Naming a worksheet

At the moment our workbook **TERMS** contains a two worksheets with the default names **Sheet1** and **Sheet 1 (2)** . We will give them the more meaningful names 'pessimistic model' and 'optimistic model'

A sheet name can be up to 31 characters long. It can contain spaces, but the following special characters **cannot** be used: [ ], /, \, ? and *

If you are not continuing from the previous unit then you will need to open the workbook **TERMS** created in Unit 1.

1   Make sure that Sheet1 is the active sheet. (Click the tab)

Open the **Format** menu and select **Sheet** then the **Rename** options.

A dialog box appears.

2   The **Name** box should already be selected. Type the name 'pessimistic model'

Click the **OK** button – the sheet name appears as the name tab.

3   Repeat this operation for Sheet1 (2), naming it 'optimistic model'.

Hint: Renaming worksheets makes the name tabs larger. This means that not all name tabs are visible at the same time. You may need to start using the arrow buttons to the left of the sheet tabs to find the sheet that you need.

Activity 2   Consolidation – check your progress

Copy the sheet 'optimistic model' (hold down the Ctrl key and drag the sheet by its tab) renaming it 'Spring Term', then make the following changes:

1   From week 3 onwards Accommodation rises to £65 a week.

2   Your parents send you £30 for your birthday in week 8.

3   You want to go to an end of term celebration in week 10. Add an appropriate amount to the 'Other' category for week 10 so that you end the Spring Term with £5.

4   Save these changes and use **Appendix 2** to check your calculations.

Activity 3   Deleting a worksheet from a workbook

From time to time you may need to discard unwanted worksheets from a workbook. We now have three worksheets in the workbook TERM1.XLS – 'pessimistic model', 'optimistic model', and 'Spring Term'. Let's assume that the first sheet, 'pessimistic model' was an original cash flow forecast that is no longer needed.

Click the name tab **'pessimistic model'** to activate it.

Open the **Edit** menu and select the **Delete Sheet** option.

A dialog box appears, warning the sheet will be permanently deleted.

Make sure that you are deleting the correct sheet, then click **OK.**

Activity 4   Independent activities

1   Copy the worksheet 'Spring Term' under new name 'Summer Term'

2   Modify the income and expenditure categories and amounts to fit your own financial situation.

3   Print out the 'Summer Term' worksheet using the File menu or the Print button.

Here are some additional hints on the use of the Print dialog box as a guide.

a.   Select **Page Setup** and use the **Page** option to print width-ways in **landscape.**

b.   Select the Print option then the **Selected Sheets** option to print the whole sheet

c.   In the **Print Preview** option check the appearance of your sheet before you print

4   Exit from Excel.

Activity 5   Consolidation – averages and percentages

In this activity we will recap on some of the skills that you have learnt and also find out how to calculate averages and percentages.

We will create a new workbook for this activity

1   Open a new workbook. If you have started a new Excel session then one is provided, otherwise open the **File** menu and select **New.**

2   Now create the worksheet shown in Figure 1 as follows.

Format the worksheet as shown:

❑   title centred across columns A – E

❑   cell labels in bold and centred

❑   values centred in cells

3   Calculate the quarterly totals in column E using the SUM function for row 4 then Edit-Fill-Down. Calculate the totals in row 9 next, using Edit-Fill-Right.

Don't just type the totals in.

4 **Save** the workbook as **INS_SLS.XLS** – remember to select the correct drive.

Cancel the Summary Information dialog box.

5 We now wish to find the average sales for each type of insurance and place them in row 8.

	A	B	C	D	E	F
1		Insurance Sales - First Quarter				
2						
3		Motor	Life	Property	Total	
4	Jan	1465	1243	2456	5164	
5	Feb	1345	1456	1987	4788	
6	Mar	1132	2310	1598	5040	
7						
8	Quarterly Average					
9	Quarterly Total	3942	5009	6041	14992	
10	% of Total					

Figure 1

Select cell **B8** and enter the formula **=AVERAGE(B4:B6)**

Click the tick box and the three cells are averaged. (1314)

Use **Edit-Fill-Right** to average Life, Property and Total categories too.

Now centre the row 8 values three values in their cells.

7 Next we will express the quarterly totals – cells B9 to D9 – as fractions of the total sales – cell E9.

Select cell **B10** and enter the Formula **=B9/$E$9**

Click the tick box.

The quarterly total for motor insurance is shown as a decimal fraction of the overall quarterly total – the value 0.26 is displayed in the cell

8 **Explanation of the formula.**

a. The / sign represents division.

b. **Absolute and Relative References.** So far all the cell references that you have been using are *relative* references. This means that the references of cells used in a formula are relative to the location of the cell where the formula is placed. This allows Excel to automatically adjust the cell references in formulae when cells are copied, as we have seen. However this would not work for the percentages that we have just calculated as they must all be based upon one fixed cell – E9. We do not want this cell value to be adjusted when we use the Fill Right command. The dollar signs in front of the column and row number make it into an *absolute* reference and prevent this happening.

9   Percentages.

Now to turn this into a percentage.

Make sure that cell **B10** is still selected.

Open the **Format** menu and select **Cells** then the **Number** tab.

Click the **Percentage** option in the **Category** box.

Select the format **0.00%** from the **Format Codes** box. Click **OK**.

10   Motor insurance is now shown as 26.29% of total sales.

Use the **Edit-Fill-Right** command to show Life and Property as percentages too.

11   Finally add a text box to the worksheet, explaining its function.

The Text Box tool is provided on the Standard Toolbar – see the tool bar key at the end of this unit.

Click the Text Box tool – the pointer changes to cross hairs.

Locate the screen pointer on the top left-hand corner of cell **B12**.

Drag across and down to cell **E14**. The text box is now drawn.

Enter the text, 'This worksheet shows a sales analysis of the three major insurance categories.'

You will see that the text wraps automatically to the size of the box.

Hint: Remove an unwanted box by clicking the border to select it. Then select Clear from the Edit menu.

12   Compare your worksheet to Appendix 3.

13   Save and close the workbook.

Activity 6   Automatic formatting of worksheets

Excel's AutoFormat feature allows you to format your worksheets automatically, offering 17 built-in formats to choose from. This allows you to format either a range of cells or a complete worksheet in attractive, standardised formats, thereby saving the time and effort of designing your own.

1   Open the workbook **INS_SLS.XLS**.

Select all the cells in the worksheet.

2   Open the **Format** menu and select **AutoFormat**

A dialog box appears showing a sample worksheet.

3   **Reviewing the Formats.**

Take some time to select each of the various formats listed in the table; the sample worksheet changes to illustrate each format selected.

4   Now select the **Classic 3** format and then **OK.**

Your worksheet is converted to the format chosen, but you will probably not be happy with its appearance, e.g. the columns are too wide.

5   **Undoing a Format Change.**

Open the Edit menu and select Undo AutoFormat – your worksheet is restored to its previous format.

Hints. Always use Undo immediately after making any unwanted change. If not then Select Format-AutoFormat, then scroll down the Table Format list and select the None option then OK. You may find that the original formatting has disappeared. If all else fails then closing the worksheet without saving it will undo any disastrous mistakes – but you will also lose any other changes made since the worksheet was opened or saved.

6   **Selecting a Format.**

Make sure that the worksheet cells are still selected and open the AutoFormat menu again.

Select the **Classic 3** format from the table and then click the **Options** button.

Six **Formats to Apply** are offered at the bottom of the dialog box; initially all options are selected. Try deselecting and reselecting all of them and notice their effect on the sample. When a format is deselected, such as Border or Alignment, the present formats continue to apply.

7   Now deselect the **Font, Alignment** and the **Width/Height** options then click OK.

The worksheet is reformatted in the Classic 3 format, minus the options that we have deselected.

Restore the worksheet to its original format – see section 5 above.

8   We could choose to save these changes using Save, but we won't bother in this instance. Close the workbook without saving.

Summary of commands and functions

Notes

Menu commands show the menu name first, followed by the command to choose from the menu, e.g. Edit-Clear means open the Edit menu and select the Clear command.

Menu commands

Edit-Clear-All	Delete cell contents
Edit-Delete Sheet	Delete selected worksheet
Edit-Fill-Right	Copy selected cells into selected right hand columns
Edit-Undo	Undo previous operation
File-Close	Close current workbook
File-Exit	Exit Excel
File-New	Open new, blank workbook
File-Open	Retrieve an existing workbook
File-Page Setup	Amend page settings for printing
File-Print	Print worksheet
File-Save	Save current workbook
Format-AutoFormat	Apply Excel built-in format
Format-Sheet-Rename	Rename Selected Sheet

Functions

=AVERAGE()	Average range of cells

Standard toolbar

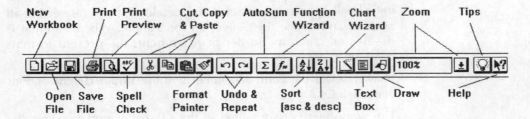

Formatting toolbar

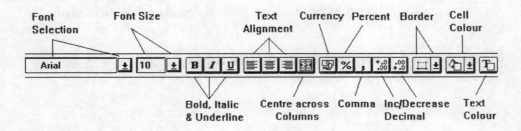

Creating some simple charts

Skills to be learned — **Activity**

Skills to be learned	Activity
AutoFormat – using	4
Chart – creating	2
Chart size – altering	3
ChartWizard – using	2
Column chart – creating	2
Moving chart components	9
Pie chart – creating	5
Retrieving a chart	8
Saving a chart	8
Windows – re-arranging	6

Previous skills needed to tackle this unit

Skill	Covered in Unit
How to create a simple worksheet	1 and 2
How to create a chart	5

Introduction

In earlier units we covered some important worksheet skills – including entering data and using formulae to calculate and printing. In the next 4 units we're going to use charts and graphs to present the worksheet data in a more visual way.

Excel uses a special feature called **ChartWizard** which guides you through a series of simple steps and lets you create a wide variety of different chart types – line graphs, pie charts, bar charts etc. You can either **embed** a chart in your worksheet or create it as a separate **chart sheet**.

We will be looking at all these approaches and finding out how to alter and format charts for the best results.

Activity 1   Creating some chart data

1   If you are starting a new Excel session then open Excel as before; you will see a blank worksheet window.

2   We need some worksheet data before we can produce charts. Create the following simple worksheet shown in Figure 1. It shows the number of holidays sold by a travel company for various European countries.

EUROSLS.XLS

	A	B	C	D	E	F
1	Sunfilled Holidays					
2			Holidays Sold - Europe			
3						
4		1st Quarter	2nd Quarter	3rd Quarter	4th Quarter	Total
5						
6	Italy	85	99	200	93	477
7	Spain	150	246	355	145	896
8	Portugal	120	180	300	123	723
9	Greece	168	277	320	162	927
10	France	70	120	250	110	550
11						
12	Total	593	922	1425	2940	3573
13						

Sheet1 / Sheet2 / Sheet3 / Sheet4 / S

Figure 1

Format it as shown, i.e. data centred in columns, column widths adjusted, and headings and labels in bold.

3   Next total the first column in cell B12, using a formula or the Auto Sum button.

4   Copy this formula to the next 3 cells. (C12-E12)

5   Calculate the totals across in a similar way.

As a check the grand total for all holidays should be 3573. If not check your data and your formulae!

6   Now save the workbook as **EUROSLS.** When the Summary dialog box appears enter some information, eg title and subject

We can now use this worksheet to create a variety of charts.

Activity 2   Creating a chart using ChartWizard

ChartWizard allows you to create simple charts using 5 steps:

1.   Select the cells you wish to use in the chart

2.   Select the type of chart – bar, column, pie chart etc.

3.   Choose a format for the for chosen chart type – 3D, stacked etc

4.   Specify the axis, data series etc.

5.   Add titles and legend.

Dialog boxes guide you through these 5 steps. At each step you have the option of cancelling, getting help, going back a step, or going on to the next step.

First we will create a pie chart of the first quarter's sales:

1   Select the cell range **A6 – B10.** (ie 10 cells in all)

Open the **Insert** menu and select **Chart**

Select the **As New Sheet** option – see Figure 2.

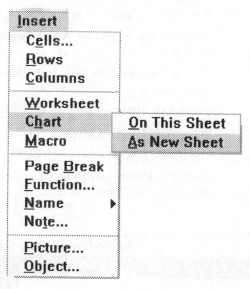

Figure 2

2   The first ChartWizard dialog box is displayed –

ChartWizard – Step 1 of 5

Step 1 allows you to confirm or change the range of cells (A6-B10) that you wish to chart. Check them – notice that they are shown as absolute references – with dollar signs inserted. If they are incorrect then amend them or press the Cancel button and start again.

Hint: You can drag the dialog box to one side by its title bar in order to view the worksheet better.

If correct click the **Next** button to go to –

ChartWizard – Step 2 of 5

Step 2 allows you to choose the chart type. Click Column then the Next button to go to –

ChartWizard – Step 3 of 5

Step 3 displays alternative formats for the chart type that you chose in step 2. Select format 1 then the Next button to go to –

ChartWizard – Step 4 of 5

Step 4 previews the final chart. Click the **Back** button to return to Step 3 and then select chart format **6**.

Click the **Next** button to return to Step 4. (you can retrace your steps as often as you wish)

Click the **Next** button again to go to –

ChartWizard – Step 5 of 5

Step 5 allows you to add titles and a legend to your chart.

Click the **No** Button for **Add a Legend –** our column chart will not need one .

Click the **Chart Title** box and enter ' 1st Quarter Holiday Sales' – this is added to the preview box.

In the **Axis Titles – Category (X)** box add the title 'Country'

In the **Axis Titles – Category (Y)** box add the title 'Number Sold'

The dialog box should now look like Figure 3:

Click the **Finish** button and the Chart is displayed; it is given the default name Chart1

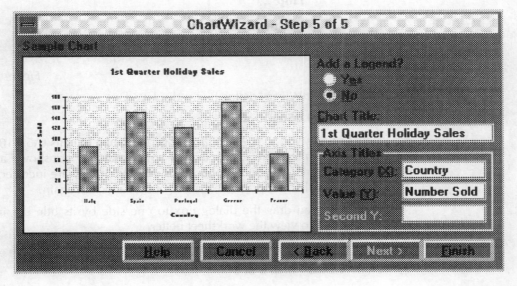

Figure 3

Activity 3   Re-sizing the chart

When a chart is first created its size is independent of the window size, with a result that the chart and the titles may be too small. The View menu offers two options to resize a chart.

1   First maximise the chart window if necessary.

   Open the **View** window and select the option **Sized with Window.** The Chart expands to fill the window space available.

2   Alter the Window size – the chart size automatically changes too.

   Open the **View** menu and select **Full Screen.** The chart can be seen at maximum size.

3   Repeat step 1 and the Sized with Window option is **deselected** – it is no longer 'ticked'. Now reduce the Window size and you will find that part of the chart may no longer be visible.

4   Open the **View** menu and select the **Zoom** option – a dialog box opens allowing you to specify a particular chart size, independent of window size. (this option is unavailable while the **Sized with Window** option is selected)

   Try out various scales – the larger the scale the more detail you can read, but the less the amount of the chart that will fit in the window.

   Finally try out the **Fit Selection** option, this fits the chart to the window size available.

5   Now deselect the **Full Screen** option and reselect the **Sized with Window** option.

   Note: Don't worry about the chart toolbar for the moment – it can be dragged out of the way using its title bar.

Activity 4   Explanation of the chart

Excel has plotted a standard column chart, based on the data contained in cells A6 to B10. Let's study chart and worksheet for a few moments, and see how Excel plots a chart; key terms that you should remember are in bold:-

a.   The 5 columns on the chart show the values of the 5 worksheet cells that you selected – cells B6 – B10,

   Each value is called a **data point.**

   In this simple chart there are 5 data points forming a data series – the holidays sold for each country – and 5 corresponding columns on the chart.

b.   The columns are charted on the **Y** or **vertical** axis, also called the **value** axis.

c.   The **X** or **horizontal** axis shows the 5 categories; for this reason the X axis is also referred to as the **category** axis.

Excel takes the text labels for each row – Italy, Spain etc – and places them on the X axis as category names.

Activity 5   Changing the chart type using autoformat

Although we have plotted the worksheet data as a column chart, we can convert it to another type of chart at any time. You can click the ChartWizard button, or you use the AutoFormat option, which offers you a range of built-in formats to choose.

1   Make sure that Chart1 is still the active document, i.e. overlaying the worksheet.

Open the **Format** menu and select **AutoFormat.** A dialog box opens, offering you a choice of chart types – select **Pie** from the **Galleries** menu

You are offered a choice of several pie chart formats.

Format 1 is already selected

2   Select **OK** – the chart is re-plotted as a pie chart.

Pie charts are good for showing the relative contributions of various elements to the total 'pie'. This can be shown as a number or as a percentage. However, there are now no X or Y axes so the coloured sections need a key or **legend** to explain them.

3   **Adding a Legend.** Open the **Insert** menu and select **Legend.**

The legend appears on the chart, surrounded by a selection rectangle.

Press the **Esc** key to remove it

Activity 6   Moving between chart and worksheet

1   The pie chart **Chart1** and the worksheet **Sheet1** are two separate documents.

At the moment the chart overlays the worksheet – it is the 'active window'

Click the sheet tab for Sheet1, it overlays the chart to become the active window.

Note.   If the sheet tabs are not visible then maximise the workbook window – see Unit 1, Activity 2. if necessary.

2   Let's now make the two windows smaller so that we can see chart and worksheet alongside each other – see Figure 4.

EUROSLS.XLS:1			
	A	B	C
1	Sunfilled Holidays		
2			Holidays Sold - E
3			
4		1st Quarter	2nd Quarter	3rd
5			
6	Italy	85	99
7	Spain	150	246
8	Portugal	120	180
9	Greece	168	277
10	France	70	120
11			
12	Total	593	922

Sheet1

EUROSLS.XLS:2 [Group]

1st Quarter Holiday Sales

- Italy
- Spain
- Portu;
- Greec
- Franc

Chart1 / Sheet1

Figure 4

First make the chart the active window.

Now open the **Window** menu and select the **New Window** option.

Excel opens a second window so that more than one workbook document can be seen at the same time

Open the Window menu again; two documents are listed at the bottom of the menu – **EUROSLS.XLS:1** and **EUROSLS.XLS:2**. At the moment they are both copies of the pie chart.

3   Click the sheet tab for **Sheet1** to make it the active window.

4   **Arranging Windows.**

Windows offers several ways of viewing both windows at the same time.

Open the **Window** menu and select **Arrange.** The Arrange Windows dialog box appears.

Select the **Arrange-Cascade** option then the **Windows of Active Workbook** option. Click **OK.**

The two windows are arranged in an overlapping pattern. Click on the border of each window – this is a quick way to move from one window to another.

Open the **Window-Arrange** menu again.

This time select the **Arrange Vertical** option (and the **Windows of Active Workbook** option if necessary) The two windows are displayed side by side – see Figure 4 above.

5   **Re-sizing the Windows.**

Click each window in turn – it becomes the active window. If necessary you can move each window by dragging the title and re-size the chart or the worksheet by dragging the sides. Do not overdo this with the chart as its dimensions can become rather 'squashed'.

6   **Troubleshooting.**

Note that sheet tabs are available for both windows. If the chart or the sheet have disappeared check that Sheet1 and Chart1 are the active windows.

Activity 7   Re-plotting a chart

1   Now that Chart and Worksheet are both displayed side by side we can show the dynamic relationship between them.

Click the worksheet to activate it

2   Select cell **B7** and amend the number of Spanish holidays to **500.**

Press **Enter.** The pie chart also changes to reflect this.

3   Open the **Edit** menu and select **Undo Entry.**

The pie chart returns to its previous shape.

Activity 8   Saving and retrieving a chart

1   Open the **File** menu and select **Save.** The chart is saved under its default name Chart1, as part of the workbook EUROSLS.XLS.

Note: If you have had several tries at creating charts then the default chart name will be Chart2, Chart3 etc. Deleting an unwanted chart is the same procedure as for a worksheet – Open the Edit menu and select Delete Sheet. Make sure that the correct sheet is selected as the deletion cannot be undone.

2   To check this open the **File** menu and select **Close.** A dialog box may prompt you to save any changes to Sheet1, the other document in the workbook. If so, click the **Yes** button and exit.

3   Now again open the workbook EUROSLS using the File menu – you may notice that it is listed at the bottom of the File menu. The last 4 documents that you have used are listed in this way.

Activity 9   Moving pie chart segments

1   Makes sure that Chart 1 is the active sheet in the workbook.

Activate the pie chart by clicking it.

2   Place the screen pointer on the segment denoting Portugal and click once – 'handles' appear on the segment.

3   Now drag the segment slightly away from the rest of the pie chart – this can be used for emphasis.

4   Press the Esc key to turn off the handles.

Troubleshooting: Use the **Edit – Undo** option to reverse any mistake you make.

If you double click on the pie then you may call up the Format Data Point dialog box. If so cancel it and try again.

Activity 10 Adding values to a chart

It can be difficult to judge the relative proportions of the pie chart segments unless the values are added. The Insert menu allows us to add the actual values to pie segments. (and other types of chart)

1   Open the **Insert** menu and select **Data Labels.**

2   The dialog box offers a number of options – try each one in turn.

Finally select the option **Show Percent.** Your pie chart will resemble Figure 5.

1st Quarter European Holiday Sales

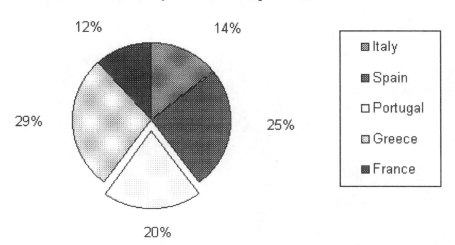

Figure 5

3   If you are not proceding directly to the next unit then use the File menu to save and close your workbook

Summary of commands

Note

Menu commands show the menu name first, followed by the command to choose from the menu, e.g. Edit-Clear means open the Edit menu and select the Clear command.

Format-Autoformat	Select pre-formatted chart type
Insert-Chart	Create a new chart
Insert-Data Labels	Label chart values
Insert-Legend	Add legend to chart
View-Fit Selection	Chart fits window size available
View-Full Screen	Sheet increases to full screen size
View-Sized With Window	Re-size chart to window size
Window-Arrange	Arrange layout of windows
Window-New Window	Open extra window

Further chart types and skills

Skills to be learned	Activity
Arrow – adding	2
Colours – changing	4
Copying a chart	10
Formatting a chart	2
Legend – adding	6
Line chart – creating	5
Moving chart components	1, 7
Naming a chart	9
Non-adjacent cells – charting	8
Patterns – changing	4
Printing a chart	3
Text – adding	2
Titles – adding	6

Previous skills needed to tackle this unit

Skill	Covered in Unit
How to create a simple worksheet	1,2
How to create a chart	5

Introduction

You now know how to create some simple charts. In this unit we will be learning how to print charts and more on how to alter and improve their appearance. We will also be naming and copying charts.

Activity 1   Moving and re-sizing chart items

Whenever you change a chart you may want to alter the size and layout of its component parts, eg pie segments, segment labels, title or legend.

You can do this quite easily with the mouse – first click the item that you want to work on to select it, then use the mouse to drag on. Any item in a chart can be selected in this way.

Hint: You will find that it takes a little practice to select the right item – particularly when they are close together. Persevere and remember these simple rules:

❐ An item is not selected unless it is enclosed in selection 'handles'

❐ Click elsewhere or press the Esc key to remove selection handles

❐ Undo an incorrect operation straightaway, using the Edit-Undo option

❐ Single click not double click

Note. If you are starting a new Excel session then you will need to open the Workbook EUROSLS created in the previous unit. Make sure that Chart 1 is the active sheet.

1   First experiment and click the various parts of the chart in turn to select them – pie segments, segment labels, title or legend.

Now click on the Legend box – it is surrounded by a selection rectangle upon which are a number of square 'handles'

2   Move the screen pointer onto the the top left handle and the pointer changes to a double-headed arrow – see Figure 1.

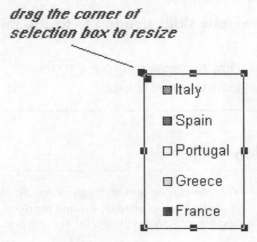

drag the corner of selection box to resize

Figure 1

Drag the selection handle to make the legend slightly larger.

3   Click the outside edge of the pie chart until it is surrounded by the selection rectangle – this can be tricky – make sure that the whole

pie is selected not just the individual segments or labels – see Figure 2.

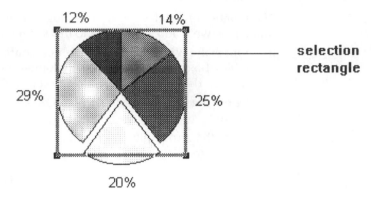

selection
rectangle

Figure 2

Now make the pie chart slightly larger by0 dragging the selection handle on the bottom right corner.

4   Now click the title until it is surrounded by the selection rectangle and move it up the window. (nb the title cannot be resized by dragging – see next activity for formatting text)

Next click in front of the word 'Holiday' in the title – an insertion point is placed there.

Insert the word 'European' – the title is amended.

Activity 2   Formatting a chart

We are going to format the pie chart further to improve its appearance .

1   Make sure that the pie chart is still the active sheet.

2   **Changing Text Fonts and Style.**

First we will make the title more prominent.

Move the screen pointer onto the title and click once – it should be enclosed by a selection rectangle.

Open the **Format** menu and select **Selected Chart Title** – the Format dialog box appears.

Click the **Font** tab in the dialog box and you are offered a range of fonts, sizes and styles.

Choose **Helvetica** font (or another font if this is not available)

Alter the size to **14** Point.

Select **Bold,** then **OK.**

The title will now change – click the title again to deselect it.

Note. Bold and Italic options are also available on the toolbars

3   **Adding Text and Arrows.**

The number of holidays sold for Portugal seems rather low for this quarter, so we'll add a comment to this segment.

a.   Open the **View** menu and select **Toolbars** – the Toolbars dialog box allows you to display further toolbars in addition to the two defaults which are already selected.

Select the **Drawing** toolbar plus **OK** – it is displayed on your chart.

Click the arrow button – it is the downwards-pointing arrow – see figure 3.

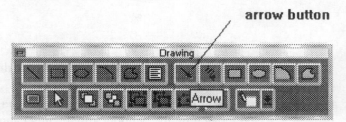

Figure 3

b.   The screen pointer changes to a cross; drag to draw the arrow, as shown in Figure 4 below.

If you make a mistake then make sure that the arrow is still selected and press the **Delete** key.

c.   Adding text to the arrow is simple; type the comment 'What went wrong?'

The comment appears in the Formula Bar at the top of the screen.

e.   Click the Tick Box next to the Entry Box.

The comment now appears on the screen enclosed by handles.

f.   Place the screen pointer *on the selection rectangle itself but not on one of the handles* and drag the text to move it next to the arrow.

g.   Now try re-sizing the text; assuming that the text is still selected, click the **Bold** button. If you wish to experiment with further styles or colour then use the Format menu as you did in section 2 above.

h.   If you have made a serious mistake you can delete selected text with the Delete key and start again.

4   **Independent Activity.**

Using the techniques you have just learnt format the percentage labels on the pie chart.

5   If you are happy with the changes – compare your chart with Figure 4 – then save them, if not use the Edit-Undo option.

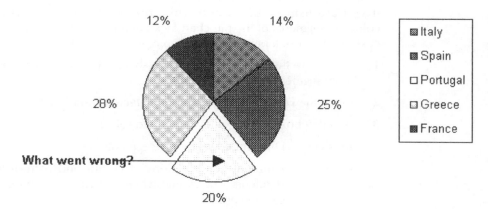

1st Quarter European Holiday Sales

Figure 4

Activity 3   Printing a chart

1   Make sure that the Chart1 is the active sheet.

Open the **File** menu and select **Print.** (you can also use the Print button on the Standard Toolbar).

Troubleshooting: If the Print option is dimmed it is unavailable, check that you have completed any operations – the tick box should not be displayed in the Formula bar

2   A Print dialog box opens;

First select the number of copies.

If you wish to check the page setup or the printer setup then take the appropriate option on the File menu.

Now click the **Preview** button – the Print Preview screen shows the chart as it will appear on the printed page.

To see more detail use either click the part of the image that you wish to enlarge or use the **Zoom** button.

If you are satisfied click the **Print** button, otherwise the **Close** button.

3   If nothing happens then check that :-

☐   The printer is switched on – both at the mains and on the printer!

☐   The Online Switch on the printer is on.

☐   The cable from the computer to the back of the printer is connected.

☐   The paper supply/feed trays are OK.

Activity 4   Changing chart patterns and colours

If you are using a black and white printer you may find that the coloured segments of the pie chart lack contrast when printed, in which case you can use a pattern rather than a plain block of colour.

1   Make sure that Chart1 is the active sheet. Click a segment to select a pie segment – the handles appear.

2   Open the **Format** menu and select **Selected Data Point.**

3   A dialog box appears, allowing you to select :-

Border   Different edges for the segments

Area   Different combinations of colour and pattern for the segments – black and white patterns are best for mono-chrome printers.

Select suitable combinations and click **OK.**

4   Save the changes to the pie chart.

Activity 5   Creating line charts

We are going to use data in the worksheet to create another type of chart – the line chart. Line charts are good for showing trends over time.

1   Make sure that the workbook EUROSLS is open. Make sure that Sheet 1 is the active sheet.

2   Let's compare the sales for Italy and Spain for the 4 quarters.

Select cells **A4** to **E7,** a block of 20 cells.

3   Open the **Insert** menu and select **Chart.**

4   Select the **As New Sheet** option. The Chart Wizard 'Step 1 of 5' dialog box is displayed. Check that the cell range selected is correct, then click the **Next** button.

5   Select Line from the 'Step 2 of 5' dialog box then click the **Next** button.

6   Select format 1 from the 'Step 3 of 5' dialog box and press the **Next** button.

7   Click the **Next** button on the 'Step 4 of 5' dialog box.

8   On the final dialog box click the **No** button for the **Add Legend** option and click the **Finish** button. The line chart appears with the default name Chart2.

9   Open the **View** menu and select the option **Sized with Window.** The line chart expands to fill the window – enlarge the window if necessary.

It lacks a legend and titles because we did not use ChartWizard to add them; however we can do this at a later stage, in our next Activity.

Activity 6   Adding chart titles and legend

The Insert and Format menu offers different ranges of options, depending whether a chart or worksheet is the active sheet. We will try out some of them in this activity

1   Make sure that the line chart created in the previous activity is the active sheet. Open the **Insert** menu and select the **Titles** option.

2   Select **Chart Title** from the Titles dialog box and click the **OK** button.

3   A title box appears at the top of the chart. Simply type 'Sales for Italy and Spain' and press **Enter** – the text is placed in the title box.

4   Now open the **Insert** menu and select the **Titles** option again. This time select the option **Value (Y) Axis.**

Type the title 'Holidays Sold' and press Enter.

5   Repeat the above operations to add the title 'Current Year' to the X axis.

6   Use the **Insert** menu again to add a legend.

Activity 7   Re-positioning titles and legend using the format menu

You can drag titles and legends to new positions with the mouse, but the Format menu offers further options which we will try out now.

1   Click the title for the Y axis, 'Holidays Sold' to select it.

Open the **Format** menu and select the option **Selected Axis Title.**

2   The **Format** dialog box opens, click the **Alignment** tab. You are offered various options – see Figure 5. – select the horizontal orientation option then click **OK**

3   The title 'Holidays Sold' is now displayed horizontally – more readably but it may overlap the chart itself. You can select the title then drag it and/or re-size it if this is a problem. You can see in Figure 6 that it is also possible to split the title over two lines – see if you can work out how!

4   **Independent Activities.**

a.   Select the legend and experiment with the Format menu to change its style and alignment.

b.   Use the **AutoFormat** option on the **Format** menu to try out other Line Chart types – return to type 1 when you have finished.

c.   Finally print the line chart and compare it to Figure 6.

horizontal orientation
selected

alignment option
selected

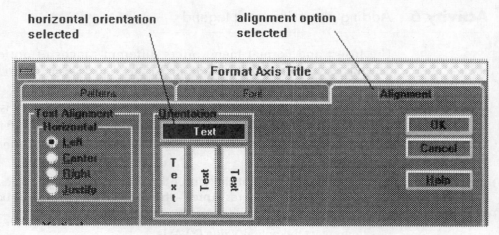

Figure 5

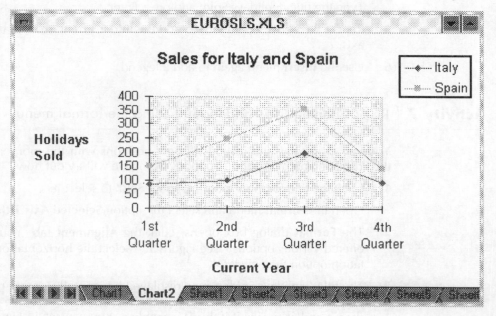

Figure 6

Activity 8 Charting non-adjacent cell ranges

Sometimes you may wish to chart data from different parts of a work-sheet. Using the Ctrl key we can select cell ranges that are not adjacent and base charts on them, eg those for Italy and France in our present workbook.

1 Make sure that Sheet 1 is the active sheet. Select the column head-ings **A4** to **E4.**

2   Now hold down the Ctrl key and select the 4 quarters sales for for Italy – cells **A6** to **E6.**

Repeat these operations for the row for France – cells **A10** to **E10**.

3   Now create another line chart, using ChartWizard as before, adding a legend.

Your chart should resemble Figure 7.

4   Add a suitable title to the chart – see previous Activity .

This chart has the default name Chart3 (or a later number if you have created other charts)

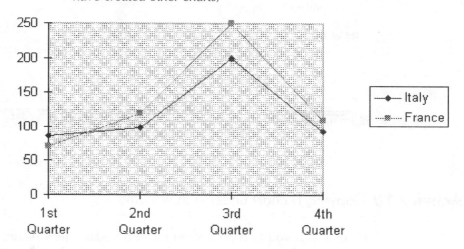

Figure 7

Activity 9   Naming charts

At the moment the workbook **EUROSLS.XLS** contains a worksheet with the default name **Sheet1** , plus 3 charts with the default names:

Chart1 – the pie chart created in Unit 5.

Chart2 – the line chart (Italy and Spain) created in activity 5

Chart 3 – the line chart (Italy and France) created in activity 8

(your documents may be numbered differently, depending on how many other sheets and charts you have created)

We will give them the more meaningful names. A chart name, like a sheet name, can be up to 31 characters long. It can contain spaces, but the following special characters **cannot** be used: [ ], /, \, **?** and *

1   Make sure that **Sheet1** is the active sheet – the sheet tab should be selected.

Note: If the sheet tabs are not visible then you may need to maximise the document window. Open the Format menu and select Sheet then the Rename options.

A dialog box appears.

2   Select the **Name** box and type the name **Euro Hols Data.** Click the **OK** button – the sheet name appears on the name tab.

3   Repeat this operation: Activate the chart sheets in turn

Name the pie chart **PIE1** and the line charts **LINE1** and **LINE2** respectively – the sheet tabs at the bottom of the screen should now resemble Figure 8.

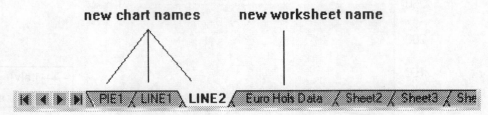

Figure 8

Activity 10 Copying a chart under a new name

Excel allows you to copy a sheet under a under a new name. We will do this and then modify the copy, leaving the original unchanged.

1   Click the name tab for **Line2** to make it the active window.

2   Hold down the **Ctrl** key and then use the mouse pointer to drag the name tab along past the next name tab – the cursor changes to an icon marked with a + sign.

3   The place where the copy will be placed is marked with a small triangle.

Release the mouse button then the Ctrl key and the copy is made – the name tab is marked **LINE2 (2)**

Troubleshooting: If you let go the Ctrl key too soon then you may merely have moved Sheet1 to a new position. In this case use the mouse on the name tab to drag it back to its original position and try again.

4   Now use the **Format** menu to rename the copy **LINE3.**

5   If you are not proceding directly to the next unit then use the File menu to save and close your workbook

Summary of commands

Note

Menu commands show the menu name first, followed by the command to choose from the menu, e.g. Edit-Clear means open the Edit menu and select the Clear command.

File-Print	Print Chart
Format-Selected.....	Format selected chart element
Format-Sheet-Rename	Name a chart sheet
Insert-Chart	Create a new chart
Insert-Titles	Create axis or chart title
View-Toolbars	Show or hide a tool bar

Further chart operations

Skills to be learned	Activity
Area chart – creating	3
Bar chart – creating	7
Chart axes – altering	1,5
Column chart – creating	7
Combination chart – creating	8
Deleting a chart	2
Gridlines – adding	6
Removing chart components	4

Previous skills needed to tackle this unit

Skill	Covered in Unit
How to create a simple worksheet	1 and 2
How to create a chart	5

Introduction

In this unit we look at chart axes and chart values in more detail. We will also create bar, column, area and combination charts.

Activity 1 Re-scaling a chart axis

On the line chart LINE2 (and the copy LINE3) the values for Italy and France are very close at some points, making them difficult to read. This is because the scale is not the best one for the range of values on the chart. We can change this default scale.

Note. If you are starting a new Excel session then you will need to open the Workbook EUROSLS.

1   Make sure that LINE3 is the active window.

Move the screen pointer onto the vertical axis and click it to select it – selection handles appear on the axis.

2   Open the **Format** menu and select **Selected Axis;** a dialog box appears.

Select the **Scale** tab – the dialog box now resembles Figure 1.

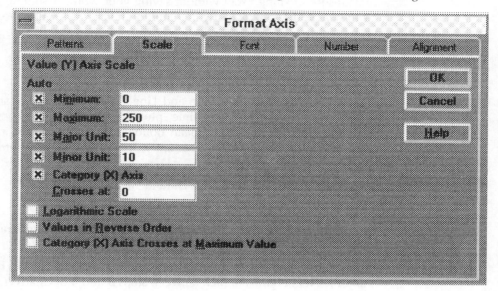

Figure 1

3   The axes and scales on charts are calculated automatically – hence the check marks in the auto boxes – from 0 to 250, the minimum and maximum values.

Type **50** in the **Minimum** box and click **OK.**

4   The chart is replotted to show the new range from 50 to 250, the scale is also plotted in smaller divisions, making values easier to compare.

Open the **Edit** menu and choose the **Undo** and **Re-do** commands to review this.

5   Open the **File** menu and select **Save** to save the changes.

Activity 2   Deleting a Chart

Let's assume that you wish to use the re-scaled chart LINE3 and discard LINE2. You can delete this chart from the workbook

1   Click the name tab for **LINE2** – check that it is now the active chart.

2   Open the **Edit** menu and select the **Delete Sheet** option.

3   A dialog box warns you that the sheet will be permanently deleted.

Check that the correct sheet is selected then click **OK.**

The sheet is now deleted – check that the name tab has disappeared.

Troubleshooting: If you have deleted the wrong sheet there is still a last resort – exiting Excel without saving your work. Assuming that you save your work regularly then not too much work will be lost.

Activity 3   Area Charts

So far we've covered Column, Pie and Line Charts. Area charts show both the amount of change over time, plus the sum of these changes. For example, in the case of European holidays we are not only interested in the performance for each country, but its individual contribution to the total holidays sold.

1   Make the worksheet **Euro Hols Data** the active window.

Select cells **A4** to **E10**, i.e. all countries, all quarters.

2   Create a new chart as before using ChartWizard, selecting **Area** as the chart type.

There are a number to choose from, try them all, ie use the **Back** and the **Next** buttons to flick between steps 3 and 4 of ChartWizard

3   Now select the area chart type 5 that labels both countries and quarters. You will not need a legend for this type of chart so deselect this option.

4   When you finish ChartWizard use the **View – Sized with Window** option to enlarge the chart to the size of the window.

Now add a suitable title in bold; also embolden the labels for the X axis and the 4 quarters – see Figure 2.

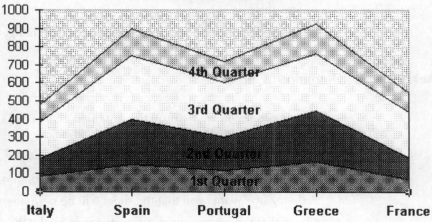

Figure 2

5   Name the chart AREA1 (see Unit 6, Activity 9)

Activity 4   Adding and removing chart values

You can remove a a range of values from a chart without needing to re-plot it; it is simply a matter of selecting that part of the chart and deleting it. Conversely you can add a range of values to a chart simply by copying and pasting from the worksheet to the chart.

1   Make sure that **AREA1** is the active chart.

2   **Removing Chart Values.**

Click once on the area for the 3rd quarter (not on the name), it should now have a number of selection handles; the formula for the cell range is confirmed in the Formula Box at the top of the window – see Figure 3.

The formula looks more complex than it really is because for each cell in the range plotted – D4 to D10 – Excel includes both the sheet name 'Euro Hols Data' and the $ symbol, indicating an absolute reference.

Troubleshooting: Make sure that you select the whole area, not the area label; press the Esc key to deselect – or simply click the correct part of the chart. Double clicking calls up a dialog box – simply click the Cancel button.

3   Now press the **Delete key** and Quarter 3 is removed (the **Edit – Undo** Clear command will reverse it if you make a mistake)

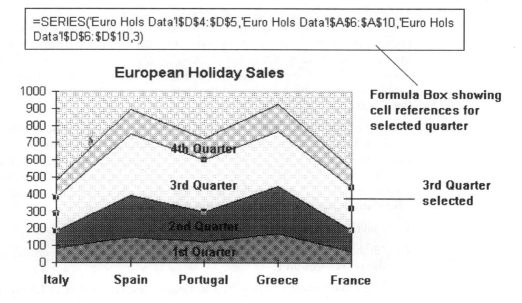

=SERIES('Euro Hols Data'!$D$4:$D$5,'Euro Hols Data'!$A$6:$A$10,'Euro Hols Data'!$D$6:$D$10,3)

Figure 3

4   **Adding Values to a Chart.**

Click the name tab for the sheet Euro Hols Data to make it the active window.

Select the cell range **D4 – D10**, ie for the 3rd quarter that we have just removed.

Open the **Edit** menu and select **Copy**.

5   Now make **Area1** the active window.

Open the **Edit** window and select **Paste**.

The range of values for the 3rd quarter is pasted back into the chart, but in an incorrect position.

6   **Changing the position of a Data Series.**

Click the top of the chart so that the whole chart is selected – enclosed in a selection box.

7   Open the Format menu and select the option **1. Area Group**.

When the Format Area Group dialog box appears, click the **Series Order** tab.

The dialog box allows you to select the 3rd Quarter and move it to its correct position. Do this, then click **OK**.

The 3rd Quarter is now restored to its correct position – compare it to Figure 2.15 above. You may need to re-size the window.

Activity 5   Reversing the chart axes

Study the chart AREA1 carefully; it shows the 5 countries as the categories (along the X or category axis) and the holidays sold in each quarter as the values (along the Y or value axis). However it could be equally useful if the axes were reversed, ie if each quarter formed the categories along the X axis, and the number of holidays the values on the Y axis.

When it plots a chart Excel assumes that you want fewer data series than categories as this is easier to read. In the worksheet 'Euro Hols Data' 5 rows and 4 columns of data were charted, (excluding cell labels) so the columns B to E become the values plotted and the rows 6 – 10 the categories. We can get reverse this using ChartWizard either by creating a new chart or by modifying an existing one

1   Make sure that **AREA1** is the active sheet.

2   Click the **ChartWizard** button on the Standard Toolbar – see key at the end of this unit.

3   The ChartWizard dialog box appears – notice that it is labelled 'Step 1 of 2'.

As we are modifying rather than creating a new chart only 2 of the usual 5 steps are offered. Click the **Next** button.

4   ChartWizard – Step 2 of 2 is displayed; at the top of the dialog box you can opt to display the data series (ie the worksheet values) either in rows, or as currently, in columns, the default arrangement.

5   Experiment with each setting noting the effect on the area chart shown; we have in effect 2 views of the same data:

Data Series in Columns – the countries are the categories, the values for the quarters are plotted on the value axis.

Data Series in Rows – the quarters are categories , the values for the countries are plotted on the value axis.

These techniques can be applied to other chart types.

6   Finally select **Data Series in Rows** and click **OK** – the area chart should now look like Figure 4.

7   **Independent Activity**.

Copy AREA1 to a new sheet, renaming it AREA2 and re-create the first view, showing the data series in columns – see Figure 2 above.

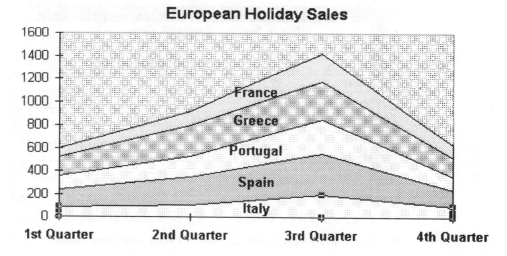

Figure 4

Activity 6   Adding gridlines

Adding gridlines to a chart can help us to read off the values more clearly.

1   Make sure that the chart AREA1 is the active window.

Open the **Insert** menu and select **Gridlines.**

2 A dialog box opens. Select **Major Gridlines** for both the Category Axis and the Value Axis. Click **OK.**

Gridlines can be deleted or modified by repeating the above steps.

3 Close the EUROSLS Workbook.

Activity 7 Bar charts and column charts

Bar charts show data values as a series of horizontal bars, column charts show values as vertical columns. A bar or column on a chart represents a single number on the worksheet. Both are suited to showing the relative sizes of 2 or more items; column charts are often used for showing change over time, bar charts are often used to compare the sizes of items at one point in time.

1 To produce these charts we're going to use another worksheet – see Figure 5.

Create it in a new workbook – open the **File** menu and select **New** – and save it as BOOKSLS.

	A	B	C	D	E
1		Book Sales - Current Year			
2					
3	Month	No. Sold	Revenue	Advertising	
4	Jan	850	2011	300	
5	Feb	1010	3155	425	
6	Mar	1175	3550	500	
7	Apr	1430	4356	750	
8	May	1710	5150	800	
9					

Figure 5

2 Select cells **A3 – D6** and create a new chart as follows:

3 Open the **Insert** menu and select **Chart – As New Sheet.**

Follow the ChartWizard steps as before, selecting bar chart, format number 6.

Open the **View** menu and select **Sized with Window.**

4 The chart produced is the standard clustered bar chart, showing each month's values as a separate set of bars – see Figure 6.

5 Name the bar chart BAR1. (Double click the sheet tab)

6 Return to sheet 1 making sure that cells A3 to D6 are still selected create a second bar chart.

This time select the 3rd type of bar chart – stacked bars.

Save it as BAR2 – see Figure 7.

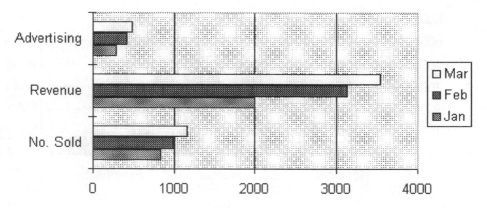

Figure 6

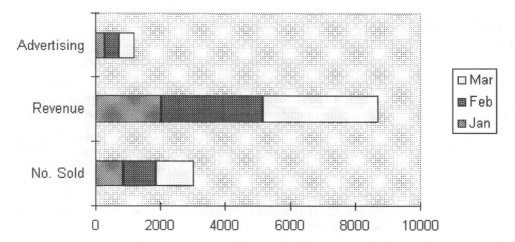

Figure 7

7   Each bar is the sum of the 3 smaller bars. This allows us to see the contribution of each month to the 3 months total for revenue, sales and advertising.

8   Independent Activity – Column Charts.

Make sure that cells **A3** to **D8** are selected and use ChartWizard to experiment with different types of column chart.

Try to produce the column chart shown in Figure 8 – you will need to reverse the axes in order to show the 5 months as the values on the Y axis and Sales, Advertising and Revenue as categories on the X axis. (see activity 5)

Save the sheet as COLUMN1.

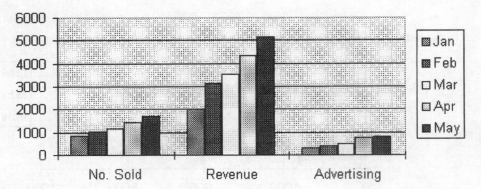

Figure 8

Activity 8   Adding overlays – combination charts

1   Make sure that worksheet Sheet 1 is the active sheet.

2   Make sure that cells **A3** to **D8** are selected and use ChartWizard to create a standard column chart. This time accept the default axis settings so that the months are the categories on the X axis.

3   Move the screen pointer to one of the columns representing Advertising and click – all 5 bars represent Advertising are now selected.

4   Open the **Format** menu and select **AutoFormat**

    Select Combination chart, Format 1 from the ChartWizard dialog boxes; the data series for advertising is now plotted as a line chart – see Figure 9.

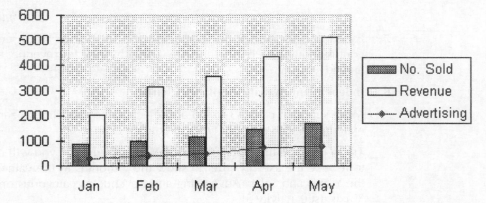

Figure 9

5   This type of chart is called a combination chart, and is useful for emphasising relationships between different data series – in this case the correlation between advertising, sales and revenue. Sales and revenue are still rising whilst the money spent on advertising has started to level off.

6   Save the sheet as **COMB1**.

Now use AutoFormat again to experiment with the other combination charts offered.

7   If you are not proceding directly to the next unit then use the File menu to save and close your workbook.

Summary of commands

Note

Menu commands show the menu name first, followed by the command to choose from the menu, e.g. Edit-Clear means open the Edit menu and select the Clear command.

Edit-Copy...Paste	Copy data from worksheet to chart
Edit-Delete Sheet	Delete a chart sheet
File-Save	Save workbook
Format-Autoformat	Select pre-formatted chart type
Format-Selected.....	Format selected chart element
Insert-Chart	Create a new chart
Insert-Gridlines	Add gridlines to chart
View-Sized With Window	Re-size chart to window size

Standard Toolbar

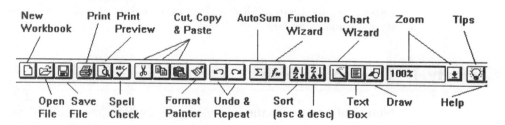

Formatting Toolbar

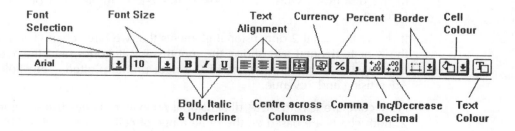

Using 3D charts

Introduction

To round off your knowledge of charts we will be creating three dimensional charts. The third dimension offers extra opportunities to present the data and show the chart from a variety of angles. We will also be looking briefly at embedding a chart in a worksheet, rather than creating it on a separate sheet.

Activity 1   Creating 3D charts

Note.   If you are starting a new Excel session then you will need to open the Workbook BOOKSLS. Make sure that Sheet1 is the active sheet.

In this activity we will be building our first 3-D chart, based on the data in the BOOKSLS worksheet. Look at the 2-D column chart below – Figure 1.

It shows the usual 2 dimensional elements that we have charted so far; the X or horizontal axis shows the months as categories, and the Y or vertical axis shows the values of the data points plotted – No Sold, Advertising and Revenue.

Now compare it with the 3 dimensional equivalent beneath it – Figure 2. Both charts are based on the same range of cell values – A3 to D8 – but Figure 2 offers a third axis – the **Z** axis.

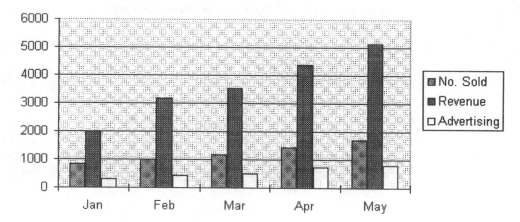

Figure 1

The **X axis** remains the category axis as before.

The **Y axis** (also called the *depth* or *inward* axis) now shows No. Sold, Revenue, and Advertising as three data series.

The **Z axis** is now the value axis, showing the value of the data points.

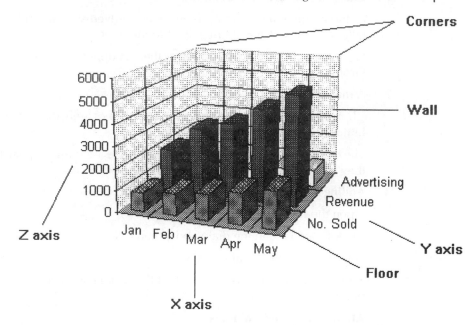

Figure 2

The 3-D chart is plotted on a base floor against background *walls,* meeting at *corners.* The 3-D chart can be rotated against this background giving you different views of the data.

Note: Some of Excel's 3-D charts, eg the 3-D pie and 3-D bar charts, simply use the third dimension to add depth to the 2-D version, but do not chart a third dimension.

1   Make sure that workbook **BOOKSLS** is open and Sheet1 the active sheet.

2   Make sure that cells **A3 to D8** are selected and use ChartWizard to select a **3D** column chart, Format 6.

3   At ChartWizard – Step 4 of 5 do not change the default axis settings. Press the **Next** button.

4   At ChartWizard – Step 5 of 5, press the **Finish** button.

5   The 3-D chart is now created – open the **View** menu and select **Sized with Window.** Your chart will now resemble Figure 2 above. Name the chart sheet 3-D COLUMN using the Format-Sheet-Rename command.

Activity 2   Formatting a 3-D chart

The Insert and Format options offer the same range of options that we have already used for previous 2-D charts. Similarly the ChartWizard button allows you to change the chart type and other parameters.

1   **Changing the order of Columns.**

At the moment the columns representing Advertising are hidden by taller columns. We will bring them to the front.

Open the **Format** menu and select the last option – **1 3-D Column Group**.

2   A dialog box appears – click the Series Order tab.

Click **Advertising** in the **Series Order:** box, then the **Move Up** button.

The Advertising columns move forward one column. Repeat until they move to the front of the chart, then click **OK.**

3   **Adding a Chart Title.**

Open the **Insert** menu and select **Titles.**

Click **Chart Title** in the dialog box, then **OK.**

Enter the title 'Book Sales Analysis'.

You can change the position of the title by dragging with the mouse pointer.

4   **Altering Text and Columns.**

The principle is exactly the same as for 2-D charts. It is a matter of:

❑   clicking what you wish to modify, eg title, column, axis, grid-lines – selection handles appear.

❑   opening the **Format** menu and selecting the first option, **Selected......**

❑   then making your choices using the dialog boxes provided.

Activity 3   Changing the viewing angle of a 3-D chart

In a 3-D chart you can vary the angle at which you view the data. This allows you to emphasise different characteristics of the the chart.

You can do this either by direct chart editing – clicking the axis and dragging – or by using the Format menu. We will practise the second method as it is more precise.

1   Make sure that the chart 3-D COLUMN is still the active chart.

Open the **Format** menu and select the option 3-D **View.**

2   The following dialog box appears – see Figure 3

Move the screen pointer onto the title bar of the of the dialog box and drag it to one side so that you can see the effects of the changes on the chart

Read the following explanations carefully and follow the instructions:

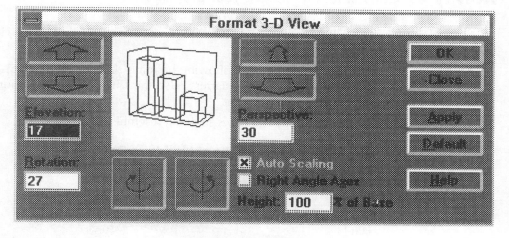

Figure 3

Elevation is the height (in degrees) at which you view the columns; it can vary from 0 to 44 degrees in a column chart. Make a note of the present setting.

Click the **Up** and **Down** arrow buttons above the **Elevation** box and watch the angle of elevation change in the dialog box.

Click the **Apply** button and the changes are reflected in the column chart itself. Finally return the Elevation box to its previous setting by pressing the **Default** button.

Perspective is the three dimensional depth of the chart. The figure in the box (between 0 to 100) is the ratio of the front of the chart to the back. Make a note of the present setting.

Click the perspective arrow buttons above the **Perspective** box and watch the perspective change. Click the **Apply** button and the changes are reflected in the column chart itself. Finally return the Perspective box to its **Default** setting.

Rotation rotates the chart about its vertical axis. Make a note of the present setting.

Click the rotation arrow buttons next to the **Rotation** box and watch the angle of rotation change. Click the **Apply** button and the changes are reflected in the column chart itself. Finally return the Rotation box to its **Default** setting.

Height % of Base alters the height of the chart relative to the base.

Amend the default figure to 50, then click the **Apply** button to see its effect.

Click the **Default** button to restore the original setting.

3 Finally click the **Close** button to close the dialog box.

Activity 4   Consolidation – check your progress

1 Open the workbook EUROSLS and open the worksheet **Euro Hols Data.**

Create a 3-D area chart showing holidays sold for the Italy, Spain and Portugal for all 4 quarters. Use the ChartWizard techniques used in previous activities.

Modify the chart as follows so that it resembles Figure 4.

Number of Holidays Sold

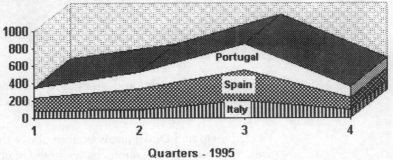

Figure 4

Hints: Name the chart 3-D AREA
Add titles.
Embolden the chart text.
Alter the patterns of the 3 areas.

2 Open the workbook BOOKSLS. Add a further column to the work-sheet, showing advertising as a percentage of revenue for each month.

Create a percentage line chart showing this relationship; name the chart LINE 1 Compare it with the chart shown below – Figure 5.

Hints. Add titles and axis labels as shown.

Embolden the text.

Add the % to the data points on the line – first select the line then use the Format- Selected Data Series option

Embolden and move the percentage labels as shown.

Activity 5 Embedded charts

So far we have created separate chart documents. Excel also allows us to create embedded charts which form part of the worksheet. It is simply a matter of selecting the Insert-Chart-On This Sheet option. This is useful if you want to view or print a chart and worksheet on the same page.

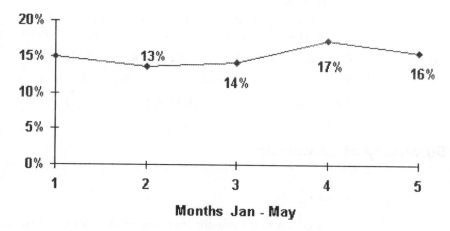

Figure 5

1 Open the worksheet **INS_SLS.**

Maximise the worksheet window.

2 Highlight the cell range **A3** to **D6.**

3 Open the **Insert** menu and select **Chart,** then the **On This Sheet** options.

4 Move the screen pointer back onto the worksheet – it is now chart-shaped.

Drag the screen pointer across an empty area of worksheet, e.g. cell range **F3** to **H11.** (press down the **Shift** key as well if you want the embedded chart to be square)

5   Chart Wizard – Step 1 of 5' is displayed.

(At each step you have the usual options of cancelling, getting help, going back a step, or going on to the next step)

Accept the range of cells offered by clicking the **Next** button.

'Chart Wizard – Step 2 of 5' is displayed.

Choose **Bar**

Click the **Next** button.

'Chart Wizard – Step 3 of 5' is displayed.

Choose Format 1 and click the **Next** button.

'Chart Wizard – Step 4 of 5' is displayed.

Click the **Next** button.

'Chart Wizard – Step 5 of 5' is displayed.

You can add Legend and titles at this stage.

Do this and click **Finish.**

6   The embedded chart is created; it can be moved or re-sized using the selection handles. Chart and worksheet can be selected in turn by clicking.

7   To edit the chart double click it; the dialog box will then be displayed and the chart can be edited as if it were a separate document.

8   A chart can be deleted – select it and press the Delete key.

9   You can save or print the chart now as part of the worksheet.

10   Exit from Excel, saving any changes.

Summary of commands

Note

Menu commands show the menu name first, followed by the command to choose from the menu, e.g. Edit-Clear means open the Edit menu and select the Clear command.

Format-3D View	Change viewing angle
Format-Selected.....	Format selected chart element
Insert-Chart-On This Sheet	Create an embedded chart
View-Sized With Window	Re-size chart to window size

Standard Toolbar

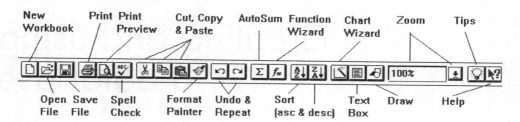

New Workbook   Print   Print Preview   Cut, Copy & Paste   AutoSum   Function Wizard   Chart Wizard   Zoom   Tips

Open File   Save File   Spell Check   Format Painter   Undo & Repeat   Sort (asc & desc)   Text Box   Draw   Help

Formatting Toolbar

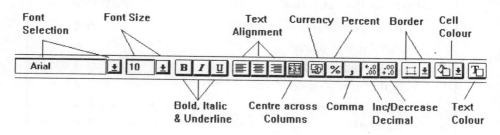

Font Selection   Font Size   Text Alignment   Currency   Percent   Border   Cell Colour

Bold, Italic & Underline   Centre across Columns   Comma   Inc/Decrease Decimal   Text Colour

unit 9

Creating and using a database

Introduction

In earlier units we have covered worksheets and charts, the first two components of Excel. This unit covers the third component, databases.

Businesses use databases to store and retrieve records of all types – customers, employees, goods in stock, etc. The software package used to create and run a database is called a database management system or DBMS.

Figure 1 is an example of a simple database that records the customer orders. We can use it to introduce certain key database terms.

	A	B	C	D	E
	Order No.	Order Date	Co.Ref	Co. Name	Value
2	14000	10-Mar	1453	Wilson Garages	3200.00
3	14001	08-Mar	2413	Patel Industries	1466.00
4	14002	11-Mar	1453	Wilson Garages	98.76
5	14003	11-Mar	1289	Marsden Products	4456.00
6	14004	10-Mar	2413	Patel Industries	567.00
7	14005	11-Mar	955	Tilley Transport	1678.00
8	·14006	10-Mar	2375	Patel Kitchens	55.54
9	14007	09-Mar	1453	Wilson Garages	2654.00
10	14008	12-Mar	2245	Goldfield Stables	123.85
11	14009	12-Mar	1289	Marsden Products	1652.54

Figure 1

Record   There is an entry for each order. Each entry is called a *record* and takes up a row.

Field   Each record contains the same 5 *fields* or items of information – Order No, Order Date, Co. Ref, Co. Name and Value. Each field takes up a column. The first row of the database contains the *field names,* the other rows contain the actual data – the field *values.*

Database   At the moment our database consists of a *range* of 10 records.

Excel is primarily a spreadsheet and does not offer all the features of a special-purpose DBMS such as Access or Paradox, but you can perform straightforward database tasks such as:

❐   finding individual records

❐   adding new records

❐   editing existing records

❐   deleting records

More complex tasks are also possible, such as sorting records into a different order, or extracting all records meeting a particular search criterion.

Database rules in Excel

Database size   A database can be as large as the entire worksheet, but cannot occupy more than one worksheet.

Fields/Field names   A database can contain up to 256 fields.

The first row of the database must contain the field names.

Field names must consist of letters only, not numbers, blank cells etc.

Field names can be up to 256 characters long and must be unique

Records   A database can contain up to 16,383 records. Every record must have the same fields, but fields can be left blank.

Do not enter extra blanks at the start of fields.

Capitalization   Excel ignores upper or lower case when searching or sorting   the database, so you may use either, e.g.'SMITH', 'smith' or 'Smith'.

Activity 1   Building the database

It is essential to plan the structure of a database before you create it. The information that you need will determine what fields you include. For example, Figure 1 shows a database set up to keep track of customer orders. We therefore need to know not only the customer details – name and reference code – but also the order details – date, reference code and value. Each of these information items is given its own field and can be processed separately.

Notice that we also have implicitly decided what **not** to store e.g. the customer address – this would probably be stored in a customer data-base rather than an orders database.

1   **Inserting the field names.**

First open a new blank workbook, then enter the 5 field names shown shown in Figure 1. (cells **A1 – E1**)

Use the right arrow key to move across the columns.

Widen the columns where necessary, and centre and embolden the field names.

2   **Entering the data.**

First complete columns C and D – the **Co. Ref** and **Co. Name** fields as shown in Figure 1.

Next enter the order values in column E, the Value field. Don't enter .00 after a value if there are no pence, so for example in the case of cell **E3** just enter the value 1466.

3   **Formatting the Fields.**

Now we will format the values to 2 decimal places

Select the 10 value fields – cell range **E2** to **E11**.

Open the **Format** menu and select the **Cells** option.

When the dialog box appears click the **Number** tab if necessary.

Select the **0.00** option from the **Format Codes** list and click the **OK** button.

4   Creating a Data Series.

The Order no. field is a numeric sequence – increasing by 1 for every new order record. We can use the Fill Series command when numbers or dates in adjacent cells increase (or decrease) by a constant factor.

Enter the start value 14000 in cell **A2**, then select the whole range, **A2** to **A11**.

Open the **Edit** menu and select the **Fill** then the **Series** options.

A Dialog box appears, make sure that the following options are selected, as shown in Figure 2.

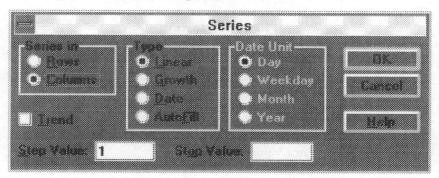

Figure 2

Series in columns   the data series will occupy a column

Linear   the progression will be linear

Step value 1   the numbers will increase by 1 each time (for weekly dates you would step value 7)

5   Click the OK button and the column is filled with the order numbers 14000-14009.

6   **Entering the Order Date.** Excel allows dates to be entered in a variety of formats and in most cases will automatically assign the correct date format.

Enter the first date field as **10mar** and press **Enter.** Excel automatically converts it to the date format 10-Mar (if it doesn't then check what you have entered)

Enter the remaining field values in a similar way.

Hint: Look at the status bar at the top of the screen as you do this. Irrespective of the date format in the cells Excel displays dates in a numeric format, e.g. 3/10/96.

7   Finally centre the field values for the **Order No, Order Date** and **Co. Name** fields.

The database should now resemble Figure 1 above.

8   Save the worksheet as **ORDERS** and the workbook as **DATABASE.**

You will see that it is assigned the usual worksheet extension .XLS.

Activity 2   Sorting the database

A common business need is to present the same information in a variety of ways, eg in order number sequence, (as at present) or in customer name sequence. Sorting involves rearranging the records in a new physical sequence, and speeds up search time once a database gets over a certain length. The field used to sort the database is called the **sort key** or **key field**; we can sort the database in order of any field or fields.

Rules and hints for sorting

Sorting will work with any range of worksheet cells, not only databases.

Order of Sorting: field values are sorted in the following order;

❑   Numbers
❑   Text
❑   Logical Values
❑   Error Values
❑   Blanks

You can always undo an unsuccessful sort by selecting **Undo Sort** from the **Edit** menu, provided that you do so immediately.

Note: All the fields in the database, ie all columns, must be included in the sort, otherwise any fields omitted from the sort will remain in the same sequence and become attached to the wrong records.

1   Let's sort the customer orders into date sequence first.

Select cells **A1** to **E11** – all fields, all records, including the field names in the header row.

Open the **Data** menu and select **Sort.**

The Sort dialog box appears.

If necessary, locate the screen pointer on the title bar and drag the dialog box down so that the database is visible.

2   Complete the dialog box as follows using Figure 3 as a guide.

> **Sort by:**   At the moment the first field name, Order No, is selected.
>
> Click the down arrow button on the **Sort By** box – a field list is displayed – select **Order Date.**
>
> Leave the **Ascending** button on – earliest dates first.

Then by: Ignore the next two boxes, we are only sorting by one field.

My list has: Leave **Header Row** selected – the field names in row 1 will not be included in the sort

The screen should now resemble Figure 3.

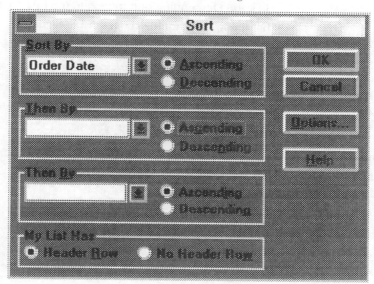

Figure 3

Click the **OK** button and the ten records are sorted in a new sequence – date order.

Hint: A sort can be changed by either selecting Undo Sort from the Edit menu, or by another sort operation.

3 Consolidation – resorting records.

Make sure that the cell range A1 to E11 are still selected.

Using sections 1 and 2 as a guide, sort the ten records by Co. Name.

Notice that strict alphabetical sequence is followed, the record for Patel Industries is placed before Patel Kitchens.

4 Sorting by more than one key.

Let's sort the records in reverse date sequence, within Co. Name. This means that all the records for, e.g. Wilson Garages, are grouped together, with the latest orders displayed first. This involves two keys – Co. Name as the **primary** key and Order Date as the **secondary** key.

Make sure that the entire database range is selected as before and issue the Sort command.

Complete the Sort dialog box as follows, using Figure 4 as a guide:

a. Ensure that **Co. Name.** is still selected in the first **Sort By:** box.button.

b. Now click the first **Then By:** dialog box then the down arrow key next to it.
   Select **Order Date** from the field list.

c. Click the Descending button next to the first **Then By:** box.
   The dialog box should now resemble Figure 4.

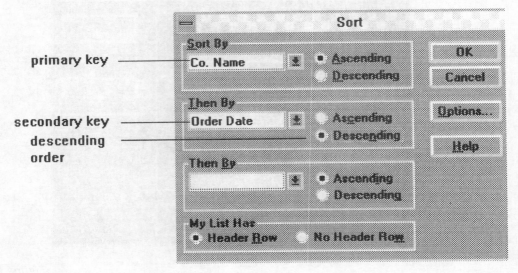

Figure 4

d. Finally click the **OK** button.

e. Click on the worksheet to remove the selection highlighting from the database – it should resemble Figure 5.

	A	B	C	D	E
1	Order No.	Order Date	Co.Ref	Co. Name	Value
2	14008	12-Mar	2245	Goldfield Stables	123.85
3	14009	12-Mar	1289	Marsden Products	1652.54
4	14003	11-Mar	1289	Marsden Products	4456.00
5	14004	10-Mar	2413	Patel Industries	567.00
6	14001	08-Mar	2413	Patel Industries	1466.00
7	14006	10-Mar	2375	Patel Kitchens	55.54
8	14005	11-Mar	955	Tilley Transport	1678.00
9	14002	11-Mar	1453	Wilson Garages	98.76
10	14000	10-Mar	1453	Wilson Garages	3200.00
11	14007	09-Mar	1453	Wilson Garages	2654.00

Figure 5

5   **Consolidation**

Try sorting the order records as follows:

a.   In descending order of value, i.e. largest orders first.

b.   By Co. Ref. in ascending date order – compare your result with Appendix 4.

Activity 3   Creating new fields by calculation

We are going to add two new fields to the database:

a.   The **VAT** field will hold the 17.5% VAT to be added to the value of an order.

b.   The **Total** field which will hold the VAT field added to the order value field.

These new fields will both be calculated by formulae in the usual way.

1   Make sure that the Workbook database is open and worksheet **ORDERS** is selected.

Add the two new field names, **VAT** and **Total,** to cells **F1** and **G1.**

Centre them in their cells.

2   VAT is 17.5% of Value; move to cell F2 and apply the formula **=E2*0.175** (* is the multiplication sign) Remember to press Return.

Now copy this formula to the rest of the VAT fields using the **Edit-Fill-Down** command.

3   Now calculate the first **Total** field by adding the **Vat** field to the **Value** field, using a formula. Fill down again.

4   Format the two new fields to 2 decimal places, using the **Format-Cell-Number** command.

5   Calculated fields can be searched and sorted in the same way as any other fields. To demonstrate this, sort the database by the Total field (ascending order)

Your database should now resemble Figure 6.

Activity 4   Database maintenance using a data form

Obviously all databases need updating as information changes; records will need adding, deleting and amending. You can use a special Excel data form to simplify the searching and updating process.

1   Make sure that the ORDERS worksheet is selected.

There is no need to select the whole database in order to search or maintain it; simply make sure one of the cells in the database is selected.

Select cell **D2.**

Order No.	Order Date	Co.Ref	Co. Name	Value	VAT	Total
14006	10-Mar	2375	Patel Kitchens	55.54	9.72	65.26
14002	11-Mar	1453	Wilson Garages	98.76	17.28	116.04
14008	12-Mar	2245	Goldfield Stables	123.85	21.67	145.52
14004	10-Mar	2413	Patel Industries	567.00	99.23	666.23
14001	08-Mar	2413	Patel Industries	1466.00	256.55	1722.55
14009	12-Mar	1289	Marsden Products	1652.54	289.19	1941.73
14005	11-Mar	955	Tilley Transport	1678.00	293.65	1971.65
14007	09-Mar	1453	Wilson Garages	2654.00	464.45	3118.45
14000	10-Mar	1453	Wilson Garages	3200.00	560.00	3760.00
14003	11-Mar	1289	Marsden Products	4456.00	779.80	5235.80

Figure 6

2   Open the **Data** menu and select the **Form** command.

A data form is displayed. On the left hand side of the form are shown the field names and field values for the first record. The form always shows the number of the current record displayed, Number 1 of 10 – see Figure 7.

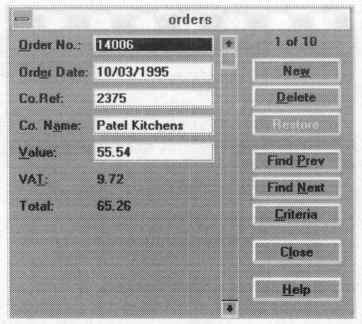

Figure 7

3   Let's carry out some key database tasks using the command buttons on the right hand side of the data form:

Find Next button   click this to scroll forward in the database a record at a time.

Notice how the field values change as the Record Counter displays the current record – 2 of 10, 3 of 10 etc.

Find Prev. button   Click this to scroll backwards in the database.

Scroll Bar   Moves between records more rapidly.

Move to the last record in the database – 10 of 10.

Delete button   click it once.

A message warns you that 'Displayed record will be deleted permanently'. Click the Cancel button (records deleted with a data form cannot be restored, so make sure that you really want to delete the whole record before deleting it).

Criteria button   allows you to locate records by named criteria. You will be learning this in more detail in later sections.

4   Try these simple searches now:

a.   Scroll back to the first record and click the **Criteria** button. A blank record is displayed.

Enter your first criterion, **Patel,** in the Co. Name field – the data form now resembles Figure 8 – then click the **Find Next** button.

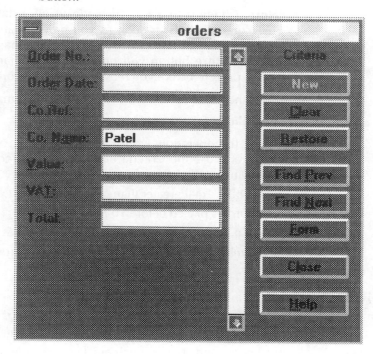

Figure 8

101

The first record matching this search criterion is displayed; press the **Find Next** button again to view any further matches.

There are 3 records in all. Notice that both Patel companies are located – we would need to enter the complete company name to narrow the search further.

A 'bleep' informs you when the last matching record is displayed.

Press the **Find Prev.** button to scroll back again.

b. Press the **Criteria** button again. Patel is still displayed in the Co. Name field.

Press the **Value** field and enter the second criterion **<1000**

Press the **Find Next** button.

Two records match the combined criteria, i.e. company name = Patel *and* order value less than £1000.

Click the **Criteria** then the **Clear** button to remove the search criteria, then the **Form** button to return to the Data form.

5 **Editing data.**

The first 5 data fields can be edited, but the two new calculated fields, **VAT** and **Total,** cannot be changed. Their data is produced by formulae which cannot be overwritten. This is why the data in these 2 fields is not enclosed in boxes – see Figure 7.

Using the data form find the record for order number 14005 and amend the Co. Ref to 965.

Note. Changes to a record made using a data form are saved **permanently** as soon as you move to another record, even though no specific Save command has been given. The **Restore** button will only undo the change providing you press it before you move to another record.

6 Press the **Close** button to exit from the data form.

7 **Consolidation.**

Using the operations you have just learned, open the data form again and use the Criteria button to locate records matching the following conditions:

a. Order Total greater than or equal to 3000 (>=)

b. Orders placed before 10-Mar (<)

c. Co. Ref = 1289

Remember to clear previous criteria before starting the next search.

Activity 5   Adding subtotals to a database

We can total up the values of the orders for each customer using the subtotal command. This is much quicker and easier than using the SUM function. We can also outline the database and just display the subtotals.

1   Make sure that the ORDERS worksheet is open for use. Make sure that one of the cells in the database is selected, ie active.

    Use the **Sort** command to sort the database by Co. Name order – see Activity 2.

2   Open the **Data** menu and select **Subtotals.** The whole database is selected and a dialog box opens. Complete the entries as follows, using Figure 9 as a guide.

At Each Change in:	Select the Co. **Name** field from the list box – we want subtotals for each company.
Use Function:	Leave this as **SUM,** the default – we want to add the value of orders
Add Subtotal to:	Make sure that **Total** is selected – this is the field value we want to add.

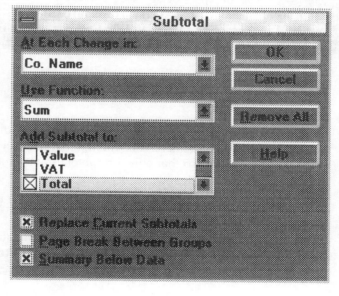

Figure 9

3   Click the **OK** button your database should resemble Figure 10 following. After each customer a new row is inserted, holding the customer name and the value of their orders subtotalled.

    At the end of the table a grand total for all orders is displayed – you may need to scroll down to see this.

4   **Outlining.** At the top left hand corner of the screen are three small buttons, labelled 1, 2 and 3.

    Click on button **2.** The records are hidden, and only the subtotal and grand total are displayed

    Click on button **1.** Only the grand total is displayed.

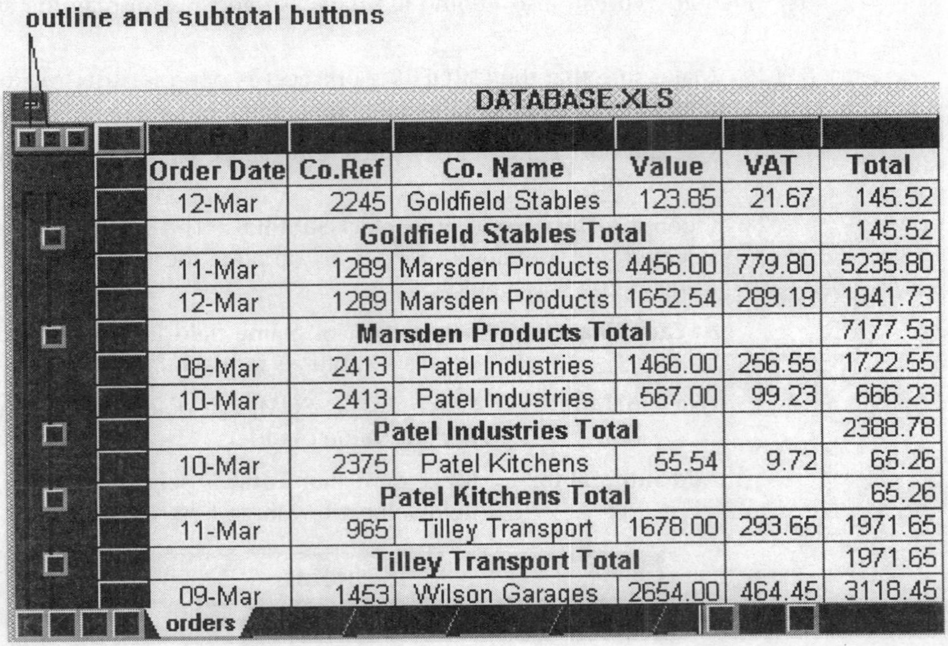

outline and subtotal buttons

Order Date	Co.Ref	Co. Name	Value	VAT	Total
12-Mar	2245	Goldfield Stables	123.85	21.67	145.52
		Goldfield Stables Total			145.52
11-Mar	1289	Marsden Products	4456.00	779.80	5235.80
12-Mar	1289	Marsden Products	1652.54	289.19	1941.73
		Marsden Products Total			7177.53
08-Mar	2413	Patel Industries	1466.00	256.55	1722.55
10-Mar	2413	Patel Industries	567.00	99.23	666.23
		Patel Industries Total			2388.78
10-Mar	2375	Patel Kitchens	55.54	9.72	65.26
		Patel Kitchens Total			65.26
11-Mar	965	Tilley Transport	1678.00	293.65	1971.65
		Tilley Transport Total			1971.65
09-Mar	1453	Wilson Garages	2654.00	464.45	3118.45

DATABASE.XLS

orders

Figure 10

Click on button **3**. The records, subtotals and grand totals are all displayed.

Now experiment with the **minus** buttons displayed down the left side of the screen. You will find that you can hide individual groups of records so that only the subtotals are displayed. The button now displays a '+' sign.

Click the button again and the records are displayed as they were before.

5   **Removing Subtotals.** Open the **Data** menu and select **Subtotals**. When the dialog box appears click the **Remove All** button. The database is now displayed without subtotals.

Activity 6   Simple database searches

The data form that we used in Activity 4 has limited search facilities. It can only display one record at a time, and we cannot use 'or' conditions such as ' > 1000 or < 2000 ' in a data form field. AutoFilter allows you to do this by setting up the search criteria on the worksheet itself. You can also combine 2 search criteria using either 'AND' or 'OR'.

1   Make sure that the ORDERS worksheet is open for use. Make sure that one of the cells in the database is selected, ie active.

2   Open the **Data** menu and select **Filter,** then the **AutoFilter** option.

Arrow boxes appear next to each field name in the database.

Click each arrow in turn and you will see that they contain lists of all the values for that particular field.

3   **Searching by Individual Field Values.**

Click the arrow button next to the **Co. Name** field – a list appears.

Select Wilson Garages – only the records for this company are selected.

Click the arrow button again and select **(all)** – you may have to scroll through the list. All the records are redisplayed.

Hint: If you find that you cannot restore all the records then open the **Data** menu and select **Filter,** then the **Show All** option.

4   **Building your own Searches.**

Let's say that you want to display all records for the 9th or the 11th March. This involves building your own custom search.

Click the down arrow on the **Order Date** field and select **(Custom...)** from the list.

A dialog box appears. Complete the entries as follows, using Figure 11 as a guide.

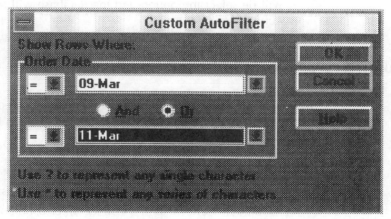

Figure 11

You have 4 list boxes to complete plus an 'And' or an 'Or' button to select.

a.   Leave the = sign as it is.

d.   Click the down arrow on the first Order Date box and select the date **09-Mar**

c.   Click the **'Or'** button.

d.   Click the next arrow box and select an = sign

e.   Click the final arrow box and select the date **11-Mar.**

Finally click the **OK** button and the 4 records that meet the search criteria (9th March or 11th March) are selected – the rest are hidden – see Figure 12.

	A	B	C	D	E	F	G
1	Order N	Order Da	Co.R	Co. Name	Valu	VA	Tota
	14003	11-Mar	1289	Marsden Products	4456.00	779.80	5235.80
	14005	11-Mar	965	Tilley Transport	1678.00	293.65	1971.65
	14007	09-Mar	1453	Wilson Garages	2654.00	464.45	3118.45
	14002	11-Mar	1453	Wilson Garages	98.76	17.28	116.04

Figure 12

5   Click the arrow button on the Order Date field again and select **(all)** – you may have to scroll through the list. All the records are redisplayed.

6   **Independent Activity.**

Use the arrow box on the Order No. field to select records with order numbers between 14005 and 14009.

Hints. You will need to search for numbers >= 14005 and <= 140009. Refer to Appendix 5 for guidance on the dialog box entries if necessary. 5 records should be selected.

7   Open the **Data** menu and select the **Filter-AutoFilter** option. This will de-select the option and the database will revert to its normal appearance.

Summary of commands and functions

Menu commands show the menu name first, followed by the command to choose from the menu, eg Edit-Clear means open the Edit menu and select the Clear command.

Commands

Data-Filter-AutoFilter	Search a database using AutoFilter
Data-Filter-Show All	Cancel filter condition and show all records
Data-Form	Search a database using a data form
Data-Sort	Sort selected cells
Data-Subtotals	Subtotal a database
Edit-Fill-Series	Create a data series

Searching and extracting records

Skills to be learned	Activity
* and ? operators – using	1.1
AND operator	1.11
Comparison operators – using	1.8
Database Functions – using	3
Defining a database	1.2, 2.1
Extracting Records	2
Function Wizard – using	3.4
OR operator	1.11
Search criteria – using	1.4
Wildcard operators – using	1.1

Previous skills needed to tackle this unit

Skill	Covered in Unit
Starting Excel	1
Basic mouse, menu and Windows operations	1
Creating a simple worksheet	1
Database terminology	9

Introduction

In the previous unit we have learnt some simple sorting and database search skills. This unit shows you more advanced ways of retrieving and extracting records from a database. It also shows you how to use functions to summarise database information.

Activity 1   More advanced searches

If you need to use more complex search criteria then even AutoFilter may not be adequate. Excel offers an Advanced Filter option that allows you to search on more than two fields, and offers a wider range of operators than those offered by AutoFilter.

1. We will conduct these searches using a new database that holds details of voluntary helpers who act as guides, gardeners, drivers etc. at heritage sites in various areas.

	SURNAME	FORENAME	AREA	JOB	AGE	AVAILABILITY
	Morrison	James	Winton	Driver	33	12-Jul
	Cohen	Harry	Wimborne	Gardener	65	13-Jul
	Wilson	John	Ringwood	Guide	34	20-Jul
	Sutton	Tony	Winton	Driver	39	23-Jul
	Sutton	Linda	Poole	Canteen	54	22-Jul
	Smith	Louisa	Poole	Kitchen	50	26-Jul
	Goldfield	Chris	Boscombe	Guide	34	30-Jul
	Muir	Sue	Wimborne	Warden	43	30-Jul
	Ali	Kate	Redhill	Warden	16	30-Jul
	Burton	Judy	Mudeford	Kitchen	68	02-Aug
	Pierce	Karen	Poole	Guide	20	02-Aug
	Maycock	Ray	Wallisdown	Gardener	40	04-Aug
	Povey	Malcolm	Downton	Driver	25	30-Aug
	Baker	Tony	Ringwood	Canteen	66	05-Aug

Open a new workbook and save it as HELPERS.

Create and format the worksheet as shown above.

Note: Make sure that the records are exactly as shown; it will be important in checking your search results

2. **Defining the Database.**

The first step is to define and name the worksheet cells as a database.

Select all the cells **A1** to **F15**, ie the 14 records plus the field headings on row 1.

Open the **Insert** menu and select the option **Name** then the **Define** option.

A dialog box appears. Enter the name DATABASE as shown in Figure 1.

Click the **OK** button.

The name DATABASE identifies the first row of cells as field names.

The database is now defined.

3. **Defining the Search Criteria.**

Select all the 6 field names in row 1.

Open the **Edit** menu and select **Copy.**

Select cell **A17,** then select **Paste** from the **Edit** menu – the cells are copied across row 17.

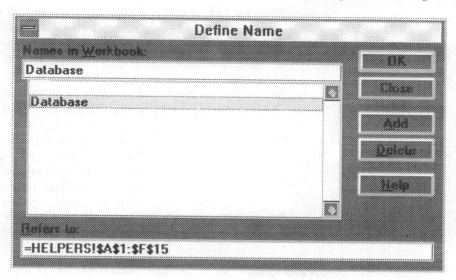

Figure 1

Notes on defining search criteria:

a. These cells form your **criteria range** – the field names that you use as search criteria.

b. You don't have to use a Copy command to copy the field names from the database, you can type them if you wish.

c. You don't need to include all the field names in the criteria range, only those that you intend to use in your search.

d. The criteria range may be located at any convenient place on the worksheet – usually close to the database you are searching.

4   Entering the Search Criteria.

The first row of cells (row 17) contains the field names, the next row of cells, row 18, are for you to enter your search criteria.

You merely enter your criteria under the field that you want to search.

Let's select all the records for drivers first.

Enter the search term **Driver** in cell D18 underneath the field name **Job** (don't worry about capital letters, the search is not case sensitive)

Remember to press Enter or click the tick box to enter this search term.

5   Using Advanced Filter.

Open the **Data** menu and select the **Filter** then the **Advanced Filter** options.

The Advanced Filter dialog box is displayed – complete it as follows, using Figure 2 as a guide:

Action: Filter the List, in place. Leave this option selected; the search will 'filter out' or hide records that do not match the search criterion 'Driver' and only show the matching ones.

List Range: You must specify the range of cells for the database you are searching. Modify them if not. Check that the cell references are the same as in Figure 2 below (the $ signs are important and indicate an absolute reference – see Unit 4, Activity 5.8 if necessary) This can be done either by keying them in or dragging the mouse across the cell range to select it.

Criteria Range: This is the cell range holding your search criteria – see section 4 above. Check that the cell references are the same as in Figure 2 below. Modify them if not.

Ensure that no other options are selected on the dialog box, then click **OK.**

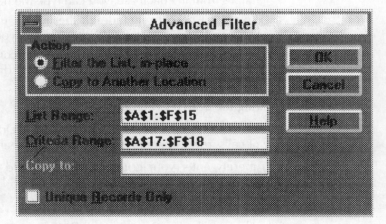

Figure 2

The 3 records for the drivers are selected. If not repeat the above steps, checking the cell references very carefully

6   Open the **Data** menu and select **Filter** then the **Show All** option..

This ends the search and displays the whole database again

7   Now add a further search criterion, **Winton** in cell **C18** and press **Enter.**

Use the **Advanced Filter** option again; only two drivers match the second criterion; the other record is filtered out.

8   Comparison Operators.

The following 6 operators can be used in searching the database:

=	equal to (not needed on its own)
<	less than
>	greater than
<>	not equal to
<=	less than or equal to
>=	greater than or equal to

9   Use them to make the following three searches:

All helpers living in Wimborne (no operator needed)

All helpers aged 50 or over

Poole helpers available before 25th July.

Search hints

Erase previous search conditions using the **Edit-Clear** command or the **Backspace** key.

Press **Enter** after entering the search criterion.

Use the **Data-Filter-Show All** command to show all the records before starting the next search.

If no records are selected check:

that the search criteria are correct,

entered under the correct field name,

the cell coordinates in the Advanced Filter dialog box are the same as in Figure 2.

10   Wildcard Searching.

The * and ? characters can be used as 'wild cards' to stand for one or more characters.

Try the following three searches:

a.   Enter ***ton** as a search condition in cell C18.

Records for both Winton and Downton are located. The * character can substitute for any combination of adjacent characters.

b.   Enter the search condition **L?nda** under the forename field.

If we are unsure if the forename 'Linda' is spelled with a 'y' or an 'i', the ? character can be used to substitute for a single character.

The record for Linda Sutton will be located.

c. Enter the search condition **Wi** under the Area field.

Records for both Wimborne and Winton are located, i.e. there is no need to use a wildcard character if you can supply the starting characters of the search criterion.

Restore all 15 records as before and remove all the search criteria from row 18.

11 'And' vs. 'Or'

When we used more than one search criterion we have implicitly used the **AND** condition; ie both conditions needed to be met for a record to be retrieved, e.g. Poole area AND available 25th July.

We also need to search using the **OR** condition, e.g. Poole or Ringwood area, age under 20 or over 40. To do this involves entering the search criteria in different rows

Let's retrieve records for areas Boscombe or Ringwood.

Enter **Boscombe** in the first cell below the Area criterion – cell **C18.**

Enter **Ringwood** in the second cell below the Area criterion – cell **C19.**

12 Next we need to amend the criteria range as our criteria now occupy 2 rows.

Use the **Data-Filter-Advanced Filter** commands as before – the dialog box is displayed.

Select the **Criteria Range:** box and amend it to the references shown in Figure 3.

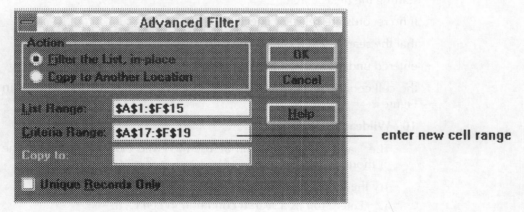

enter new cell range

Figure 3

Click **OK** – the 3 records who match either search condition are selected. Restore all 15 records as before.

13 We can now make a more complex search – Guides for Ringwood or Wardens for Redhill.

The logic is (guide **AND** Ringwood) **OR** (warden **AND** Redhill).

Enter the search criteria as shown in Figure 4.

Run Advanced Filter and 2 records that match both sets of criteria will be selected.

	A	B	C	D	E	F
2	Pierce	Karen	Poole	Guide	20	02-Aug
3	Maycock	Ray	Wallisdown	Gardener	40	04-Aug
4	Povey	Malcolm	Downton	Driver	25	30-Aug
5	Baker	Tony	Ringwood	Canteen	66	05-Aug
6						
7	**SURNAME**	**FORENAME**	**AREA**	**JOB**	**AGE**	**AVAILABILITY**
8			Ringwood	Guide		
9			Redhill	Warden		

Figure 4

14   Independent Activities.

Try the following searches:

a.   All helpers over 60 or under 21.

b.   Any Guide available before 21 July or after 1st August. (you will have to enter the job criterion twice – on both rows)

Activity 2   Extracting records from the database

Once a database gets to a certain length, it can become unwieldy to use. In this situation we might find it useful to copy or extract selected records to another part of the worksheet and work with them separately.

We will use the ORDERS database, created in Unit 9, to practise this.

We will use Advanced Filter; the commands are very similar to ones we used to search the HELPERS database.

1   Define the Database.

Open the Workbook DATABASE then the worksheet **ORDERS** and select the whole database, including the field names.

Open the **Insert** menu and select the **Name** then the **Define** options.

The Name dialog box appears.

Enter the name DATABASE and click **OK** – see Figure 1 above. The name DATABASE identifies the first row of cells as field names.

The database is now defined.

Note: The worksheet cells should be re-defined as a database every time it is opened for use in case records have been added or deleted.

2   Define the Search Criteria.   Select all the field names in row 1.

Open the **Edit** menu and select **Copy.**

113

Select cell **A13,** then select **Paste** from the **Edit** menu – the cells are copied across row 13.

3   **Set up Field Headings for the extracted Records.** Copy the field names once again; this time to row 17 – see Figure 5 as a guide. The extract range, like the criteria range, requires a row of field names matching those in the database.

	A	B	C	D	E	F	G
8	14005	11-Mar	965	Tilley Transport	1678.00	293.65	1971.65
9	14007	09-Mar	1453	Wilson Garages	2654.00	464.45	3118.45
10	14000	10-Mar	1453	Wilson Garages	3200.00	560.00	3760.00
11	14003	11-Mar	1289	Marsden Products	4456.00	779.80	5235.80
12							
13	Order No.	Order Date	Co.Ref	Co. Name	Value	VAT	Total
14							<1000
15							
16							
17	Order No.	Order Date	Co.Ref	Co. Name	Value	VAT	Total
18							

Figure 5

4   **Enter the Search Criteria.** Let's extract all records totalling less than £1000.

Select cell **G14** and enter the criterion **<1000**

5   **Define the Criterion and Extract Ranges.** Open the **Data** menu and select the **Filter-Advanced Filter** options. The Advanced Filter dialog box opens.

a.   Click on the Copy to another Location button.

b.   Check the cell references in the **List Range:** box with Figure 6. These cells define the database range. Amend them if necessary.

c.   Select the **Criteria Range:** box and check the cell references shown with Figure 6. These cells define where we will enter our search criteria.

d.   Select the **Copy to:** box and check the cell references shown with Figure 6. These cells define where the records will be copied to.

e.   Finally click the **OK** button.

Four records matching the search criterion (Total < 1000) are extracted from the database and placed below the field headings in row 17. You may need to scroll down to see them.

Note. Any data in cells that are already underneath the field names of the extract range will be overwritten by the extracted data. It will be permanently lost, as you cannot undo an extract operation (unless you exit the worksheet without saving it). So either be careful where you place the extract range, or limit it to a definite number of rows. This can be done by selecting that number of rows in addition to the field names when you define the extract range.

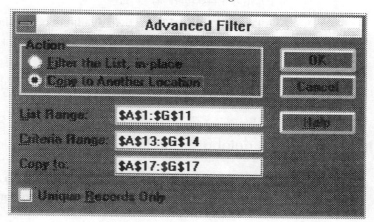

Figure 6

6   **Independent Activity.**

Clear the search condition from cell **G14** and the extracted records from row 18 and below. Do **not** delete the field headings from row 17.

Now extract all the records where the order date is on or before 10-Mar. 5 records should be extracted.

Hint: Remember to click on the **Copy to another Location** button again – see section 5a above – the cell coordinates should remain unchanged .

7   **Extracting Partial Records.**

Instead of extracting all the fields in the record, you may wish to extract certain fields only, eg Co. Name, Value,VAT and Total.

Clear the search condition, and the extracted records as before .

Clear the three field names **Order No, Order Date** and **Co.Ref** from cells **A17** to **C17.**

Enter the search criterion **>0** in cell **E14** (all records match this condition and will be extracted)

Now select the **Data-Filter-Advanced Filter** command as before.

The dialog box appears; delete the current entry from the the **Copy to**: box and enter the cell references **$D$17:$G$17** The references can be either keyed in or by dragging with the mouse across these 4 cells.

All 10 records are extracted and copied, but only the 4 fields that you specified.

8 **Consolidation.**

Open the **HELPERS** worksheet and extract the following records:

All members aged 50 or over

All members aged 50 or over available on or after 26-Jul.

The surname, area and job fields only for members from Poole (you will need to define a new extract range).

Remember to use the **Data-Filter-Show All** command to restore all the records when you have finished.

Activity 3   Using database statistical functions

You have already used the Excel functions SUM and AVERAGE in previous activities. A function is a built-in, predefined formula; Excel provides a large number of them, some of which we will be using in future units.

Excel offers a number of special database functions, e.g. DSUM, DAVERAGE, DMIN, DMAX. Rather than operating on a whole range of cells as the ordinary statistical functions SUM, AVERAGE, MIN and MAX do, you can use them to select particular records on which to operate. For example, in the ORDERS database you can find not only the average order value, but the average order value for a particular customer, or since a certain date.

Taking DSUM as an example, database functions have the form:

DSUM(database,"field",criteria) :

database is the name of the database range that you have defined using the Name command – see Activity 1.1

field is the field whose values you wish to sum eg VAT.

criteria is the criteria range that you define using the Advanced Filter dialog box – see Activity 1.5.

You can either type the function yourself or use FunctionWizard to guide you through the steps. The latter is better if you don't use functions very often as their syntax can be quite complex.

A fuller list of database functions is given at the end of this unit.

1 Open the Workbook DATABASE and the worksheet ORDERS if necessary. First we will check that the database and criteria ranges are correctly set – see Activity 1 above.

Open the the Insert menu and select **Name-Define** – the dialog box appears.

Click on the name **Database** and check in the **Refers to** box that the database range is set to $A$1:$G$11

Click on the name **Criteria** and check in the Refers to box that the criteria range is set to **$A$13:$G$14**

Reset these ranges if necessary and click **OK.**

2   Now remove the extract range used in Activity 2.7, ie both the field headings in row 17 and the records underneath it.

3   Now let's designate a section of the worksheet for several database functions.

Starting in cell **A16,** enter the cell titles shown in Figure 7. Centre and embolden them.

	A	B	C	D	E	F	G
9	14007	09-Mar	1453	Wilson Garages	2654.00	464.45	3118.45
10	14000	10-Mar	1453	Wilson Garages	3200.00	560.00	3760.00
11	14003	11-Mar	1289	Marsden Products	4456.00	779.80	5235.80
12							
13	Order No.	Order Date	Co.Ref	Co. Name	Value	VAT	Total
14							
15							
16	No of Orders	Avg. Value	Total Value	Total Vat	Min. Total		

Figure 7

4   **Using Function Wizard.**

Let's use the DSUM function to total up the VAT that Wilson Garages have to pay on their orders.

First enter the search term **Wilson Garages** in cell **D14.**

Now select cell **D17** – this is where the database function will be entered.

Click the Function Wizard button – it is on the Standard toolbar and marked with **fx**

5   The dialog box Function Wizard – Step 1 of 2 appears.

Select **Database** from the **Function Category** list.

Select **DSUM** from the **Function Name** list.

Click the **Next** button.

6   The dialog box **Function Wizard – Step 2 of 2** appears.

Complete it as shown in Figure 8.

Enter **Database** in the **Database** box (this is the name of the database – see section 1)

Enter **Vat** in the **Field** box – this is the field to be summed.

Enter **Criteria** in the **Criteria** box – this is the name of the criteria range.

Click the **Finish** button.

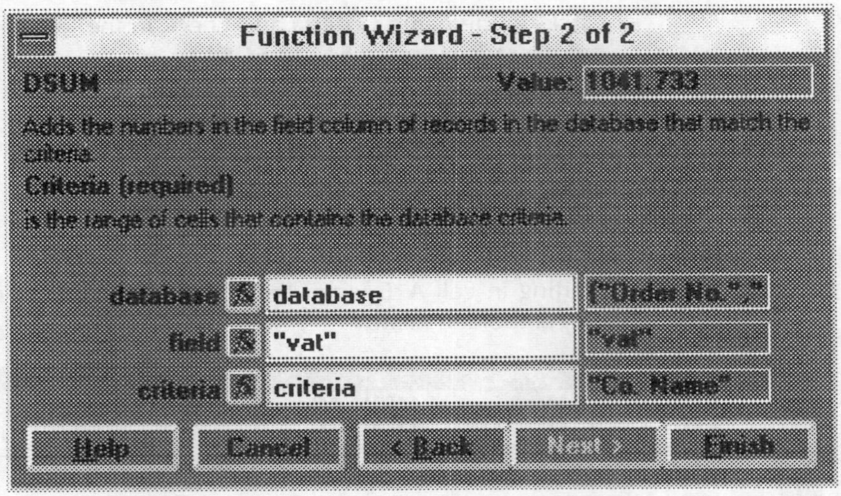

Figure 8

7   The total Vat on orders for Wilson Garages is placed in cell D17.
     (1041.73) the formula **=DSUM(database,"VAT",criteria)** appears in the
     Formula Bar.

     Error Messages. If you get an error message then check that each name
     is spelt correctly and the field name entered in double quotes. You can
     edit it in the Formula Bar.

8   **Consolidation – Function Wizard**. Select cell C17, then click the Func-
     tion Wizard button.

     Use the **DSUM** function to calculate cell the total value of invoices for
     Wilson Garages.

9   **Entering Functions Directly. I**n cell A17 we will use the DCOUNT
     function to count the number of orders for Wilson Garages:

     Select cell **A17** then enter the formula:

        =DCOUNT(database,"total",criteria)

     Error Messages. If you get an error message then check that the field
     name is spelt correctly and entered in double quotes. You can edit it in
     the Formula Bar.

     Check that you have placed the = sign, commas and brackets correctly.

     Notice also that there are no spaces in the formula, and that you can use
     upper or lower case.

10   Activate cell **B17** next and use the DAVERAGE function to calculate the
     average value of an order for Wilson Garages.

     The formula is, **=DAVERAGE(database,"value",criteria)**

11   Cell E17 uses the DMIN function to find the order for Wilson
     Garages with the lowest value.

     Enter the formula **=DMIN(database,"value",criteria)**

12 Using the **Format** menu, format the cells **A17** to **E17** to 2 decimal places.

13 We have now created a number of database function formulae and can select any search criteria to apply them to particular records.

Clear the search condition **Wilson Garages** from cell **D14.**

Enter **2413** in cell **C14** as a search criterion; the values in all the formulae cells change to reflect the totals for this company's orders.

Reading across row 17, 2 orders are counted, their average value is £1016.50, etc.

14 **Consolidation – Search Criteria.** Every time the search criteria in row 14 are changed the formulae immediately recalculate the results.

Enter the following search criteria, *remembering to clear previous search conditions before you do*:

a. Order numbers 14005 onwards.

b. Orders with VAT amounts less than £250.

c. Orders totalling less than £1000 or more than £5000 (you will need to reset the criteria range to use an 'OR' condition – see activity 1).

Summary of commands and functions

Note

Menu commands show the menu name first, followed by the command to choose from the menu, e.g. Edit-Clear means open the Edit menu and select the Clear command.

Commands

Data-Filter-Advanced Filter Filter	Search database using Advanced
Data-Filter-Show All	Show all records in database
Insert-Name-Define	Define cell range as database

Database functions

Database functions have the form:

[FUNCTION](database,"field",criteria) :

database is the database range that you have defined.

field is the field name or cell reference in the database on which the function operates and must be enclosed in double quotes.

criteria is the criteria range that you have defined.

DAVERAGE	Average a numeric field
DCOUNT	Count number of records
DMAX	Find maximum
DMIN	Find minimum
DPRODUCT	Multiply
DSTDEV	Calculate standard deviation
DSUM	Add
DVAR	Calculate variance

Copying workbooks

Introduction

The next few units show you how to link several workbooks together. Excel allows you to link workbooks together, so that you can share and exchange data between them. This has a number of advantages:

a.   Although you could create several smaller worksheets within one large workbook, there are cases where separate workbooks are better. For example it may also be more convenient for several workbooks to be created independently and combined and summarised later.

b.   You can edit the linked workbooks as a group; changes made to one workbook will be reflected in the others.

c.   The Excel windowing facility means that several workbooks can be open in memory at once so that you can see the results of any changes.

A typical linking application is the departments or branches of a company. The same type of financial or numeric data is recorded for each, and they are combined into an overall summary.

We will create a set of simple profit forecasts for a group of three hotels – Greenlands, Whiteways, and Blueskies – and combine them into an overall summary.

Activity 1   Creating a template workbook

1   We will first create a master workbook, copy it and then customise it for each hotel.

Start Excel and open a new workbook.

	A	B	C	D	E
1			BUDGET - FIRST QUARTER		
2					
3		JAN	FEB	MAR	TOTAL
4	No. of Rooms				
5	No. of Days	31	28	31	
6	Occupancy Rate	0.7	0.6	0.65	
7	Av. Rate per Room	40	40	40	
8	Total Room Revenue	0			
9	Estim. DOP - Rooms	0			
10	Estim. Food Revenue	0			
11	Estim.DOP - Food	0			
12					
13	Total Operating Profit	0			

Figure 1

2   Enter the data shown in Figure 1, using the following notes as a guide:

Row 4.   No. of Rooms. Leave this blank as the number of rooms available will vary between hotels/months.

Row 5.   The number of days in the month. Enter 31 etc as shown.

Row 6.   Occupancy Rate   (not every available room is let) Enter as 0.7 (i.e. 70%) for Jan, 0.6 for Feb etc. as shown.

Row 7.   Av. Rate per Room. This is £40, the average charged per room per day, excluding food. Enter this for cells B7 to D7. *Do not enter a £ sign.*

Rows 4 to 7   above hold all the variables, the remaining rows are all based on **formulae.** Remember to begin every formula with an '=' sign.

Row 8.   Total Room Revenue is the product of the first 4 cells, so the formula is **=B4*B5*B6*B7.** Enter this formula in cell **B8.** It will show a value of 0 at the moment until row 4 is completed.

Row 9.   Estimated DOP – Rooms. The direct operating profit or DOP is estimated as 40% of Total Room

Revenue – cell **B8**. Enter the formula **=B8*0.4** in cell **B9.**

Row 10.   The Estimated Food Revenue is 45% of the Total Room Revenue. Enter the formula **=B8*0.45** in cell **B10.**

Row 11.   The Estimated Direct Operating Profit – Food is estimated as 45% of the Estimated Food Revenue. Enter the formula **=B10*0.45** in cell **B11.**

Row 13.   Total Operating Profit is the operating profits for food and for rooms added together, i.e. **=B9+B11**
Enter this formula in cell **B13.**

Activity 2   Filling right and formatting the worksheet

Now that we have created the data and formulae for Jan we need to copy them across to the other 2 months and to create the quarterly totals in column E.

After formatting the workbook will look like Figure 2 and serve as a template for other workbooks.

	A	B	C	D	E
1			BUDGET - FIRST QUARTER		
2					
3		JAN	FEB	MAR	TOTAL
4	No. of Rooms				0
5	No. of Days	31	28	31	90
6	Occupancy Rate	0.7	0.6	0.65	
7	Av. Rate per Room	40.00	40.00	40.00	
8	Total Room Revenue	0.00	0.00	0.00	0.00
9	Estim. DOP - Rooms	0.00	0.00	0.00	0.00
10	Estim. Food Revenue	0.00	0.00	0.00	0.00
11	Estim.DOP - Food	0.00	0.00	0.00	0.00
12					
13	Total Operating Profit	0.00	0.00	0.00	0.00

Figure 2

1   **Filling Right.** Select the row of cells **B8** to **D8.**

Open the **Edit** menu and select **Fill** then the **Right** option. The formula is copied into cells C8 and D8.

Now select the block of cells **B9** to **D13** and repeat the Fill Right operation. Now all the formula are copied for the 3 months.

2   We will create the totals in the TOTAL column by adding across the 3 months.

Select cell **E5** then click the **Autosum** button (on the tool bar marked with the Sigma symbol, like a capital M on its side)

Cells **B5** to **D5** are outlined, and the correct formula **=SUM(B5:D5)** appears in the cell.

Click the 'tick' button on the Formula Bar and the formula is entered. The total days in the quarter (90) are displayed in cell **E5**.

3   Now repeat this SUM operation for cells **E8** to **E11** and cell E13. (do not add the Occupancy Rate or the Rate per Room – these cannot sensibly be summed)

Finally do it for cell **E4**.

4   As a check that your formulae are correct, enter the figure **100** in cell **B4**.

Your Total Operating Profit should be **52,297.** If not you will need to check the formula and the data entered.

Erase this entry once you have checked it. (press the Delete key)

5   Finally format the worksheet as follows, using the Format-Cells menu.

Format the cells holding numeric data to 2 decimal places. (not rows 3 to 5)

Embolden the Titles and cell labels and centre the headings.

Widen column A if necessary.

The worksheet should now resemble Figure 2 above.

6   Save the workbook as BUDGMAS. When the Summary dialog box appears enter a note to remind you that this is the template for all the hotel profit forecasts.

Activity 3   Copying workbooks

You now have an empty matrix, it can be copied to create forecasts for the 3 hotels. The three hotels will be called Greenlands, Whiteways, and Blueskies. To do this we need to create 3 copies of the workbook, plus an extra copy to hold the summary figures. There are two ways to do this, you can either use the Save As command to save the workbook BUDGMAS under different names, or you can copy and paste the cells from BUDGMAS into a new empty workbook. We will try both methods

1   Make sure that the BUDGMAS workbook is still open.

Open the **File** menu and select **Save As** – a dialog box appears.

The **File Name** box contains the current name BUDGMAS; enter the new name **GREEN,** check the drive letter and click the **OK** button. The original workbook BUDGMAS is copied under the new name GREEN and then closed, leaving the GREEN workbook displayed.

2   Now repeat this operation, saving the workbook GREEN under the name WHITE – we now have workbooks for the two hotels Greenlands and Whiteways.

3   We'll use another method to create the third worksheet.

       Select all the worksheet cells, i.e. **A1** to **E13** in Sheet 1 of the Workbook White.

       Open the Edit menu and select **Copy.**

4   Open the File menu and select **New.**

       When the new blank workbook appears, open the **Edit** menu and select **Paste.**

       Widen the columns if necessary.

       Save this workbook as **BLUE** – don't bother to complete the Summary dialog box.

5   We now need to create a 4th copy of BUDGMAS to hold an overall summary of the totals of the 3 other workbooks. This time copy the *title and cell labels only, not the data and formulae,* to a new worksheet, ie cell ranges:

       A1 to **E3** – the titles and heading,

       A4 to **A13** – the row labels.

       Hint: You will need to repeat steps 3 and 4 twice; you can use the Window menu to move between the two workbooks.

6   Save the workbook as **SUMMARY1.**

       We now have 4 copies of the original template workbook BUDGMAS – GREEN, WHITE and BLUE for the 3 hotels and SUMMARY1.

7   Save and close all the workbooks that remain open, using the **File-Close** option.

Summary of commands and functions

Note

Menu commands show the menu name first, followed by the command to choose from the menu, e.g. Edit-Clear means open the Edit menu and select the Clear command.

Commands

      Edit-Fill-Right   Copy selected cells to selected right hand columns

Linking workbooks

Skills to be learned	Activity
External ranges – linking	4
Linking formulae	2.3
Multiple workbooks – displaying	1
Opening linked workbooks	3.4
Workbooks – linking	2
Workspaces – creating	3

Previous skills needed to tackle this unit

Skill	Covered in Unit
Starting Excel	1
Basic mouse, menu and Windows operations	1
Creating a simple worksheet	1
Using simple formulae and formatting	1 – 3

Previous workbooks needed

The 4 workbooks GREEN, WHITE, BLUE and SUMMARY1, created in the previous unit.

Introduction

Now that we have created the 3 workbooks in the previous unit we can use the summary workbook to link and summarise the totals that they contain. We will also save them as a combined workspace file.

Activity 1   Opening and displaying multiple workbooks

In this activity we will practice different ways of displaying and viewing multiple worksheets.

1 **Opening Multiple Workbooks.**

We need to open the 4 workbooks GREEN, WHITE, BLUE and SUMMARY1.

Open the File menu. As Excel lists the 4 last documents used, the workbooks are probably listed at the bottom of the menu. Open each one in turn.

If a workbook is **not** listed at the bottom of the File menu then take the **Open** option, and select the workbook name from the **File Name** list. If you can't find it then check that you are using the correct drive and/or that the correct diskette is in the drive.

2 **Handling Multiple Workbooks.**

There are several ways of arranging the 4 workbook windows on screen using the Window-Arrange menu.

Open the **Window** menu and take the **Arrange** option – a dialog box appears.

Click the **Cascade** option then **OK**.

You should now be able to see the overlapping edges of the 4 worksheets – see Figure 1.

If you can only see one worksheet then you probably need to use the Restore button to reduce the window size.

SUMMARY1.XLS					
BLUE.XLS					
GREEN.XLS					
WHITE.XLS					
	A	B	C	D	E	F
		BUDGET - FIRST QUARTER				
		JAN	FEB	MAR	TOTAL	
No. of Rooms					0	
No. of Days		31	28	31	90	

Figure 1

3 To practise moving between worksheet windows do either of the following :-

 a. Click on the edge of a worksheet, or

 b. Use the Window menu to select the worksheet by name – this is useful if you cannot see the worksheet

 Hints. After a while the arrangement may become jumbled and worksheets become hidden, if so open the Window menu and take the **Arrange-Cascade** option again.

 If a workbook appears blank check that the correct sheet, Sheet1, is active and that the correct cells are displayed (press the Ctrl and Home keys together)

4 Open the **Window** menu and take the **Arrange** option again.

This time click the **Tiled** option then **OK.**

The workbooks are arranged side by side on the screen – see Figure 2

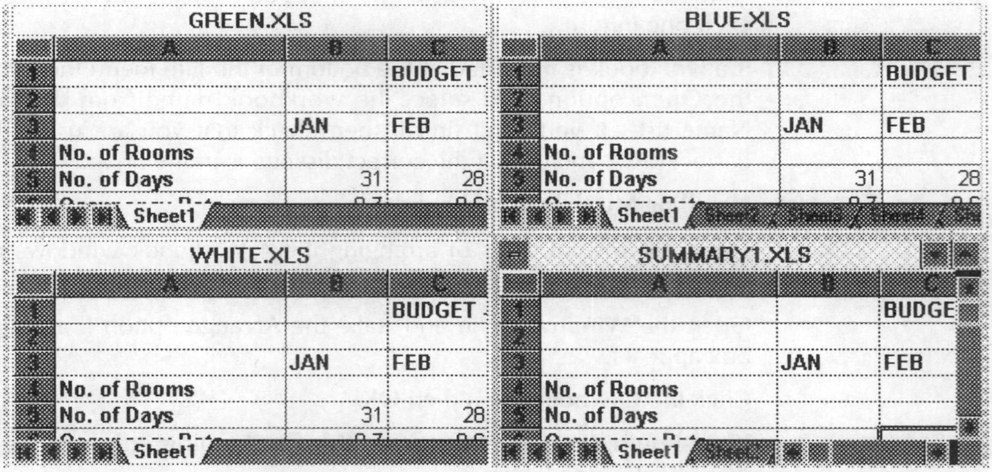

GREEN.XLS		
A	**B**	**C**
1		BUDGET
2		
3	JAN	FEB
4 No. of Rooms		
5 No. of Days	31	28

Sheet1

BLUE.XLS		
A	**B**	**C**
1		BUDGET
2		
3	JAN	FEB
4 No. of Rooms		
5 No. of Days	31	28

Sheet1 Sheet2 Sheet3 Sheet4

WHITE.XLS		
A	**B**	**C**
1		BUDGET
2		
3	JAN	FEB
4 No. of Rooms		
5 No. of Days	31	28

Sheet1

SUMMARY1.XLS		
A	**B**	**C**
1		BUDGE
2		
3	JAN	FEB
4 No. of Rooms		
5 No. of Days		

Sheet1 Shee

Figure 2

It doesn't matter if your workbooks are in a different order to that shown in Figure 2.

Click on each workbook in turn – it becomes the active workbook.

5 **Now activate each workbook in turn and enter the number of rooms for each hotel in row 4 as follows :**

	Jan	Feb	Mar
GREEN	55	48	55
WHITE	72	66	75
BLUE	92	88	95

Hint: If row 4 is not visible then you can use the scroll bars to scroll it into view. Alternatively use the Maximise button to temporarily enlarge the workbook. When you have finished click the Restore button to restore the tiled view – see Figure 3.

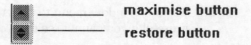 **maximise button**

restore button

Figure 3

Activity 2 Linking workbooks with formulae

1   We can now use the workbook SUMMARY1 to link the workbooks using external references.

We want to create a formula that adds together the contents of cell B4 for the 3 hotels and places them in cell B4 in the summary workbook.

Click cell **B4** in the **SUMMARY1** workbook; this activates both the worksheet and the cell.

2   **Type the formula** = WHITE.XLS!B4+BLUE.XLS!B4+GREEN.XLS!B4 in this cell.

This linking formula contains external references to 3 different workbooks. (each external reference must consist of the full name of the external workbook, plus the cell reference, both separated by an exclamation mark)

Click the tick box in the Formula Bar and the number of rooms for January at the 3 hotels is placed in cell B4 in workbook SUMMARY1.

The total should be 219 – if not check the data you have entered – see Activity 1.5 above – or the cells in the formula above.

Hint : An error message indicates that the formula is wrongly typed. If the formula is correct then Excel will add brackets around the three extenal cell references.

3   **Copying Linking Formulae.** Now click the **Maximise** button in the SUMMARY1 workbook if necessary.

Select cells **B4** to **D4,** then use **Edit-Fill-Right** to copy the formula to cells **C4** and **D4.** The linking formulae, with their external references, are copied to the 2 other cells.

Now select the cell range **B4** to **B11** and select the **Edit-Fill-Down** options.

Next select the cell range **B5** to **D11** and select the **Edit-Fill-Right** options.

Now select cell range **B6** to **D7** and press the **Delete** key to clear their contents. (Rows 6 and 7 – the Occupancy Rate and Av. Rate per room cannot meaningfully be summed and should be left blank).

The SUMMARY1 workbook should now resemble Figure 4 – check the totals.

A	B	C	D	E
		BUDGET - FIRST QUARTER		
	JAN	FEB	MAR	TOTAL
No. of Rooms	219	202	225	
No. of Days	93	84	93	
Occupancy Rate				
Av. Rate per Room				
Total Room Revenue	190092	135744	181350	
Estim. DOP - Rooms	76036.8	54297.6	72540	
Estim. Food Revenue	85541.4	61084.8	81607.5	
Estim.DOP - Food	38493.63	27488.16	36723.38	
Total Operating Profit				

Figure 4

4 Format the cells to include commas, using the Format-Cells menu; the columns may need to be widened to accommodate this new number format. (a row of hash symbols – ##### – indicates a cell that is too narrow)

5 **Independent Activity.** Create the totals in row 13 and column E.

Check your totals with Figure 5 below.

A	B	C	D	E
		BUDGET - FIRST QUARTER		
	JAN	FEB	MAR	TOTAL
No. of Rooms	219.00	202.00	225.00	646.00
No. of Days	93.00	84.00	93.00	270.00
Occupancy Rate				0.00
Av. Rate per Room				0.00
Total Room Revenue	190,092.00	135,744.00	181,350.00	507,186.00
Estim. DOP - Rooms	76,036.80	54,297.60	72,540.00	202,874.40
Estim. Food Revenue	85,541.40	61,084.80	81,607.50	228,233.70
Estim.DOP - Food	38,493.63	27,488.16	36,723.38	102,705.17
				0.00
Total Operating Profit	114,530.43	81,785.76	109,263.38	305,579.57

Figure 5

6 Use the Window-Arrange to view the 4 workbooks in tiled display again.

Changes made to any three of the supporting workbooks – WHITE, GREEN, or BLUE – will be reflected in the summary or dependent workbook SUMMARY1.

Try the two following 'what if' experiments :-

a. At the moment the group's Total Operating Profit for January is £114,530.43. The target is £120,000

Amend the Av. Rate per Room for **Jan.(B7)** to 42 for each of the three workbooks in turn.

Now activate the **SUMMARY1** workbook and look at cell B13 – the target is now achieved.

b. The occupancy rate for March for Greenways Hotel drops to 60% (amend cell **D6** on the **GREEN** workbook to **0.6**) – will the quarter's total operating profit still exceed 305,000 for the three hotels?

Now look at cell **E13** in the SUMMARY1 workbook – the target is still achieved.

Activity 3   Saving linked workbooks as a workspace

Linked workbooks need to be saved in the correct sequence otherwise the links between them may be lost. The dependent workbook SUMMARY1 must be closed and saved last – after the three supporting workbooks – WHITE, GREEN, and BLUE.

If you close the dependent workbook first there is a danger that any external formula may be lost. To make this easier all 4 linked workbooks can be saved and opened again under one group name, called a **workspace** in Excel. As well as making it easier to save and retrieve, a workspace will also preserve the arrangement of the workbooks on screen so that you can continue from where you left off last time.

1   Click the **Restore** button if necessary to return to the tiled layout for the 4 workbooks.

2   Open the **File** menu and choose **Save Workspace.** A menu box appears, offering you the default name RESUME.XLW.

Type the workspace name **HOTELS** and check the drive – I assume that you will want to save it to diskette so make sure that the **Drives** box shows a: and click **OK.** The 4 workbooks are saved under the workspace name HOTELS – the extension .XLW is automatically added. If the workbooks have changed you will be prompted to save each one first – do so.

Note: It will take some time to save all 4 workbook files to diskette under the workspace name HOTELS, as all the links must be saved too.

3   Now exit Excel, saving the workbooks if prompted to do so.

4   Start Excel again. It is not necessary for all the linked workbooks be open for the links to operate.

Open the **File** menu – at the bottom the workspace file HOTELS is listed, but so are the individual workbooks as well – they can still be opened as separate files.

To make this point open one of the supporting workbooks, WHITE.XLS.

Amend the Occupancy Rate for Feb. to **0.66.**

Save and **Close** the workbook.

5   Now open the SUMMARY1 workbook; a message appears, "This Document Contains Links. Update Links?'

Click the **Yes** button and observe the totals for Feb.

They are updated to reflect the changes made in the supporting workbook, WHITE.XLS.

6   Save and Close the workbook SUMMARY1.XLS.

Activity 4   Linking external ranges

In the previous activities we linked workbooks using formulae with external references – references to cells in other workbooks (see Activity 2, section 2)

Another way of achieving the same result is to use the Paste Link command. This ensures that when the original workbook changes the copy changes also.

To demonstrate this we will copy some of the totals from the SUMMARY1 workbook to a new workbook SUMMARY2.

1   Open the workbook **SUMMARY1.** Enlarge it if necessary so that all the cells are visible. If you get the message ' This document contains links. Re-establish links?' then click the **OK** button.

2   Open the **File** menu and select **New.** A new blank workbook is displayed.

Open the **File** menu and select **Save as.**

When the Save as dialog box appears type the workbook name **SUMMARY2** and check the drive – If you will want to save it to diskette make sure that the **Drives** box shows a: and click **OK.**

3   The Summary dialog box is displayed next. In the Title box enter 'Selected totals from SUMMARY1'

Click **OK** – the workbook is now saved as SUMMARY2.

4   Now open the **Window** menu and select **Arrange** then the **Cascade** option.

The edges of both workbooks are visible. Click the edge of **SUMMARY1** so that it is on top.

We are going to copy rows 9, 11 and 13 which hold the summaries of the operating profits for the quarter.

5   Select the row of cells **A9** to **E9**.

Open the **Edit** menu and select **Copy.**

Now click the workbook **SUMMARY2** to select it (or use the Window menu)

Select cell **A3.**

Open the **Edit** menu and select **Paste Special** – a dialog box appears – click the **Paste Link** button.

The 4 cells are copied from SUMMARY1 to SUMMARY2 – note the linking formula in the Formula Bar at the top of the worksheet.

6   Now repeat the above operations twice more to copy rows **11** and **13** from the **SUMMARY1** workbook to rows 4 and 5 respectively of the **SUMMARY2** workbook.

7   Now, using Figure 6 below as your guide, format the SUMMARY2 workbook as follows:

Widen the columns to fit the data (a row of hash symbols – ##### – indicates a cell that is too narrow) add the column headings, centre and embolden them, format the numbers to two decimal places with commas.

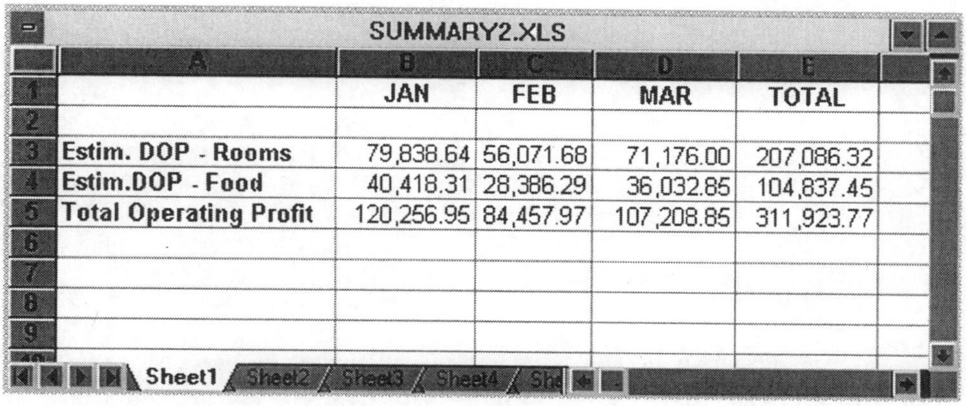

SUMMARY2.XLS					
	A	B	C	D	E
1		JAN	FEB	MAR	TOTAL
2					
3	Estim. DOP - Rooms	79,838.64	56,071.68	71,176.00	207,086.32
4	Estim.DOP - Food	40,418.31	28,386.29	36,032.85	104,837.45
5	Total Operating Profit	120,256.95	84,457.97	107,208.85	311,923.77
6					
7					
8					
9					

Sheet1 / Sheet2 / Sheet3 / Sheet4 / Sh

Figure 6

8   Now **Save** and **Close** the 2 workbooks SUMMARY1 and SUMMARY2.

9   Let's test the links now; open the workbook **GREEN.XLS** and amend the the number of rooms for March to **80.**

Save and **Close** the workbook.

10   Now open the workbook **SUMMARY1.** A message appears, "This Document Contains Links. Re-establish Links?'

Click the **Yes** button and note down the grand total in cell **E13**

They are updated to reflect the changes you have just made to the supporting workbook, GREEN.XLS.

11   Now open the workbook **SUMMARY2** and note the grand total in cell **E5** – it has automatically changed to reflect the updates that have taken place in SUMMARY1.

12   Finally **Save** and **Close** both workbooks.

Summary of commands and functions

Note

Menu commands show the menu name first, followed by the command to choose from the menu, e.g. Edit-Clear means open the Edit menu and select the Clear command.

Commands

Edit-Paste Special-Paste Link	Link copied cells in two workbooks
File-Save Workspace	Save workbooks as a linked group
Window Arrange	Arrange windows on screen

Creating and using tables

Introduction

Excel allows you to build data tables of various types. We will be experimenting with two types:

Input Tables hold data based on variables and formulae held in the worksheet, eg Figure 1 below shows a table of mortgage repayments based on different interest rates.

Lookup Tables work the other way round; the table is already created and you use a formula to look up values in it – see Figure 6 below.

Activity 1   *One-input tables*

We have seen in previous activities how we can perform 'what if' analysis by substituting different values in formulae. If we want to test a range of values it is quicker to hold them in a data table rather than change them one by one.

1   We will set up a one-input table first, which sets up a range of values for one variable – the mortgage interest rate.

Open a new workbook and create the worksheet shown in Figure 1 as follows:

	A	B	C
1		Mortgage Repayments Schedule	
2			
3	Interest Rate	10%	
4	Repayment Term	240	(enter term in months)
5	Amount Borrowed	50000	
6			
7	Possible Interest	Repayment p.m.	
8	Rates		
9	9.00%		
10	9.25%		
11	9.50%		
12	9.75%		
13	10.00%		
14	10.25%		
15	10.50%		
16	10.75%		
17	11.00%		
18			

Figure 1

Widen the columns and centre and embolden the title and cell labels as shown.

Use a data series to produce the range of percentages in column A as follows:

Enter **9.00%** in cell **A9** – the percentage sign must be entered.

Open the **Edit** menu and select the **Fill** then the **Series** option.

The Fill dialog box is displayed, enter the values as follows using Figure 2 as a guide.

Click **Columns** in the **Series in** box.

Enter the step value of **0.25%** in the **Step Value** box.

Enter the stop value of **11.00%** in the **Stop Value** box.

Finally click **OK.**

2   Enter the interest rate as **10%** in cell **B3** – the percentage sign must be entered.

Enter the repayment term as **240** in cell **B4.** (240 months = 20 years)

Enter the amount borrowed as **50000** in cell **B5.**

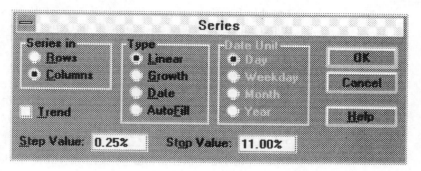

Figure 2

Format cells **B4** and **B5** to number format **0.00,** using the **Format-Cells-Number** command.

Select cell **B8** and open the **Format** menu. Select the **Edit-Cells** then the **Border** option to outline the cell. This will emphasise where the result is to appear.

Save the workbook as **MORTGAGE.**

3   **Naming Cells.**

Instead of referring to cells by their row and column references, we can name them and use their names in formulae and functions. Names can be shorter and easier to remember than cell references.

Select cell **B3,** then open the **Insert** menu and select the **Name** then the **Define** option. A dialog box appears with a default name already inserted.

Simply overtype with the name **RATE,** then click **OK.**

Similarly give cell **B4** the name **TERM,** and give cell **B5** the name **AMOUNT.**

We will use these cell names in the formula that follows.

4   **Setting up the PMT Formula.**

We will use the PMT function to calculate the monthly repayments. The Help facility (press F1 then the Search button) will tell you more about this function; it is used to calculate payments made at regular intervals at fixed interest rates, such as mortgages.

The syntax is, **=PMT(interest,term,principal)** where interest is the interest rate, term is the repayment term, and principal the amount borrowed.

Select cell **B8** and enter the formula   **=PMT(rate/12,term,-amount)**

Rate is divided by 12 as we want the monthly repayment and the – sign will express the amount as a positive rather than a negative number.

The monthly repayment of **482.52** is now displayed in cell B8, based on the values entered in cells **B3** to **B5.**

Troubleshooting: If your formula is correct then Excel converts it to upper case – a useful indicator: If not check the cell data and the formula.

5   **Creating the One-input Table.**

To find out the effect on the monthly repayments if the interest rate changes, we can create a table, based on the interest rates in cells A9-A17.

Select cell range **A8** to **B17.**

Open the **Data** menu and select the **Table** option; a dialog box appears.

Select the **Column Input Cell** box and enter the cell reference **B3.** Click **OK.**

You have defined the cell range A8 – B17as an input table and cell B3 as the cell where data will be entered – the varying interest rate.

6   The repayment figure is shown in cell **B8** as before. However different monthly repayments, based on different rates of interest, are now shown in cells **B9** to **B17,** and can be compared with cell B8.

Format the table entries to 2 decimal places, using the **Format-Cells-Number** command.

7   **Consolidation.**

Amend the interest rate in cell **B3** to **9%,** and the amount borrowed in cell **B5** to **70000.**

The new repayment is shown in cell B8 – **629.81** per month.

At what interest rate would you start to pay more than £700 per month?

8   **Adding Further Formulae to the One-input table.**

We can create another table on the same worksheet, showing the effect of changing interest rates on another variable – the total cost of the loan.   This is the monthly repayment multiplied by the term of the loan – see Figure 3 below.

Put the title **Total Repaid** in cell **C7.**

Enter the formula **=B8*TERM** in cell C8.

Now select the cell range **A8** to **C17** (the new table range)

Open the **Data** menu and select the **Table** option – a dialog box is displayed.

Select the **Column Input Cell** box and enter the cell reference **B3.** Click **OK.**

You have created a second table in column C, showing the total amount repaid over the period of the loan.

	A	B	C
1		Mortgage Repayments Schedule	
2			
3	Interest Rate	9%	
4	Repayment Term	240	(enter term in months)
5	Amount Borrowed	70000	
6			
7	Possible Interest	Repayment p.m.	Total Repaid
8	Rates	629.81	151,153.96
9	9.00%	629.81	151,153.96
10	9.25%	641.11	153,865.63
11	9.50%	652.49	156,598.04
12	9.75%	663.96	159,350.83
13	10.00%	675.52	162,123.64
14	10.25%	687.15	164,916.09
15	10.50%	698.87	167,727.82
16	10.75%	710.66	170,558.46
17	11.00%	722.53	173,407.65

Figure 3

9 Format the table values **C8** to **C17** to number format **#,##0.00** and centre them.

Select the **Cells** then the **Border** option to outline cell **C8**. This will emphasise where the result is to appear.

The worksheet will now resemble Figure 3.

10 **Consolidation.** Alter the interest rate to 10.5%, the term to 360, and the amount borrowed to 65,000.

    a. What is the total amount repaid?

    b. What is the monthly repayment?

11 Save and close the workbook.

Activity 2   Two-input tables

The one-input data table used in the previous activity is one-dimensional; it can only show table values based on one input variable – the interest rate. Although we built a second table to show the total amount repaid, it was still based on this same variable.

In this activity we will use a two-input table to calculate salespersons' monthly commission – see Figure 4 below. It uses a two-dimensional table or matrix; one variable – monthly sales – is in column B, the other, the commission rate, is in row 5. We will create a table that will use both variables to calculate commission, eg £50,000 sales at 5% commission rate.

A	B	C	D	E	F
	MONTHLY COMMISSION TABLE				
	Commission Rates				
	0	5%	6%	7%	8%
	50,000				
	60,000				
Monthly Sales:	70,000				
	80,000				
	90,000				

Figure 4

1   Start a new workbook and enter the information shown in Figure 4. Format it as shown.

   Hint: If you wish use the Data Series command to create the percentages in row 5 and the sales figures in column B. (see Activity 1)

2   The commission earned is the commission rate multiplied by the monthly sales.

   The formula must be entered where the row and column variables intersect in cell B5.

   Select cell **B5** and enter the formula **=B3*B4**

   You may wonder why cells B3 and B4 have been chosen. In fact we won't be entering any values in these cells. This is because in this example the two-input table provides the full range of values we are interested in. (unlike the previous example of the one-input table) However the table needs to use two cells when it calculates its values. We nominated B3 and B4, but could use any empty cells outside the table.

3   Now select cells that the table will fill, i.e. cell range **B5** to **F10**.

   Open the **Data** menu and select **Table** – the Table dialog box appears.

   Enter **B3** in the **Row Input Cell** box and **B4** in the **Column Input Cell** box.

   Click **OK.**

   The commission table is calculated, equivalent to 25 separate calculations – see Figure 5 below. This makes the table a valuable tool.

   Save the workbook as **COMMISS.XLS.**

	A	B	C	D	E	F
2						
3			Commission Rates			
4						
5		0	5%	6%	7%	8%
6		50,000	2500	3000	3500	4000
7		60,000	3000	3600	4200	4800
8	Monthly Sales:	70,000	3500	4200	4900	5600
9		80,000	4000	4800	5600	6400
10		90,000	4500	5400	6300	7200
11						
12	Enter No. of Months:					
13						

Figure 5

4   **Consolidation.**

We will adapt the table so that we can calculate the commission for a number of months.

Enter the label in cell **A12** – see Figure 5 above.

Now format cell **B12** with a border as shown – see previous activity if necessary.

Amend the table formula in cell **B5** to include cell **B12** in its product, ie =B3*B4*B12

Now enter **6** in cell **B12** – the table is recalculated, showing the commission earned for 6 months at various interest rates.

5   Save and close the table.

6   **More Information on tables.**

Move or delete a table. Select the whole table and then select Clear from the Edit menu. (or press the Delete key)

Modify a table. Select the whole table and choose the Table command from the Data menu.

Extend the range of a table. Enter the extra values then proceed as for modify.

Activity 3   Lookup tables

The table values in the previous activities are generated using variables and a formula. The user inputs a number of variables, e.g. mortgage amount, term, etc, then the Table command builds a table based around one or more of them. A lookup table involves the reverse procedure; the table is already created and you look up a value in it. Lookup tables can be used to hold various types of fixed information that can be 'looked up' from another part of the worksheet, e.g. rates of pay, credit ratings or addresses.

Look at Figure 6 below.

	A	B	C	D	E	F
1				Order Discount Look-up		
2						
3	Cash Order					
4	Order Value:					
5	Discount					
6	Net Value			Order Value	Cash	Credit
7				0	5%	0%
8	Credit Order			500	10%	5%
9	Order Value:			1000	15%	10%
10	Discount			5000	20%	15%
11	Net Value			10000	25%	20%
12						

Figure 6

In columns D to F is a table to look up customer discounts, based on the order value – from £0 to £10,000 – and the type of order (cash or credit). As the discount rates in the table do not follow any obvious numeric sequence, using a formula to generate them would be difficult.

You can use two lookup functions to get data from a table, HLOOKUP and VLOOKUP:

HLOOKUP is used if the lookup values are arranged horizontally in a row. The syntax is **=HLOOKUP(x,range,index)**

VLOOKUP is used if the lookup values are arranged vertically in a column, as they are in the table shown above (the more usual arrangement).

The syntax is **=VLOOKUP(x,range,index)**

> **x** is the value that you want to look up; it can be entered as text, a number, or a cell reference.
>
> **range** is the range of cells forming the table.
>
> **index** tells you which column or row to look in.

Applying this to Figure 6 above:

> **x** is cell B4 where the value of the order will be entered,
>
> **Range** is the cell range D7 to F11 holding the lookup table,
>
> **Index** are columns E and F where the the lookup values are held.

Note: For the LOOKUP function to work the first column of the lookup table must consist of entries that are used to look up items of data in immediately adjacent columns. These entries must be unique and in ascending order.

1   Open a new workbook. Create the data as shown in Figure 6 above and enter an order value of **600** in cell **B4.**

2   In cell **B5** enter the formula **=VLOOKUP(B4,D7:F11,2)**

Enter it in lower case – if it is correct it is converted to upper case.

The formula means 'look up the value in cell B4, from the table in cell range D7 to F11, in the 2nd column of the table'. The lookup function searches the first column of compare values – column D – until it reaches a number equal to or higher than 600 (cell D9) It then goes back a row if it is higher (to cell D8), then goes to the second column (E) and looks up the discount of 10% (in cell **E8)**

For this reason the values in the first column of the lookup table – column D – must be in ascending sequence.

3   The discount is displayed as **0.1.** Use the **Format** command then the **Cells-Number** options. From the dialog box select **Percentage** from the category list.

Then select 0% from the list of percentage options and click **OK.**

The discount is now displayed as 10% in cell B5.

4   The formula to calculate the net value of the order (ie order value minus discount) can now be entered in cell **B6.**

Enter the formula = **B4-(B4*B5)** in this cell. The order value minus discount is shown in cell B6.

Try entering some other order values in cell B4 to test this.

5   **Consolidation.**

Now repeat these steps and enter another VLOOKUP formula in cell **B10** to calculate the discount on credit orders.

Note: You will need to modify the cell references, for the lookup value (B9) and the column number (3) where the lookup values are held.

6   Save the workbook as **DISCT1** and close it.

Summary of commands and functions

Note

Menu commands show the menu name first, followed by the command to choose from the menu, e.g. Edit-Clear means open the Edit menu and select the Clear command.

Commands

Data-Table	Create a table from selected cells
Edit-Fill-Series	Create a data series

Functions

Functions require you to supply information for their operations. These are called *arguments*. eg SUM(range) requires the argument cell range, to be added. Arguments must be enclosed in brackets. Optional arguments are shown in the lists that follow in square brackets – [ ]. These brackets are for your guidance only and should **not** be typed. Function arguments are separated by commas. The commas **must** be typed.

HLOOKUP(x,range,index)

Look up a value in a table where the values are displayed horizontally

VLOOKUP(x,range,index)

Look up values in a table where the values are displayed vertically.

x is the value that you want to look up; it can be entered as text, a number, or a cell reference. range is the range of cells forming the tableindex tells you which column or row to look in.

PMT(interest,term,principal,[,fv,type])

Gives the repayments required for a loan amount (principal) based on the interest rate and the term. Options are to enter future value and whether payment is made at the end of the period (type=0, the default) or at the beginning (type=1)

unit 14
Analysis tools

Introduction

In the previous unit we have used input and lookup tables to compare values for one or more variables. In the next few activities we will look at the special-purpose analysis tools Goal Seek and Solver. These two tools automate the process of repeated 'What if?' trials.

Activity 1   Goal Seek

The 'what-if?' abilities of Excel allow us to try out alternative values for a given situation. The first and simplest is Goal Seek; often you want to know what value a variable needs to be for a formula to equal a particular value. Goal Seek keeps changing the value of the variable until the formula achieves the target value.

1   Open the workbook **BLUE.XLS.** You will recall from Unit 12 that it calculates the quarterly operating profit for Blueskies Hotel.

We want to find out what occupancy rate for February would achieve a total operating profit of £40,000 for this month. We could keep amending the occupancy rate cell (C6) and observe the effects, but Goal Seek is easier.

2   Open the **Tools** menu and select **Goal Seek** – a dialog box appears.

If necessary move the box so that you can see column C – see Figure 1.

You would need to position the screen pointer on the title of the box, and drag it using the mouse.

	B	C	D	E	F	G	H
	JAN	FEB	MAR	TOTAL			
	92	88			Goal Seek		
	31	28					
	0.7	0.6	Set cell:	C13		OK	
	42.00	40.00	To value:	40000		Cancel	
	83848.80	59136.00	By changing cell:	C6			
	33539.52	23654.40					
	37731.96	26611.20				Help	
	16979.38	11975.04	15505.43	44459.85			
	50518.90	35629.44	46133.43	132281.77			

Figure 1

3   Complete the box as shown in Figure 1, ie:

Set cell	**C13**
To value	**40000**
By changing cell	**C6**

Make a note of the present value of cell C6 and click **OK.**

A further Goal seek Status dialog box appears reporting the solution.

The value of cell C6 is changed to **0.67** – the occupancy rate needed to reach the £40,000 goal.

4   Click the **Cancel** button now; this restores the previous value for cell C6 and all the dependent cells.

If you click OK by accident then select **Undo** from the Edit menu.

5   Now try the following Goal Seek; what average rate per room for January (cell B7) would achieve a total room revenue (cell B8) of £100,000?

6 **Consolidation.** (optional) Open the workbook **TERMS.XLS** created in Unit 2 and scroll to week 9 of worksheet Spring Term.

How large a loan would you need in week 9 to achieve a closing balance of £150?

7 Close the workbooks BLUE and TERM1 without saving any changes.

8 **Notes on Goal Seek.**

The Goal Seek Status dialog box displays two extra buttons;

Pause – allows you to pause during goal seeking

Step – allows you to continue one step at a time.

Goal seeking will only work if the cell whose value you set contains a value, not a formula.

The cell whose value you set must be related by a formula to the cell whose target value you are changing.

Activity 2 Solver

The Goal Seek tool used in the previous activity can substitute various values for a variable in a formula. It cannot determine what the 'best' ones are for your purpose.

Solver, as its name suggests, can solve certain types of problem. It will juggle with multiple values for variables and find the combination producing the optimum or target result, e.g. it can determine the most profitable mix of products, schedule staff to minimise the wages bill, or allocate working capital to its most profitable use.

Solver allows you to specify up to two hundred variables; it also allows you to put constraints on variables by specifying the limits that they can take e.g. minimum and maximum values for a machine's output or for a working week.

Solver is an Excel's most powerful analysis tool and uses complex mathematical methods to solve equations and arrive at its optimum or target values. It tries out various input values for the formulae and observes, not only the corresponding outputs, but also their rate of change. Each trial is known as an iteration.

The results of a previous iteration is analyzed and used to work out the next set of trial inputs. Solver converges on the optimum or target value by repeated iterations.

This method can be much quicker than Goal Seek, tables or manual calculations, especially if you are working with multiple variables and constraints.

However Solver poses certain problems for the user:

a. There are a fairly limited range of problems that can or need to be solved in this way.

b. For complex problems there may be more than one solution; Solver may provide the best given the range of values that you have specified, but it may not be the best overall. You may need to run Solver more than once with different ranges of values.

c. To use Solver effectively then you must thoroughly understand the nature of the problem that you are trying to solve, otherwise Solver will either fail to work altogether or give you misleading results.

We will first set up a typical Solver problem – see Figure 2.

	A	B	C	D	E	F	G	H	I	J
1		Staff Scheduling - New Branch								
2					Mon	Tue	Wed	Thu	Fri	Sat
3	Rota	Rest Days	Employees							
4			per Rota							
5	1	Mon, Tue	0		0	0	1	1	1	1
6	2	Tue, Wed	0		1	0	0	1	1	1
7	3	Wed, Thu	0		1	1	0	0	1	1
8	4	Thu, Fri	0		1	1	1	0	0	1
9	5	Fri, Sat	0		1	1	1	1	0	0
10			0							
11		Staff Allocated per Day:			0	0	0	0	0	0
12										
13		Staff Needed per Day:			14	14	16	17	20	22
14										
15		Av. Pay per Day (£)	30							
16		Wages Bill per Week:	0							

Figure 2

Your company wishes to open a new branch and needs to work out the optimum staff allocation throughout the working week of Monday to Saturday.

The numbers of staff needed each day are already known and are shown in row 13; more staff are needed towards the weekend as the branch gets busier.

Each staff member must get 2 consecutive rest days; these are staggered to produce 5 different rotas and are entered in columns A and B. So staff on rota 1 get Monday and Tuesday off, staff on rota 2 get Tuesday and Wednesday off etc.

In columns E to J this is represented as a 0 for a rest day and 1 for a working day.

You need to:

    a.   calculate how many staff need to be on each rota (cells C5-C9)

    b.   ensure that the staff allocated each day (cells E11-J11) cover the number of staff needed (cells E13-J13)

A problem will be that to achieve full staffing levels on busy days we may need to employ more staff then we need on other days.

1   First let's build the basic worksheet; start a new workbook and create the title and cell labels. Format them as shown, then enter the figures shown. (Open the Format menu then select the **Cells** then the **Number** options)

    Format cell ranges **C5** to **C9** and **E11** to **J11** as whole numbers. (all staff are full time so no fractional amounts are allowed)

2   Apply the following formulae :-

    a.   Cell **C10** is the sum of cells **C5** to **C9.** (this gives the total days worked by all staff) Format to a whole number.

    b.   Cell **C16** is the product of cells **C10** and **C15.** (ie the weekly wages bill is the total days worked multiplied by the average rate per day)

    d.   To calculate the number of staff working on each day you need to multiply column C – the number of staff working the rota – by column E – which indicates whether that rota is working on that day. Hence for Monday C5 is multiplied by E5 for rota 1, then added to C6 multiplied by E6 for rota 2 etc.

    Enter the following formula to calculate staff working on Monday in cell E11

    =($C5*E5)+($C6*E6)+($C7*E7)+($C8*E8)+($C9*E9)

    Use the **Edit-Fill-Right** command to copy this formula to cells **F11** to **J11.**

    The $ sign in the formula ensures that column C is an *absolute* reference and is copied unchanged into the new formulae. Absolute references are explained in Unit 3, Activity 5. Column E is a *relative* reference and gets adjusted to F, G, H etc. when the formula is copied to rows F,G,H, I and J. (this combination of fixed and relative references is called a *mixed* reference or address)

3   Save the workbook as **SCHEDULE**

4   Open the **Tools** menu and select **Solver.**

    The Solver Parameters dialog box appears – see Figure 3.

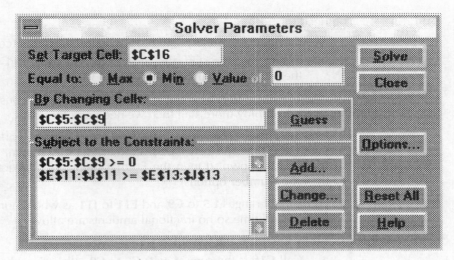

Figure 3

We wish to minimise the wages bill; complete the first part of the dialog box as follows, using Figure 3 as a guide.

Set Target Cell: Enter **C16**

Equal to buttons: Make sure that **Min** is selected and the **Value** of box is set to 0.

5   Click the **By Changing Cells** box and enter **C5:C9**

(we want to vary the cells containing the number of employees per rota to minimise the wages bill)

6   We must apply two constraints now;

a.   the number of staff per day must be >0   (i.e. not a negative number), and,

b.   the number of staff allocated on any day must meet or exceed the demand.

Click the **Add** button and a new dialog box appears – **Add Constraint.**

Add the following constraints using Figure 4 below as a guide.

Insert the cell references **C5:C9** in the **cell reference** box.

Change the relationship to >= in the middle box.

Finally click the **Constraint** box and insert **0.**

Click **OK** and you are returned to the Solver Parameters dialog box. The constraint is shown – **$C$5:$C$9>0.**

(Solver converts the cell references to absolute references)

If you have made an error then click either the Change button to edit it, or the Delete button and start again.

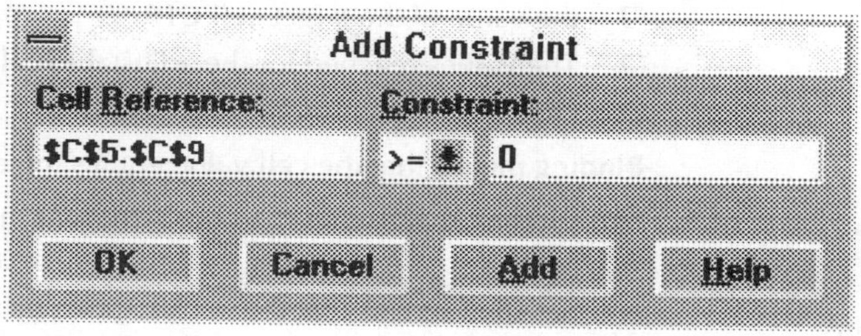

Figure 4

7   Add the second constraint in the same way – see 6b above. The constraint is **E11:J11>=E13:J13**

You have now finished your Solver parameters.

The completed dialog box should now resemble Figure 3 above.

8   Click the **Solve** button and Solver goes through a complex series of iterations until it finds the first valid solution. The worksheet figures are modified to show it.

A dialog box appears; move this aside so that you can see the solution. Solver has worked out,

a.   how many staff need to be on each rota (cells **C5** to **C9**) in order to ensure,

b.   that the staff allocated (cells **E11** to **J11**) cover,

c.   the numbers of staff needed (cells **E13** to **J13**)

You will notice that for one day – Monday – you are overstaffed by 3 people.

9   The Solver dialog box offers you the option of keeping the Solver solution or restoring the original values.

Click the **Restore Original Values** option then click **OK**.

10   **Consolidation.**

Call up Solver again and add a third constraint – that the staff allocated for Monday should not exceed those needed. The constraint is therefore that **E11<=14**

Enter this and run Solver again – you will notice that the overstaffing has merely been transferred to another part of the week. Given the staffing needs at this branch and the rota system there is no way round this.

11   **Solver Reports.** If the Solver successful completion message box is still on the screen you may wish to generate a Solver report at this stage.

Click the **Answer** option in the **Reports** box then click **OK**.

The report is generated and stored as a separate worksheet – Answer Report 1 – in the workbook. Change to this worksheet. It summarises all the solver input data:

☐   the value of the target cell **C16**

☐   The values reached for the adjustable cells **C5:C9**

☐   How well the constraint were met –

Binding means that the cell value equals the constraint value,

Not Binding means that the constraint was met but the values were not equal,

Not Satisfied means that the constraint value was not reached.

12   Exit from the workbook and save it – the report and the latest set of Solver settings are saved too.

Activity 3   Consolidation of Goal Seek and Solver

To reinforce the previous activities we will use Goal Seek and Solver on a new example. Figure 5 below shows the profits that a company makes from three products A, B and C.

1   Open a new workbook and create the simple worksheet shown in Figure 5.

Format all the numbers to whole numbers.

Total columns B and D down, and rows 5 to 7 across.

Save the workbook as PROFITS

	A	B	C	D	E
1					
2		No of	Profit	Profit	
3		Units	pre Unit		
4					
5	Product A	100	46	4600	
6	Product B	100	53	5300	
7	Product C	100	69	6900	
8	Totals	300		16800	

Figure 5

2   **Goal Seek** (Refer back to Activity 1 for guidance if necessary)

Find out how many of product B we need to make to raise total profits from £16,800 to £20,000.

Appendix 6 shows the correct entries for the Goal Seek dialog box.

Click the **Cancel** button on the dialog box so as not to save the Goal Seek variables.

3   **Solver.** We wish to make a profit of £20,000 for the three products subject to the following three constraints, which are based on production capacity and customer demand:

The maximum number we can make of Product A is 50.

We must make at least 40 each of Products B and C.

Overall production can rise to a maximum of 350.

Enter these constraints into Solver and run it.

Refer back to Activity 2 if necessary – appendix 7 shows the correct Solver parameters to enter.

4   When the **Solver Results** dialog box is displayed click the Save Scenario button.

Save the scenario as **PROFIT1** then click OK.

You are returned to the Solver Results dialog box

Click the **Restore Original Values** option then click **OK.**

5   We will now change the above constraints and save the Solver Results as a second scenario. Repeat steps 3 and 4, changing the first constraint – the maximum number we can make of product A is raised to **60.**

Save the second scenario as **PROFIT2** and restore the original values.

6   Now save the workbook – the most recent Solver settings are saved too.

7   Carry straight on with the next activity.

Activity 4   Using Scenario Manager

Scenario Manager allows you to save different combinations of variables as named scenarios and run and print them later. In the previous activity you have saved two combinations of values generated by Solver as scenarios, but you can equally well use Scenario Manager with Goal Seek or manually generated variables.

Scenario Manager will let you store as many different scenarios as you wish; you can then view and change them, delete them and print reports showing alternative scenarios.

1   **Running Different Scenarios.**

Open the **Tools** menu and select **Scenarios.**

Select the **Profit1** scenario and click the **Show** button.

The first Solver solution is applied to the worksheet and the cell values change.

Select the **Profit2** scenario and click the Show button – the second Solver solution is applied.

Close the Scenario Manager dialog box – the values remain assigned to the cells.

2 **Printing Scenarios.**

    a.   Open the File menu and select **Print Report.**

        The Print Report dialog box appears – click the **Add** button.

    b.   The Add Report dialog box appears.

        Enter the Report Name as **PROFITS**

    c.   Move the screen pointer to the **Section to Add** section.

        Click the down arrow on the **Scenario** box.

        Select the scenario **PROFIT1.**

        Click the **Add** button

    d.   Click the down arrow on the Scenario box again.

        Select the scenario **PROFIT2.**

        Click the **Add** button

    e.   Two scenarios are added to the report – click the **OK** button.

        The Print Report dialog box appears now – check your printer is turned on and connected.

3 Click the **Print** button and the report will print; it contains the printout of both versions of the worksheet, showing the 2 different sets of values generated by Solver in the previous activity.

4 Close the workbook and Save it.

Summary of commands

Note

Menu commands show the menu name first, followed by the command to choose from the menu, e.g. Edit-Clear means open the Edit menu and select the Clear command.

Insert-Name-Define	Create a name, eg for a cell
Tools-Goal Seek	Change values of selected cell so formula achieves a specified target value
Tools-Scenarios	Run Scenario Manager
Tools-Solver	Use Solver

Functions

Introduction

It is beyond the scope of these units to deal with all of the Excel functions; many, such as trigonometric and engineering functions, have little general business application.

To use others, such as financial functions, you need some specialist background in the subject to understand the significance of the results.

Some functions we have already used, such as the simpler maths functions in Unit 2 and the database functions in Unit 10. Macro functions can only be used on macro sheets and are dealt with in later units.

The following activity reviews the various types of functions. In Activity 2 we will use some widely-used functions in worksheets. Other useful functions are listed at the end of this unit.

Activity 1 Review of Excel functions

Notes on Using Functions.

☐ Functions are ready-made formulae that perform useful calculations.

☐ They produce their result in the cell in which they are entered.

☐ Every function must start with the = symbol

☐ Functions can be entered in lower or upper case. It is a good idea to type functions in lower case – if Excel does not convert it to upper case then you know that it is incorrect,

☐ Normally a function contains no spaces

☐ Functions can form part of a formula – or another function

☐ Functions require you to supply information for their operations, called arguments. eg SUM(range) requires the argument cell range to be added.

☐ Arguments are enclosed in round brackets – () these **must** be typed.

Optional arguments are shown in the lists that follow in square brackets – [ ] These brackets are for your guidance only and should **not** be typed.

☐ Two or more arguments are separated by commas.

The commas **must** be typed.

☐ You can either type the function yourself or use Function Wizard, which lets you choose the function from the list presented and paste it into the active cell.

1 **Types of Functions.** In Excel 5 there are 11 categories of functions.

Open a new workbook.

Open the **Insert** menu and select the **Function** option.

The Function Wizard dialog box appears, listing the categories – see Figure 1

Click the first Function Category – **Most recently Used.**

In the right hand box – **Function Name** – are some of the functions we have used so far.

Click each one in turn – the syntax of the function and a brief explanation are given at the bottom of the dialog box

Click the second function category – **All.** All the functions are listed alphabetically in the right hand box.

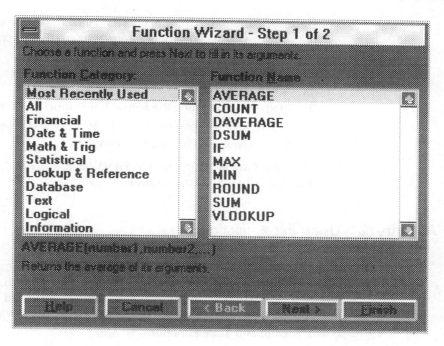

Figure 1

2 Now carry on reviewing the other Function Categories in the same way:

Financial Functions are used in the next activity.

Date and Time Functions are used in the next activity.

Mathematical and Trigonometric Functions calculate square roots, cosines etc. as well as the simpler functions such as SUM.

Statistical Functions such as average and standard deviation are used in the next activity.

Lookup Functions were used in Activities 9 to 11.

Database Functions carry out operations on database records only, e.g. summing or averaging selected records – see Unit 10, Activity 3. Some are listed in the next section.

Text Functions manipulate strings of text, e.g. finding the length or converting to upper case. A few are listed at the end of this unit.

Logical Functions test for the truth of certain conditions. A few are used in the next activity.

Information Functions test and report on cell references and contents; a few are listed at the end of this unit.

3   **Help on Functions.** The Function Wizard dialog box has a Help button; pressing it gives more information on the function currently selected.

a.   Click the **Financial** Function Category, then select **FV** and click the **Help** button.

b.   Help text explaining the Future Value function is displayed

c.   Open the **File** menu on the Help window and select **Exit**

    You are returned to Function Wizard.

4   Click the **Cancel** button on the Function Wizard dialog box. You are returned to the blank worksheet.

Activity 2   Using Excel functions

In the previous activity we reviewed the major categories of function. We shall try some of them out now, bearing in mind that these only represent a fraction of those available. Below are listed some of the functions that we will be using.

a.   **Date and Time Functions.**

Date and time functions display dates or times or calculate eg the time elapsed between two dates or times. This can be formatted to produce different date displays, eg:

NOW() displays the current date and time.

b.   **Financial Functions.**

Financial functions calculate such things as investments, repayments and depreciation. It is essential that the term of the investment, repayment etc is in the same time units as the interest rate; eg if you are,investing £5000 over 6 months at an annual interest rate of 10%, then the interest rate must be converted to a monthly rate too, eg:

FV(interest,payments,amount[pv,type])

Gives the future value of an investment, based on a fixed interest rate, the number of payments and the amount of the payment. The payments are assumed to be equal throughout. Options are to enter present value (pv) and whether payment is made at the end of the period (type=0, the default) or at the beginning (type=1)

NPV(interest,range)

Gives the net present value of an investment based on a fixed interest rate and series of cash flows within a given range.

PMT(interest,term,principal,[,fv,type])

Gives the repayments required for a loan amount (principal) based on the interest rate and the term. Options are to enter future value and whether payment is made at the end of the period (type=0, the default) or at the beginning (type=1). We have already used PMT() in Unit 13, Activity 1.

SLN(cost,salvage,life)

Calculates the depreciation of an asset using the straight-line method, based on the initial cost, its salvage value at the end of its life and the time period over which it is depreciated.

c. **Statistical Functions and Database Functions**

AVERAGE(range)

Gives the average value of a range of cells

MIN(range)

Gives the minimum value in a range of cells

MAX(range)

Gives the maximum value of a range of cells

STDEV(range)

Gives the standard deviation of a range of cells – how much they vary from the average

DAVERAGE, DMIN, DMAX, DSTDEV and DSUM are special database functions; they work in the same way as their statistical equivalents but can be used with search criteria – see Unit 10, Activity 3.

d. **Logical Functions**

IF(condition,true result,false result)

Tests a condition to see if true or false, takes one action for a true result, another for a false result.

AND(condition1,condition2,....)

Tests for all conditions being true and returns a logical True

OR(condition1,condition2,.....) tests for at least one condition being true and returns a logical True

1　We will now use some of these functions in the following worksheet, Figure 2. It monitors the performance of the shares of three travel companies over a two week period (weekends excluded).

Open a new workbook. You should be able to enter most of the worksheet for yourself. I shall concentrate on the functions.

2　**Displaying the Current Date.**

Select cell **E1** and enter the formula **=NOW()**

If a row of hash symbols (**###**) appears, widen the column.

Format it to **dd-mmm-yy** using the **Format-Cells-Number** menu.

Enter the rest of the worksheet data. Format the cell range **B4** to **D18** to 2 decimal places.

	A	B	C	D	E	F
1	Share Analysis				13-Mar-95	
2	Date	Alpha	Beta	Gamma	Changes	Share
3		Tours	Tours	Tours	in Value	Performance
4	01-Sep	19.44	50.88	123.54		
5	02-Sep	19.44	51.32	122.88		
6	03-Sep	20.65	51.36	124.55		
7	04-Sep	20.30	52.01	125.56		
8	05-Sep	19.25	52.64	125.95		
9	08-Sep	21.00	53.24	125.54		
10	09-Sep	21.35	54.25	124.54		
11	10-Sep	21.47	55.34	123.87		
12	11-Sep	20.83	55.00	127.28		
13	12-Sep	20.51	53.89	124.55		Share Increase
14						
15	Hi Val					
16	Lo Val					
17	Av Val					
18	St Dev					

Figure 2

3   Rows 15 to 17 will contain respectively the maximum, minimum and average value of the shares over the two weeks. Row 18 will show the standard deviation – the extent to which share prices have fluctuated from the average

In cell **B15** enter the function **=MAX(B4:B13)**

In cell **B16** enter the function **=MIN(B4:B13)**

4   Similarly apply the **AVERAGE** function to cell **B17**.

Apply the **STDEV** function to cell **B18**.

5   Use **Fill-Right** on the **Edit** menu to copy these functions to columns C and D.

6   Finally columns E and F are used to calculate how the three sets of shares have changed in value over the two weeks.

Add the share values for the three companies for the 1-Sep, ie add cell range **B4 – D4** and place the result in cell **E4.**

Similarly add the cell range for 12-Sep, **B13 – D13** and place the value in **E13.**

The combined value of the shares has grown between the two dates. Column E of your worksheet will now resemble Figure 3

7   In Figure 3 you will see that in cell **F13** a 'share increase' message is shown.

B	C	D	E	F
Alpha Tours	**Beta Tours**	**Gamma Tours**	**Changes in Value**	**Share Performance**
19.44	50.88	123.54	193.85	
19.44	51.32	122.88		
20.65	51.36	124.55		
20.30	52.01	125.56		
19.25	52.64	125.95		
21.00	53.24	125.54		
21.35	54.25	124.54		
21.47	55.34	123.87		
20.83	55.00	127.28		
20.50	53.89	124.55	198.94	**share increase**

Figure 3

This message is produced by the logical function **IF()** If the share values increase then this message is displayed, if not a 'share decrease' message is displayed.

Activate cell **F13** and enter the formula:

=IF(E13>E4,"share increase","share decrease")

Test the function by amending the value of cell **B13** to **14.50**

The message in cell F13 will change to 'share decrease' as the IF condition becomes false.

8 **Date Calculations.**

Dates can be added, subtracted and used in calculations.

To make this point we will calculate the time in days between the opening and closing dates.

In cell **G13** enter the label 'Time in Days'.

In cell **H13** enter the Formula **=A13-A4**

The result is 11 – the number of days. You may need to format the cell to a whole number – see section 2 above.

9 Save the workbook as **SHARES.XLS** and close it.

10 **Consolidation.** Now open a new blank workbook and try out the following financial functions :-

Future Value: You are going to save £1000 a year at 10% interest for 5 years.

Enter the following in a blank cell; **=FV(10%,5,1000)**

The result is the value of your investment after 5 years – £6,105.10. (you may need to widen the column to show the result)

Straight Line Depreciation: You have bought a PC for £1000 and estimate that in 4 years it will be worth £300. We will use Function Wizard to enter this function.

First select a blank cell in the worksheet.

Open the **Insert** menu and select **Function** – the Function Wizard dialog box appears.

Select **Financial** from the Function Category box and **SLN** from the Function name box – you may have to scroll down to find it.

Click the **Next** button – the second Formula Wizard dialog box appears.

Enter the arguments as shown in Figure 4. Notice that as each box is selected Function Wizard explains what you need to enter.

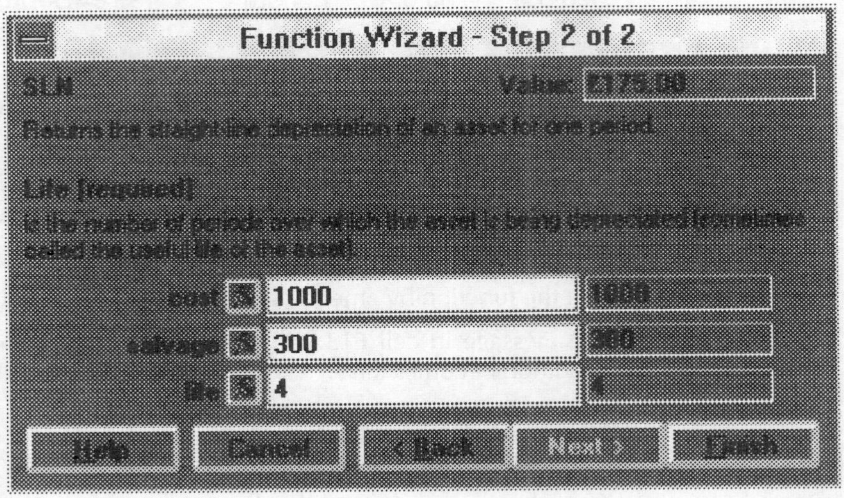

Figure 4

Finally click the **Finish** button on the dialog box.

The result is the annual amount of depreciation – £175.00.

11   Close the workbook without saving.

Summary of commands and functions

Some additional functions

Functions require you to supply information for their operations. These are called arguments. eg SUM(range) requires the argument cell range, to be added. Arguments must be enclosed in brackets.

Optional arguments are shown in square brackets – [ ]

These brackets are for your guidance only and should **not** be typed.

Function arguments are separated by commas. The commas **must** be typed.

Information functions

COLUMNS(range) counts the number of columns in a specified range

ISBLANK(value) IS functions check the type of value

ISNUMBER(value) in a cell and report TRUE or FALSE

ISTEXT(value) accordingly, depending on whether the cell is blank, text etc.

Text functions

EXACT(string1,string2) Compares two text strings. Reports TRUE if they are the same or FALSE if they differ.

LEN(string) Counts the number of characters in a text string.

Protecting and checking worksheets

Skills to be learned	Activity
Auditing Toolbar – using	2.7
Errors – tracing	2.10
Information Window – showing	2.3
Passwords – applying	1.1
Protecting Cells	1.6
Protecting worksheets	1.4
Protecting workbooks	1.9
Worksheet – auditing	2

Previous skills needed to tackle this unit

Skill	Covered in Unit
Starting Excel	1
Basic mouse, menu and Windows operations	1
Creating a simple worksheet	1
Using simple formulae and formatting	1 – 3

Previous Workbooks needed

The workbooks GREEN, WHITE, BLUE, SUMMARY1and SUMMARY2, created in units 11 and 12.

Activity 1 Protecting worksheets and workbooks

Excel offers various levels of protection. You can protect a worksheet or a workbook from being opened; this is vital if the whole document is confidential. You can also protect a workbook or a worksheet from being changed; this is important if it contains sensitive data or formulae which must not be deleted, amended or overwritten. Similar protection is available for individual ranges of cells, as well as charts and macro sheets.

1   Protecting a Workbook.

Open the workbook **SUMMARY2.** It contains profit forecasts that we might want to keep confidential.

If a message appears, "This Document Contains Links. Re-establish Links?' then click the **Yes** button.

Open the **File** menu and select **Save as.**

When the dialog box appears click the **Options** button. Various types of security are offered, make the following entries:

Always Create Backup:

> Leave this option blank, clicking it will create a backup copy of the old version of your workbook every time that you save it.

Protection Password

> Enter the password J MUIR The password will be invisible on the screen, hidden by a row of asterisks
>
> Entering a password in this box prevents the document from being opened unless the password is entered first.
>
> A password may be up to 15 characters long – numbers, letters, spaces or symbols.

Warning: If you forget the password you cannot unprotect the document; you must also remember to match the case – upper or lower – that you use.

Write Reservation

> Enter the password J MUIR Entering a password in this box prevents any changes to the document being saved unless you know the password. If you do not know it the changed document must be saved as a new document under a new name. This is useful for protecting documents from being overwritten.

Read-Only Recommended

> Leave this box blank – selecting this box will prompt (but not compel) users to open the worksheet as read-only. This alerts users if a document should not be changed unless necessary.

Finally click **OK.** You will be prompted to re-enter both passwords to confirm them.

Now click **OK** on the main Save as dialog box – you will be asked if you wish to replace the original SUMMARY2 workbook – click the **Yes** button.

2 Now close the SUMMARY2 workbook then open it again. Enter
   the password J MUIR when prompted to do so.

   Now change the heading in cell E1 from **TOTAL** to **TOTALS** – you
   can do this as the write-protection password lets you do so.

   Note: To remove or change the passwords you must first open the
   workbook as we have just done, then use the File-Save as-
   Options command to remove or change them. These levels
   of protection are not available for individual worksheets only
   for the whole workbook.

3 **Save** and **Close** the workbook.

4 **Protecting a Worksheet.**

   Open the workspace file HOTELS. If a message appears, 'This
   Document Contains Links. Re-establish Links?' then click the **Yes**
   button.

   This worksheet uses external reference formulae in order to extract
   data from its three supporting worksheets, BLUE, GREEN and
   WHITE. Once established the formulae should be protected from
   any amendment.

   Click on **SUMMARY1** to activate it. – if necessary use the Window-
   Arrange command to restore the tiled display – see Unit 12,
   Activity 1 above.

   Open the **Format** menu and select the **Cells** option – the **Format
   Cells** dialog box appears. There are 4 sub-menus, each selected by
   clicking a tab – see Figure 1.

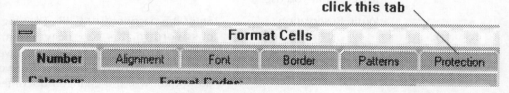

Figure 1

   Click the **Protection** tab and make sure that the **Locked** option is
   selected. (Do not select the second **Hidden** option – this hides the
   formulae)

   Finally click **OK** to return to the workbook SUMMARY1.

5 **Activating Sheet Protection.**

   Open the **Tools** menu then select the **Protection** then the **Protect
   Sheet** options.

   We won't bother with a password in this instance.

   Check that the **Contents** option is selected – this ensures that none
   of the cells can be altered (the other two options Objects and

Scenarios do not apply to SUMMARY1 and can be de-selected if you wish)

Click the **OK** option to return to the workbook.

Now try to edit any cell in the **SUMMARY1** workbook – a message informs you that the cell is locked. (to unprotect a worksheet select Tools Protection then Unprotect Sheet)

6 **Protecting Cells.**

Sometimes we do not need to protect the whole workbook or worksheet, only individual cells.

Activate the workbook **BLUE.XLS** and click the **Maximise** button.

Cells **B4** to **D7** contain numeric data that need to remain amendable. The data in the remaining rows are all based on formulae that need protecting from alteration. (this is standard practice, as a complex model may be destroyed by accidentally keying data into formulae cells)

First select cells **B4** to **D7** – the range of cells to be unprotected.

Open the **Format** menu and select the **Cells** option – the **Format Cells** dialog box appears.

Click the Protection tab – see Figure 1 above – and click the **Locked** option box to deselect it.

Finally click **OK** to return to the workbook BLUE.

7 Now repeat the operation in section 5 above to protect the whole worksheet.

Check that cells **B4** to **D7** are protected by attempting to alter them. You will find that it is possible. Experiment if you wish, but restore the original values.

Now try to amend a cell containing a formula – a message informs you that the cell is locked.

Finally restore the worksheet to its previous size.

8 **Consolidation.**

Repeat steps 5 to 7 above to protect the workbooks GREEN.XLS and WHITE.XLS in a similar way.

Restore the worksheets to their previous size.

9 **Protecting a Workbook.**

Sections 1 and 2 above protected a workbook from being either opened or changed. A lower level of protection is also possible, allowing you to prevent new worksheets being added or existing ones being moved.

Activate the workbook **WHITE.**

Open the **Tools** menu and select **Protection** then the **Protect Workbook** option.

The Protect Workbook dialog box appears – complete it as follows:

Do **not** enter a password.

Make sure the **Structure** box is selected – this prevents the sheets in the workbook being moved, hidden or re-named.

Make sure that the **Windows** box is selected – this prevents changes to the whole workbook – windows cannot be moved or re-sized.

Finally click **OK** to return to the workbook WHITE

10   Now open the **Edit** menu – you will see that the **Delete** and the **Move** or **Copy Sheet** options are unavailable.

Now open the **Insert** menu and select the **Worksheet** option – a message tells you that the worksheet is protected.

Notice also that the Minimise and Maximise buttons and other window sizing or closing features are hidden.

11   Finally open the **Tools** menu and select **Protection** then the **Unprotect Workbook** option. The workbook is now unprotected. However the individual worksheet – Sheet1 in the workbook WHITE – still retains its protection – see section 8 above.

12   Finally **Close** and **Save** all the workbooks.

Activity 2   Checking your worksheet

The worksheets that we have created have been fairly small, occupying no more than a couple of screens. As worksheets get larger and more complex there is a danger of design and data entry errors creeping in which can invalidate the whole model. These are surprisingly common in business. Excel has a number of tools to help you check your worksheet, some of which we have already used, eg:

Naming Cells   Naming cells and groups of cells make them easier to refer to and the worksheet more readable – see Unit 13, Activity 1.

Worksheet Protection   prevents crucial data and formulae being overwritten or deleted – see Activity 1 above.

View Document   The Print Preview option allows you to get an overview of the whole document – see Unit 3, Activity 2.

In this activity we will use the Excel Information Window and Auditing facilities. They allow you to get detailed information about individual cells.

1   Open the workbook **BLUE.** You will remember that it is one of four linked workbooks and that some of its cells have been protected from alteration – see previous activity.

2   Select cell **B13** which shows the Total Operating Profit for January.

Open the **Tools** menu and choose **Options.**

Select the **View** tab if necessary.

A dialog box appears – in the **Show** section click the **Info Window** button then the **OK** button.

3   An Information window appears, giving the cell reference and formula, you can re-size and/or move this window if you wish.

A new set of menus appear at the top of the screen;

Open the **Info** menu and select the following options in turn:-

Value – the cell's value is displayed, unformatted, eg to 3 decimal places

Format – all the formatting for the cell is shown, including number (0.00)

Protection – the cell's locked status is confirmed – the formula cannot be altered.

Note – displays any notes added to the cell – this is already selected

Names – displays any named areas that include this cell (there are none)

Precedents – a further dialog box appears – the Direct Only option is already selected. Click **OK.** Cells used by the formula in this cell – B9 and B11 – are listed. (the All Levels option would list any cells used in turn by these precedents)

Dependents – a further dialog box appears – the Direct Only option is already selected. Click **OK.** Cells that use this cell in their formulae are listed – cell E13 depends on this cell as it uses a formula based on it.

4   The information window now has all options selected and should now look like Figure 2.

5   Not all of the information categories apply to this cell so they can be removed.

Open the **Info** menu; all the options selected are 'ticked' at the moment.

Select the **Note** option and it disappears from the Information window.

6   **Printing and closing the cell information window.**

Open the File menu and select Print. The information window can now be printed if you wish.

Now close the Information window – open the **File** menu and select **Close.** You are returned to the worksheet.

Finally close the BLUE.XLS workbook without saving.

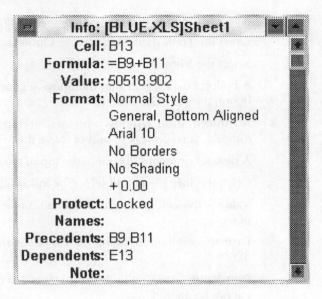

Info: [BLUE.XLS]Sheet1

Cell:	B13
Formula:	=B9+B11
Value:	50518.902
Format:	Normal Style
	General, Bottom Aligned
	Arial 10
	No Borders
	No Shading
	+ 0.00
Protect:	Locked
Names:	
Precedents:	B9,B11
Dependents:	E13
Note:	

Figure 2

7   Using the Auditing Toolbar.

Open the workbook **BUDGMAS.XLS.** This is the template model for all three hotels in the group – see Unit 11.

Open the **View** menu and select **Toolbars** – a dialog box appears.

Select the **Auditing** toolbar and click **OK** – you may have to scroll down to this option.

The Auditing Toolbar appears at the top of the worksheet – it can be dragged to a new position – see Figure 3.

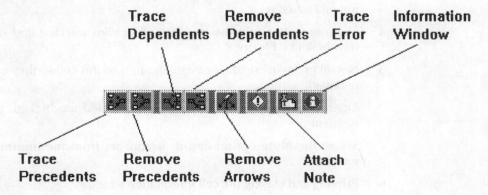

Trace Dependents   Remove Dependents   Trace Error   Information Window

Trace Precedents   Remove Precedents   Remove Arrows   Attach Note

Figure 3

Move the screen pointer over each button without clicking – an information box explains the use of each.

8   Select cell **D13** then click the **Trace Precedents** button.

Arrows make clear the cells on which the formula in cell D13 is built.

Select cell **E13** and click the Trace Precedents button again.

Finally click the **Remove All Arrows** button.

9   Now use the **Trace Dependents** button to find the dependents for cells **B6** and **B8**. Arrows will show the chain of cells which directly and indirectly depend on these buttons.

Hint: Click the Remove Dependents button to remove the last arrow.

10   **Tracing Errors:**

Select cell **B5** and enter the letter **A**. Immediately the worksheet shows a series of value errors – obviously an arithmetic formula cannot use non-numeric data, ie a letter.

Select cell **E13** then the **Trace Error** button – the source of the error is shown.

Restore the value of cell **B5** to **31** again to remove the errors.

11   Repeat step 7 above to remove the Auditing Toolbar from the worksheet.

12   **Viewing Formulae.** Let's check which cells contain formulae.

Open the **Tools** menu and select **Options.**

A dialog box appears – make sure that the **View** option is selected

Click the **Formulas** button in the **Window Options** section then **OK.**

All the formulas are displayed in the worksheet cells and can be checked..

Repeat this operation to de-select the formula option and restore the worksheet to its usual appearance.

13   Close the BUDGMAS workbook without saving it.

Summary of commands and functions

Note

Menu commands show the menu name first, followed by the command to choose from the menu, e.g. Edit-Clear means open the Edit menu and select the Clear command.

Commands

File-Save as-Options	Use various security options
Format-Cells-Protection	Protect selected cells
Tools-Options-View-Info.Window	Show information on a selected cell

Tools-Protection-Protect Sheet	Protect worksheet
Tools-Protection-Protect Sheet	Remove protection from worksheet
Tools-Protection-Protect Workbook	Protect workbook
Tools-Protection-Unprotect Workbook	Remove protection from workbook
View-Toolbars-Auditing	Display Auditing Toolbar

Macros

Previous skills needed to tackle this unit

Previous exercises needed in this unit. (Optional)

The workbook DISCT1 created in Unit 13, Activity 3.
The workbook MORTGAGE created in Unit 13, Activity 1
The workbook DATABASE created in Unit 10, Activity 1.

Introduction

This unit introduces the last main element of Excel – macros. A macro lets you save commands in a special macro sheet. The commands can then be run automatically whenever one needs to use them. Nearly any series of keyboard strokes, menu choices and mouse movements can be stored in a macro and used again when required.

There are several advantages to using macros:

Saving Time.	Issuing the same series of commands repeatedly is time consuming, a macro provides a short cut.
Reducing Error.	Long sequences of commands, mouse movements, and menu choices can be error prone. A macro achieves a consistent, correct result.
Controlling User Input.	In a commercial situation users of varying skill and knowledge may be using the same worksheet model. The designer of the model wants to prevent users destroying data, amending formulae, or modifying assumptions.

Macros also allow the designer to place limits on what users of worksheets can do; eg, to disable certain menu choices, add user instructions, error messages, custom menus and dialog boxes, and at its most complex, design a complete custom-built system.

Earlier versions of Excel used a special macro language. Excel 5 uses the Visual Basic programming language, one of the latest 'object oriented' programming languages specially developed for Windows applications. In this unit we shall be starting with some simple Visual Basic (VB) macros which automate simple tasks. In later units we shall be building a complete user application using Visual Basic macros.

Hints and Rules for Macros.

A macro is stored on a special sheet.

Many macros can be stored on one module sheet.

Macros store commands using the Visual Basic (VB) programming Language

Macros can control worksheets, charts and databases.

Every macro is saved and run under a different name. The macro name can be up to 255 characters long, must begin with a letter, and can consist of letters, numbers, full stops or underscores. Spaces are not allowed so underscores or full stops are often used instead.

Macro names are not case sensitive.

A macro can be run in several ways, it can be assigned to a special button or menu choice. It can also be assigned a shortcut key – a single letter. Pressing down the Ctrl key and keying this letter will run the macro. The letter that you assign to a macro *is* case-sensitive, eg holding down the Ctrl key and pressing small e would run a particular macro; pressing Ctrl and capital E would not. This gives you a potential 52 shortcut key combinations. However many are already used by Excel as keyboard alternatives to menu or button choices, eg Ctrl-S to save. It is best not to use these.

Activity 1   Creating a simple macro

You can create a simple macro by using the macro recorder. Actions such as menu choices, mouse movements and keystrokes are then recorded and can be 'played back' when required.

Our first macro will automate the simple task of adding the date and time to a worksheet. Instead of entering the NOW() function every time, you can use a shortcut, say, pressing the Ctrl key and the letter e.

1   **Recording a Macro.** Open the Workbook **DISCT1.XLS.**

    Note. If you don't have this workbook then any workbook containing worksheet data will do, although you may need to adjust some of the cell references.

    Select cell **A1**

    Open the **Tools** menu and choose **Record Macro** then **Record New Macro.**

    The Record New Macro dialog box appears.

2   Enter the name **DATE_TIME** in the name box – see Figure 1.

    Press the Tab key to move to the Description box. It always contains the creation date plus the name of the author or organisation. Add the description 'Adds the Date & Time'. The dialog box should now resemble Figure 1

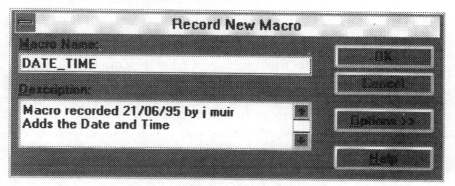

Figure 1

3   Now click the **Options** button. The rest of the dialog box appears, enter the following information using Figure 2 as a guide.

    Click the **Menu Item on Tools Menu** box – an X should appear.

    Enter **'Add Date and Time'** in the text box below – this will appear on the Tools menu)

    Click the **Shortcut Key** box. Accept the letter e in the **Ctrl+** box. (letters a – d are already used as Excel keyboard commands)

    You have now assigned a menu option on the Tools menu and the key strokes Ctrl-e to the macro DATE_TIME. These will be used to

run the macro, as we will see. (in future activities we will be
assigning macros to buttons)

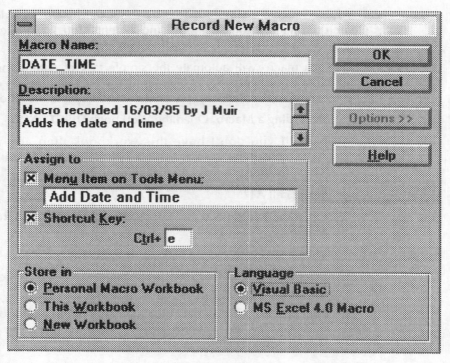

Figure 2

Now click the **Personal Macro Workbook** button.

Note: There are three ways to store macros.

a. The personal macro workbook is opened automatically when-
    ever you start Excel, and can be used to store and run
    commonly-used macros.

b. The 'This Workbook' option stores macros on a sheet with the
    rest of the workbook. This restricts using the macro to one
    workbook.

c. New Workbook stores the macros in a new workbook. If you
    use this option then you have to open the macro sheet when-
    ever you want to run the macro.

Make sure that the **Visual Basic** button is selected – this is the
macro language we will be using.

Click the **OK** button. The Recording message appears at the bottom
of the screen. And a single Stop Macro button is also displayed.

4   Recording the Macro.

We are now ready to record the macro steps. All your actions are
being recorded now, so don't issue any superfluous commands,

Enter the function **=NOW()** in cell **A1** then click the 'tick' button in the Formula Bar.

Open the **Format** menu and select Cells then the **Number** tab.

Select the **Date** category, then the format **dd/mm/yy h:mm**

Click **OK.** The date appears, correctly formatted, in cell A1 of the DISCT1 worksheet.

Click the **Stop Macro** button. The Recording message stops.

You have now recorded your first macro, DATE_TIME which automates entering the date and time. Let's see how this has been recorded.

Hint. If the column displays a row of '####' symbols then it needs to be widened to display the date.

6   Viewing the Macro Sheet.

Whenever you first open Excel the personal macro workbook is opened but remains hidden.

Open the **Window** menu and select **Unhide.** A dialog box appears.

Select **PERSONAL.XLS** then **OK.** The macro workbook appears on the screen.

The first sheet, Module1, contains the macro. It is in fact a very simple Visual Basic (VB) program, consisting of introductory comments, plus a single subroutine called Date_TIME(). This subroutine contains two VB commands:

```
ActiveCell.FormulaR1C1 = "now()"

Selection.NumberFormat = "dd/mm/yy hh:mm"
```

Open the Window menu again and select Hide – the macro workbook is hidden again.

7   Running the Macro Using the Shortcut Key.

Make sure that cell **A1** is still selected.

Hold down the **Ctrl** key and press the e key.

The hour-glass symbol will confirm that the macro is running – the time will be updated.

Unhide the macro workbook again and close it, using **Close** on the **File** menu.

Now try running the macro again (Ctrl-e). Nothing will happen. Once the special macro workbook has been closed during an Excel session it will need to be opened, before any macros can be run from it.

Now open the macro workbook PERSONAL using **File-Open** and hide it.

8   Running the Macro as a Menu Option.

Open the **Tools** menu – at the bottom of the menu is the special option **'Add Date and Time'** – see section 3.

Select this option and the macro is run from the menu.

9   Leave the DISCT1 workbook open and open the workbook MORT-GAGE.

Note. If you don't have this workbook then any workbook containing worksheet data will do, although you may need to adjust some of the cell references.

Use the Tools menu again to add the date to cell **A1.** (the special menu option **'Add Date and Time'** can be used from any worksheet)

You may need to widen the column for the date and time to display properly.

Close the MORTGAGE workbook.

10   Running a Macro by Name.

Open the **Tools** menu and select **Macro.**

Select the macro DATE_TIME and click **OK.**

The macro will run again, updating the date and time in cell A1.

11   Changing Macro Options.

We will now remove the DATE_TIME option from the **Tools** menu, you may need to do this if the number of special options gets too large, or you no longer need one.

Open the **Window** menu and select **Unhide.** A dialog box appears.

Select **PERSONAL.XLS** then **OK** – the macro workbook is displayed.

Open the **Tools** menu and select **Macro.**

Select **DATE_TIME** from the list then select **Options** – the Options dialog box appears – see Figure 2 above.

Click the **Menu Items on Tools** Menu option to deselect it – the x should be replaced by a blank.

Click **OK** – you are returned to the Macro dialog box.

Click **Close** to return to the worksheet.

Use the Window-Hide option to hide the **PERSONAL** macro workbook again.

Now open the **Tools** menu – the special menu option, Add Date and Time, has been removed. (you can still run the macro using Ctrl-e)

12 Troubleshooting – If Your Recording Fails.....

The Excel Macro Recorder will record all your commands and key strokes – right or wrong. If you make a mistake while recording a simple macro then it is best to stop recording, unhide the macro workbook PERSONAL , clear all the macro commands and start again.

13 Recap – The Steps in Recording a Macro.

❐ Activate the worksheet that the macro will control

❐ Open the Tools menu and select the **Record Macro-New Macro** options

❐ Complete the Dialog box, eg name the macro and allocate the shortcut letter

❐ Record the actions in the macro

❐ Click the Stop Macro button

Activity 2   Assigning a macro to a button

In the first activity we ran a macro in two ways – assigning it a shortcut key (Ctrl-e) and making it a special menu option. A third way to assign a macro to a button. Clicking the button will run the macro, without needing to remember key strokes or menu choices. The button can either be part of the worksheet, or placed on a toolbar.

We will create a new macro PRINT_IT that will automate the printing of part of a worksheet.

1 Open the workbook **MORTGAGE** if necessary.

> **Note.** If you don't have this workbook then any workbook containing worksheet data will do, although you may need to adjust some of the cell references.

We will create a print macro that prints the mortgage interest table held in cells A7 to C17.

2 Open the **View menu** and select **Toolbars.**

Select **Drawing** from the **Toolbars** list and click **OK**

The Drawing toolbar is displayed, click the Create Button tool – see Figure 3

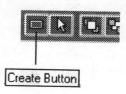

Figure 3

The screen pointer changes to cross hairs.

3   Creating the Button.

Drag the screen pointer so that the box covers cells E2 and E3.

Let go the mouse button and the button is drawn with the default name **'Button1'.** We can reposition it later if necessary.

4   Assigning a Macro to the Button.

The Assign Macro dialog box opens automatically. Use the screen pointer to drag the dialog box to one side so that cell range A7 to C17 can be seen.

Type the macro name **PRINT_MORTGAGE** then click the **Record** button.

The Record New Macro dialog box appears – click the **Options** button.

Now, using Figure 4 below as a guide, complete the dialog box as follows:

Enter the macro name as **PRINT_MORTGAGE**

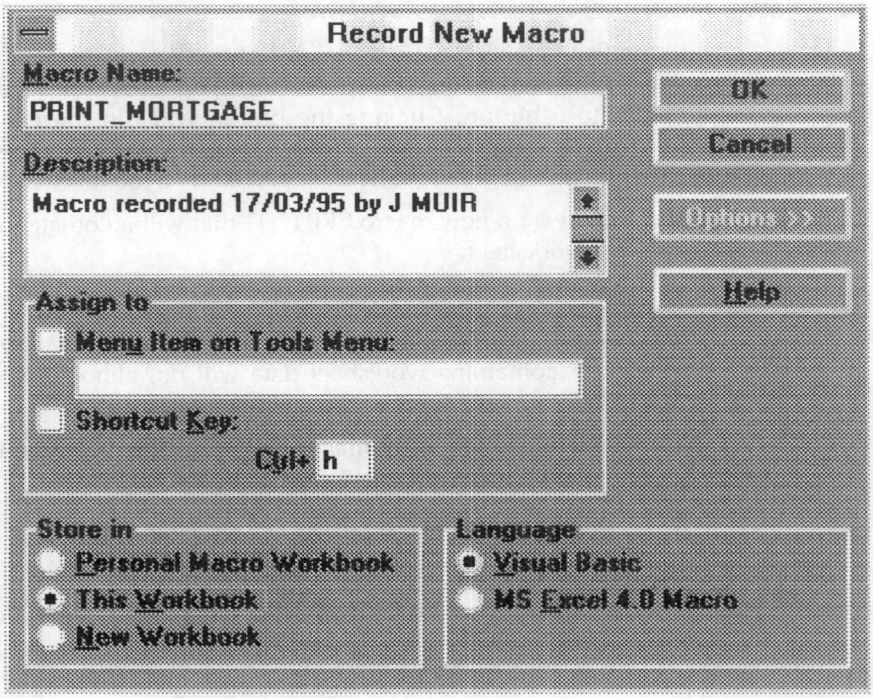

Figure 4

Leave the **Assign to** and the **Shortcut key** buttons unselected – this macro will be run from a button

Select **This Workbook** from the **Store in** options (the cells to be printed will only apply to this workbook so there is no point in storing the macro in the PERSONAL macro workbook)

Click **OK** – the macro is now assigned to the button and you are ready to start recording.

5   **Recording the Macro.**

Make sure that your printer is turned on and connected.

Open the **File** menu and select **Page Setup.**

Click the **Sheet** tab.

Click the **Print Area** box.

Enter the cell references A7:C17

Click **OK**

Open the **File** menu and select **Print;** choose 1 copy and whatever other settings you wish.

Click **OK.**

Printing will now take place; when it is finished click the **Stop Recording** button.

You have now created a print macro on a new macro sheet.

Troubleshooting – see section 11 below.

6   **Labelling the Button.**

To change the size and colour of the button, or the text that appears on it, first you must select it.

Hold down the **Ctrl** key and click the button – selection handles appear round the button.

First change the text; erase the default name then open the **Format** menu and select **Object** – a dialog box appears.

Choose **8** point from the **Size** box..

Click the down arrow button on the **Colour** box and select a colour for the text.

Click **OK.**

The button should be still selected; type the label on the button **'Click to Print'.**

Click elsewhere on the worksheet to deselect the button.

7   **Moving or Sizing the Button.**

Hold down the **Ctrl** key and click the button – selection handles appear.

To alter the size drag one of the selection handles – the screen pointer will change to a double-headed arrow.

To move the button place the screen pointer on the edge of the button – not on a selection handle – and drag. The button can now be moved (don't move the button within the print area or the button outline will be printed along with the worksheet).

Finally press the **Esc** key to de-select the button and remove the selection handles.

8   Running the Macro.

If you are happy with the appearance of your button then try running it.

Move the screen pointer on top of the button – the screen pointer becomes hand-shaped.

Click once and the worksheet should print as before.

9   Viewing the Macro:

The macro has been recorded on a module sheet in the MORT-GAGE workbook. Use the arrow keys at the bottom left of the worksheet to page through the sheets. After Sheet16 you will see a sheet tab for **Module1.**

Click this tab to view the module sheet.

Page back to the worksheet on sheet 1.

10   Save and close the macro sheet and the worksheet.

11   Troubleshooting – Information only:

If a simple recorded macro doesn't work then it is usually easiest to delete it and re-record it. (in future activities we will be learning how to de-bug and edit macros)

a   **Deleting a Button.** If you have made a mess of your button, or no longer need it, then you can delete it. Select the button as before (Ctrl- click), then open the **Edit** menu and select **Clear.**

b.   **Deleting a Macro.** If the macro doesn't work correctly then open the **Tools** menu and select **Macro.** Select the macro name then **Delete** from the dialog box.

c.   **Assigning a New Macro.** Select the button as before (Ctrl-click), open the Tools menu and select **Assign Macro.** Select **Record.**

Activity 3   Consolidation

An unavoidable limitation of the PRINT_MORTGAGE macro that we have just created is that it only applies to one specific worksheet in the workbook MORTGAGE.XLS. This is because it sets a print area that is unlikely to apply to any other worksheet, so each worksheet needs its own print macro.

1   Open the workbook DATABASE.

Note. If you don't have this workbook then any workbook containing worksheet data will do, although you may need to adjust some of the cell references.

Now, using the operations in Activities 1 and 2 as a guide, add a new macro to print off the HELPERS worksheet.

Call the macro PRINT_HELPERS and assign a shortcut key to it.

2   Create and assign a print button for this worksheet too.

3   Save and Close the Workbook.

Summary of commands

Notes

Menu commands show the menu name first, followed by the command to choose from the menu, e.g. Edit-Clear means open the Edit menu and select the Clear command.

Ctrl-[letter]	run macro using shortcut key
Ctrl-[select]	select screen button
Tools-Macro-Record New Macro	Record new macro
Window-Unhide	Show a hidden workbook window
Window-Hide	Hide a workbook window
Tools-Macro	Run, edit or delete a macro
View-Toolbars-Drawing	Display/hide drawing toolbar
Tools-Assign Macro	Assign macro to an object, eg button
Format-AutoFormat	Select automatic worksheet format
Tools-Name-Define	Assign a name to an object, eg macro

Further ways to run macros

Introduction

In Unit 17 we learnt four ways to run macros:

a. pressing shortcut keys, (Ctrl plus a letter)

b. using the Run command from the Macro menu.

c. Clicking a special button drawn on the worksheet

d. Using a special option on the Tools menu.

A fifth method is to attach a macro to a tool on a toolbar. The macro can either take over the function of an existing tool, or you can create a custom tool button. We will try the second method. We will add a tool that will format a worksheet

Activity 1 Assigning a macro to a toolbar

1   Open the workbook **INS_SLS.** We are going to select a button, add it to the standard toolbar and assign a macro to it and then record the macro.

     Note. If you don't have this workbook then any workbook containing worksheet data will do, although you may need to adjust some of the cell references.

2   **Choosing a Custom button.**

     Open the **View** menu and select **Toolbars.**

     Make sure that the **Formatting** option is selected, then click the **Customise** button.

     The Customise dialog box appears, offering a library of custom tool buttons.

     Select **Formatting** from the **Categories** list.

     Choose a suitable button tool and drag it to next to the **Bold** button on the **Formatting** Toolbar.

     Do not close the dialog box.

3   **Assigning the Macro.**

     Open the **Tools** menu and select **Assign Macro** – the Assign Macro dialog box appears.

     Type in the macro name **FORMAT_WORKSHEET** and click the **Record** button.

     The Record New Macro dialog box opens next, type in the macro name FORMAT_WORKSHEET again and click the **Options** button.

     Using Figure 1 as a guide complete the description of the macro: complete the description.

     Leave the **Assign to** and the **Shortcut key** entries blank.

     Make sure that the **This Workbook** option is selected in the **Store in** section. (the formatting macro will only apply to this worksheet)

     Click the **OK** button.

     From now on your actions are being recorded.

4   **Recording the Macro.** Select the worksheet cells holding the data, ie cell range **A1** to **E10.**

     Open the **Format** menu and select **AutoFormat.**

     Select the format Colorful 2 from the Table Format box.

     Click **OK.**

     Click the **Stop Macro** button.

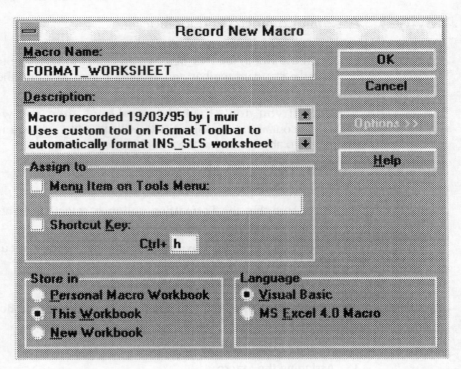

Figure 1

5   **Testing the Macro.**

First we will restore the worksheet to its normal format.

Make sure that the cell range is still selected.

Open the **Format** menu and select **AutoFormat** again.

Select the format **None** from the list box – you may have to scroll down to see it.

Click **OK** – the worksheet is now restored to its previous format.

Now click the special custom button on the Formatting Toolbar – the macro reformats the worksheet to the format previously recorded.

6   **Viewing the Macro:**

The macro has been recorded on a module sheet in the INS_SLS workbook. Use the arrow keys at the bottom left of the worksheet to page through the sheets. After Sheet16 you will see a sheet tab for **Module1.**

Click this tab to view the module sheet.

Page back to the worksheet.

7   **Troubleshooting – Information only:**

If a simple recorded macro doesn't work then it is usually easiest to delete it and re-record it. (in future activities we will be learning how to de-bug and edit macros)

a.   **Deleting a Button.** If you have made a mess of your button, or no longer need it, then you can delete it. Select the button (Ctrl-click), then open the Edit menu and select **Clear.**

b.   **Deleting a Macro.** If the macro doesn't work correctly then open the **Tools** menu and select **Macro.** Select the macro name then **Delete** from the dialog box.

c.   **Assigning a New Macro.** Select the button as before (Ctrl- click), open the Tools menu and select **Assign Macro.** Select **Record.**

8   **Deleting a Custom Toolbar Button.** (information only) Open the **View** menu and select **Toolbars.**

Use the screen pointer to drag the button off the Toolbar: When you release the mouse button the toolbar button is removed.

9   Close the Workbook INS.SLS.

Activity 2   Running a macro automatically

In the previous activity we created a button that had a macro assigned to it. Clicking the button called the macro which in turn printed part of the worksheet. It is also possible to run the macro automatically every time the workbook is opened, eg, a worksheet is formatted or printed whenever the workbook is opened.

1   Open the Workbook **MORTGAGE.XLS.**

Note. If you don't have this workbook then any workbook containing worksheet data will do, although you may need to adjust some of the cell references.

2   Open the **Insert** menu and select **Name** then the **Define** option.

3   A dialog box appears; select the **Names in Workbook** box and type the name **Auto_Open**

4   Select the **Refers** to box next.

It must contain the name of the macro that you are calling.

Type =PRINT_MORTGAGE then click **OK.**

5   Save and close the MORTGAGE workbook.

6   Now open MORTGAGE again. The PRINT_MORTGAGE macro should run automatically and the table begin to print. Cancel this if you wish.

Close the MORTGAGE workbook.

7   **Troubleshooting.** If you get an error message, check the following:

Open the **Insert** menu and select **Name-Define** again.

Check the spelling and syntax of the entries in the dialog box,

For the name **Auto_Open** to work correctly there must be no spaces and you must use the underscore (_) not the dash.

Now save and close the workbook and try again!

8   **Additional Notes**.

It is also possible to run a macro automatically when you close a workbook; use steps 1 to 5 above, but in the Name box type a name that begins with **Auto_Close**

More than one macro can be run automatically from the same workbook.

Each name must begin with Auto_Close or Auto_Open, eg Auto_Open_Print or Auto_Close_Print.

9   **Consolidation.**

Open the workbook HELPERS.XLS.

Using the above operations, make the macro PRINT_HELPERS run automatically when the worksheet is opened.

Note. If you don't have this workbook then any workbook containing worksheet data will do, although you may need to adjust some of the cell references.

Summary of commands

Notes

Menu commands show the menu name first, followed by the command to choose from the menu, e.g. Edit-Clear means open the Edit menu and select the Clear command.

Ctrl-[letter]	Run macro using shortcut key
Ctrl-[select]	Select screen button
Tools-Macro-Record New Macro	Record new macro
Window-Unhide	Show a hidden workbook window
Window-Hide	Hide a workbook window
Tools-Macro	Run, edit or delete a macro
View-Toolbars-Drawing	Display/hide drawing toolbar
Tools-Assign Macro	Assign macro to an object, eg button
Format-AutoFormat	Select automatic worksheet format
Insert-Name-Define	Assign a name to an object, eg macro

Designing a user application

Skills to be learned	Activity
Formula Bar – displaying	2.8
Formula Bar – hiding	2.3
Grid lines – displaying	2.8
Grid lines – hiding	2.3
Macro – correcting	3.6
Macro – creating	2
Macro – testing	3
Scroll Bars – displaying	2.8
Scroll Bars – hiding	2.3
Status bar – displaying	2.8
Status Bar – hiding	2.3
Toolbars – displaying	2.4
Toolbars – hiding	2.9

Previous skills needed to tackle this unit

Skill	Covered in Unit
Starting Excel	1
Basic mouse, menu and Windows operations	1
Creating a simple worksheet	1
Using simple formulae and formatting	1 – 3

Important note

Units 19 to 24 form a unified development task – they all need to be completed in order for the purchase order application to work. Unlike previous units there is no point in doing any one unit in isolation from the others, they all build on each other.

Introduction

In the previous units you created some simple macros that automated small tasks such as printing a worksheet. In this unit we are going to use macros to automate a whole application – purchase orders. Every time a

189

company orders goods it sends out a purchase order to a supplier, so it needs to maintain records of them using a database. Purchase order records will need to be added to the database, as well as edited, saved and printed.

The application may well be used by people unfamiliar with Excel, who cannot be expected to use the normal menus, commands etc. Macros are the binding material that will hold the parts of the system together and present it to the user simply. You will find that building a complete application is a lengthy painstaking process, inevitably involving much testing and some frustration. Some of this can be avoided if you plan the application properly before you start. Trial and error and experimentation can then take place within a structured framework.

Overview of the application

It is important to plan the application, at least in general outline, before starting on the worksheet and macros. Use this section to understand the various parts of the system before you start on the first activity.

1. The first screen that the user will see is a specially designed title screen – see Figure 4. This will eventually offer a custom menu at the top of the screen that replaces the standard menus. Several macros are used to display this screen, e.g. to set off normal screen defaults such as gridlines and tool bars, and to display the custom menu.

2. A custom dialog box is also designed for the user to enter purchase order details, eg Supplier Name, Quantity, Product, Price.

3. The data entered in this dialog box are transferred to a database - using a macro.

4. Users will be able to edit the data records where necessary using a standard data form. This too can be called by a macro.

5. Many of the items ordered from suppliers are standard; they are stored in a products list – see Figure 6.

6. The worksheet can thus be divided into 3 parts – shown much reduced in Figure 1.

    Part 1 is the title screen

    Part 2 is the database of purchase orders

    Part 3 is the list of products

    The fourth element is invisible to the user – this is the macro module sheet that will contain all the Visual Basic commands to run the application.

Such an application can look daunting; don't worry it can be built up and tested piece by piece. At the end you will have a worthwhile application that can be added to as needs demand.

Part 1   Title Screen

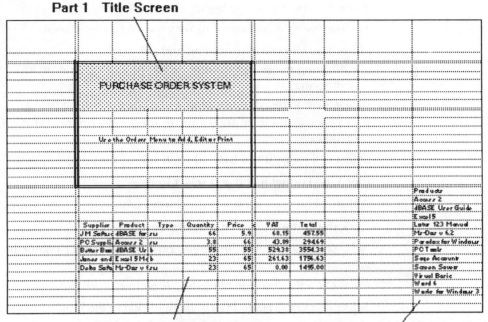

Part 2.   Purchase Order Database   **Part 3.   List of Products**

Figure 1

Programming in Visual Basic

Non-programmers need not worry unduly about the programming skills required. Rather than start with a large section of indigestible theory, programming concepts will be introduced as we go on. Space will not allow us to explore every element of Visual Basic (VB for short) which in any case is well covered in the Excel Help text.

Activity 1   Creating user screens

In this activity we will create the three parts of the purchase orders system:

    a.   the title screen – see Figure 4

    b.   the orders database – see Figure 5.

    c.   the list of products – see Figure 6.

1   Open a new workbook and maximise the worksheet if necessary.

Using Figure 2 as a guide, amend the sizes of the columns and rows as follows:

Column **A** to **17.00** wide

Columns **B** and **H** to **0.50** wide (the column letters will no longer be readable – this is OK)

Row **1** to **50.00** high

Rows 3,9 and 19 to 3.00 high.

The narrow rows and columns now form a box on screen.

Hints. You can use alter column and row sizes by either,

a.   locating the screen pointer on the row or column dividers and dragging,

b.   selecting the whole column and using the Format menu.

   You can undo mistakes using the Undo option on the Edit menu.

2   Select cell range **B3 to B19** – the left side of the box.

Open the **Format** menu and select **Cells.**

A dialog box appears; select the **Border** tab.

Click the **Outline** box in the **Border** section.

Now select a suitable line style; ou can also select colour if you wish.

Click **OK** – the first side of the box is outlined.

Select cell range **H3** to **H19** – the right side of the box.

Open the **Edit** menu and select **Repeat Format Cells.**

3   Next we can complete the horizontal sides of the box.

Repeat the above operations for the cell ranges

B3 to H3

B19 to H19.

Compare your results with Figure 2 and amend if necessary.

4   Now save the workbook as **ORDENTER.XLS**

Complete the summary box as shown below in Figure 3.

5   **Formatting the Box and Entering Text.**

Use Figure 4 below as a guide:

Select cell **C6.**

Open the **Format** menu and select **Cells.**

Click the **Font** tab

Choose **14** point **Bold** then **OK**

Now with cell C6 still selected, type the title, **PURCHASE ORDER SYSTEM** and press **Enter.**

Now select cell range **C4** to **G8.**

Centre this title across cells C6 to **G6** (use Format-Cells-Alignment-Centre across Selection)

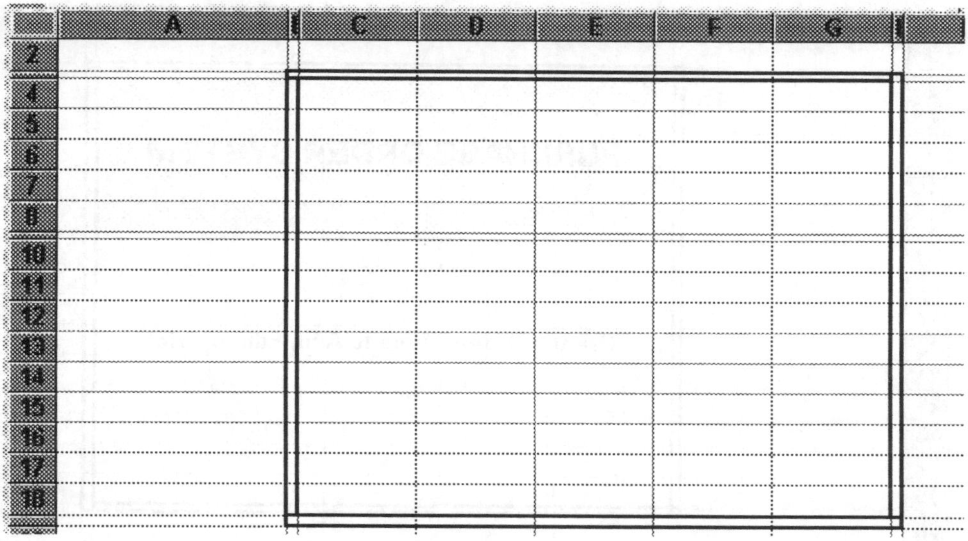

Figure 2

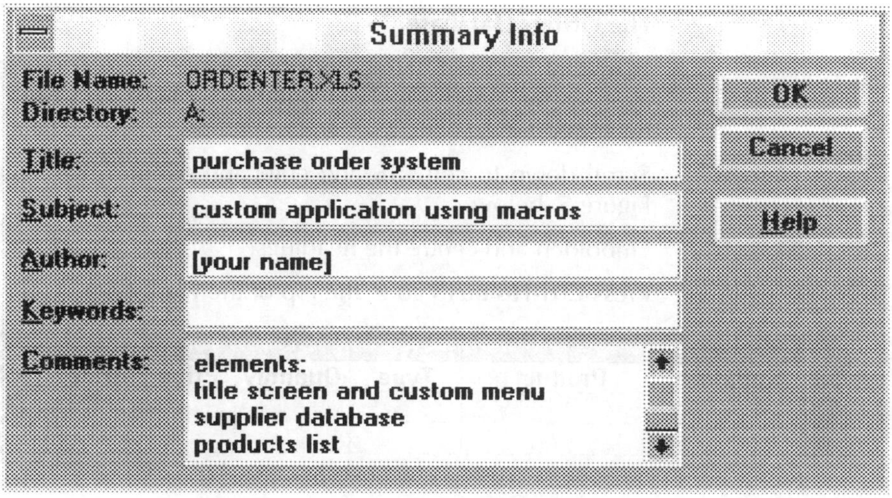

Figure 3

Open the **Format** menu and select Cells.

Click the **Patterns** tab and choose a suitable pattern.

Click **OK.**

6   Select cell **C13** and type the user message,

Use the Orders Menu to Add, Edit or Print

Embolden and centre the text as before.

Your screen should resemble Figure 4.

	A		C	D	E	F	G		I
2									
4									
5									
6				**PURCHASE ORDER SYSTEM**					
7									
8									
10									
11									
12									
13				**Use the Orders Menu to Add, Edit or Print**					
14									
15									
16									
17									
18									
20									

Figure 4

7   The Orders Database.

Now that we have defined our title screen we can create the headings for the purchase order database. These will hold records of items supplied.

Scroll down to cell **L56** and enter the column headings shown in Figure 5 below.

Embolden and centre the headings.

Press **Ctrl-Home** to go to the top of the worksheet.

	L	M	N	O	P	Q	R	S
56	**Supplier**	**Product**	**Type**	**Quantity**	**Price**	**Date**	**VAT**	**Total**
57								
58								

Figure 5

8   Creating the Products List.

We can now create the third element of the applications, the list of standard products ordered from suppliers.

Select Column **U and** widen it to about 20.00.

Enter the list of software products shown in Figure 6 in cells **U21** to **U33.**

9   Naming the Cell Range.

We need to give the range of cells holding the products a name.

Select cells **U22 – U33.**

	T	U	V	W
21	**Products**			
22	Access 2			
23	dBASE User Guide			
24	Excel 5			
25	Lotus 123 Manual			
26	Ms-Dos v 6.2			
27	Paradox for Windows			
28	PC Tools			
29	Sage Accounts			
30	Screen Savers			
31	Visual Basic			
32	Word 6			
33	Works for Windows 3			
34				

Figure 6

Open the **Insert** menu and choose **Name-Define** – a dialog box appears.

Enter the name **PRODUCT_LIST** and click **OK.**

10 Double click on the Sheet 1 tab – a dialog box appears. Rename the sheet ORDERSCREENS.

Activity 2   Macros which format screens

We now have the title and the orders database screens, plus the products list. The next step is to record macros to control them. We will create a number of small macros, each of which carries out a simple task such as turning off menus, or displaying a screen. As the macros only apply to the ORDENTER workbook they will be stored on a module sheet within the workbook, rather than in the general macro sheet PERSONAL – see Unit 17.

We will use the same recording techniques that we used in the previous units:

Remember the basic steps in creating a macro :-

❐ Activate the worksheet that the macro will control

❐ Open the Tools menu and select the Record Macro-Record New Macro options

❐ Complete the Dialog box, eg name the macro and allocate the shortcut letter

❐ Record the macro actions

❐ Click the Stop Macro button

1   Make sure that the Workbook **ORDENTER** is still open and the worksheet is currently displaying the title screen.

Press Ctrl-Home if necessary to return to the top of the worksheet.

First make sure that neither the Excel application window nor the ORDENTER document window is maximised; if so then press the Restore button(s) – their size doesn't matter at the moment.

Hint: If you're not sure of the position of these buttons, now is the time to check and experiment – not when you are recording the macro!

2   **The Title Screen Macro.**

This macro will turn off certain standard settings.

Open the Tools menu and select **Record Macro – Record New Macro.**

Click the **Options** button on the dialog box.

Using Figure 7 as a guide, complete the dialog box as follows:

```
┌─────────────────────────────────────────────────────────────┐
│  ▬                    Record New Macro                        │
├─────────────────────────────────────────────────────────────┤
│  Macro Name:                                  ┌──────────┐    │
│  Set_Title_SCREEN                             │    OK    │    │
│                                               └──────────┘    │
│  Description:                                 ┌──────────┐    │
│  Macro recorded 24/03/95 by [your name]  ▲    │  Cancel  │    │
│  displays application title and turns off     └──────────┘    │
│  menus                                   ▼    ┌──────────┐    │
│                                               │ Options   │   │
│  Assign to                                    └──────────┘    │
│   ☐ Menu Item on Tools Menu:                  ┌──────────┐    │
│                                               │   Help   │    │
│                                               └──────────┘    │
│   ☐ Shortcut Key:                                             │
│         Ctrl+ h                                               │
│                                                               │
│  Store in                     Language                        │
│   ○ Personal Macro Workbook    ● Visual Basic                 │
│   ● This Workbook              ○ MS Excel 4.0 Macro           │
│   ○ New Workbook                                              │
└─────────────────────────────────────────────────────────────┘
```

Figure 7

Name the macro **Set_Title_Screen.**

Complete the description box.

Make sure that the **This Workbook** and the **Visual Basic** options are selected.

Click **OK.**

From now on your actions are being recorded!

3   Click the **Maximise** button on both the Excel application window and the ORDENTER document window.

Click the Sheet tab for the active worksheet.

Press down the **Ctrl** and the **Home** keys together – the cursor moves to cell **A1.**

Open the **Tools** menu and select **Options.**

Click the **View** tab. (even if it is selected)

Now click on the following options in turn to de-select them:

Formula Bar

Status Bar

Grid Lines

Row and Column Headers

Horizontal Scroll Bar

Vertical Scroll Bar

Sheet Tabs

Click **OK**

4   Open the **View** menu and select **Toolbars.**

Click the Standard and Formatting Toolbar boxes to de-select them – *don't* deselect the Stop Recording box.

Click **OK**

5   Click the top left corner of the box that surrounds the title SALES ORDER ENTRY, i.e. cell **B3.**

This 'parks' the screen pointer in an inconspicuous place.

6   **Now click the Stop Recorder button**

The first macro is recorded and a new macro sheet has been added to the workbook – Module1.

Most of the usual Excel features are removed from the title screen – the user will not be needing them and it gives the opening screen a tidier appearance.

7   **Restoring the Screen Defaults.**

The second macro will reverse the effects of the first one, ie it will restore the normal screen defaults before the database screen is displayed. This is simply a matter of recording the macro again to re-select the options

Open the **Tools** menu and select **Record Macro – Record New Macro.**

Click the **Options** button on the dialog box.

Name the macro **Restore_Title_Screen.**

Complete the description box appropriately.

Make sure that the **This Workbook** and the **Visual Basic** options are selected.

Click **OK.**

From now on your actions are being recorded!

8   Open the **Tools** menu and select **Options.**

Click the **View** tab. (even if it is currently selected)

Now click on the following options in turn to select them – an 'x' will appear in each:

>   Formula Bar
>
>   Status Bar
>
>   Grid Lines
>
>   Row and Column Headers
>
>   Horizontal Scroll Bar
>
>   Vertical Scroll Bar
>
>   Sheet Tabs

Click **OK**

9   Open the **View** menu and select **Toolbars.**

Click the Standard and Formatting Toolbar boxes to select them.

Click **OK**

10   Now click the Stop Recorder button

The second macro is recorded and the Excel screen is returned to its normal appearance.

11   Save the workbook.

Activity 3   Testing macros

1   To make it simpler to move between the worksheet and the macro sheet we will re-name them and remove all the other sheets from the workbook.

Double click on the **Sheet1** tab – a dialog box appears.

Rename the sheet **ORDER SCREENS**

Click the **Sheet2** tab to select it.

Open the **Edit** menu and select **Delete Sheet.** A dialog box appears

Click **OK.**

Continue to delete the other blank sheets in the workbook – you can select several sheets if you hold down the **Ctrl** key.

Do not delete the **Module1** sheet which holds the macros – instead re-name the sheet **MACROS.**

Troubleshooting. If you accidentally delete the wrong sheet open the File menu and select **Close.** Close the workbook without saving it then open it again.

2   **Viewing a Macro.**

You should now have two sheets in your workbook; ORDER SCREENS which holds the purchase order system, and MACROS which holds the macros to control it.

Click the MACROS sheet tab – it holds the two macros.

Scroll down the sheet, the first macro **Set_Title_Screen** is shown first.

The Visual Basic code is fairly easy to understand in this simple macro – **False** indicates that a setting such as a scroll bar is turned off.

The second macro, **Restore_Title_Screen** resets the default settings to **True.**

Later on we will be adding comments to more complex macros in order to document them.

3   **Stepping through a Macro.**

It is possible to execute a macro one step at a time; this is useful for testing and debugging.

Click the Sheet tab for the **ORDER SCREENS** sheet. It is displayed.

Open the **Tools** menu and select **Macro.**

Select the macro **Set_Title_Screen** from the list.

Click the **Step** button.

The Debug window appears at the bottom of the screen – the first line of the macro should be in a rectangular selection box – you may need to scroll it into view.

Drag the window and re-size it so that you can see the worksheet screen as well.

4   Open the **Run** menu at the top of the screen and select the Step Into option.

The first line of the macro executes and the next line is selected.

Now keep repeating the Step Into command (or press the **F8** key) and notice the effect of each macro command on the worksheet settings; eventually you will step through the whole macro and the Debug window will disappear.

5   You will now need to run the Restore_Title_Screen macro.

Repeat the above steps and the title screen will return to its previous appearance.

6   **Correcting a Macro**. (Information only) If one of your macros is not working properly there are various options:

a. You can edit the macro line – this can be very difficult for a complex macro unless you fully understand its syntax – better to either,

b. Delete the whole macro and start again (select the relevant macro lines on the macro sheet and use the Clear command) or,

c. Delete the lines of the macro from the incorrect line(s) to the end, then start recording again as follows:

Select the next blank line on the macro sheet

Open the **Tools** menu and select **Record Macro.**

Select the **Mark Position for Recording** option.

Select the worksheet ORDER SCREENS.

Open the **Tools** menu and select **Record Macro.**

Select the **Record at Mark** option.

Record the actions again.

Click the Stop Recorder button.

d. Remember to test your macros after you have amended them.

7 Save and close the workbook.

Warning. Don't run a macro unless the worksheet is the active document. If you run a macro when the macro sheet is active you will get an error message and/or may end up re-formatting the macro sheet. As you cannot undo such an error you must either re-format the macro sheet manually, or exit from the macro sheet without saving it.

Summary of commands

Note

Menu commands show the menu name first, followed by the command to choose from the menu, e.g. Edit-Clear means open the Edit menu and select the Clear command.

Edit-Delete Sheet	Delete selected sheet
Format-Cells-Border	Add border to cells
Format-Cells-Pattern	Add pattern to cells
Tools-Macro	Select a macro to run, edit, delete etc.
Tools-Options-View	Turn on/off features of current worksheet
Tools-Record Macro-Record New Macro	Record new macro
View-Toolbars	Hide/show toolbars

Further application development – dialog boxes

```
Skills to be learned                        Activity
    Cells – naming                              3
    Dialog box – creating                       2

Previous skills needed to tackle this unit
    Skill                               Covered in Unit
    Starting Excel                              1
    Basic mouse, menu and Windows operations    1
    Creating a simple worksheet                 1
    Using simple formulae and formatting      1 – 3
```

Important note

Units 19 to 24 form a unified development task – they all need to be completed in order for the purchase order application to work. Unlike previous units there is no point in doing any one unit in isolation from the others as they all build on each other.

Introduction

This unit continues the development of the purchase order application begun in Unit 19. It tests the macros created so far, and shows you how to create a dialog box for the user to enter purchase order details.

Activity 1   Macros that position the screen

As the **Set_Title_Screen** macro turns off the scroll bars users will need each part of the ORDER SCREENS positioned for them. We therefore need two more macros to position the title and the database screens.

1   The Workbook ORDENTER must be open and the sheet ORDER SCREENS currently displaying the title screen.

First make sure that neither the Excel application window nor the ORDENTER document window is maximised; if so then press the Restore button(s) – their size doesn't matter at the moment.

Hint: If you're not sure of the position of these buttons, now is the time to check and experiment – not when you are recording the macro!

2   Open the **Tools** menu and select **Record Macro – Record New Macro.**

Click the **Options** button on the dialog box.

Name the macro **Position_Title_Screen.**

Complete the description box.

Make sure that the **This Workbook** and the **Visual Basic** options are selected.

Click **OK.**

From now on your actions are being recorded!

3   Click the **Maximise** button on both the Excel application window and the ORDENTER document window.

Press down the **Ctrl** and the **Home** keys together – the cursor moves to cell **A1** – the 'home' Position.

Click the top left hand corner of the box surrounding the title – cell **B3** – to park the cursor.

Click the Stop Recorder button now.

The third macro is recorded.

4   Test the macro as follows:

Open the **Tools** menu and select the **Macro** option

Select the macro name from the list and click the **Run** button.

5   We need a fourth macro to position the database screen.

As before make sure that neither the Excel application window nor the ORDENTER document window is maximised; if so then press the Restore button(s)

Hint.   You may wish to try out the series of actions in section 7 before you record them.

6   Open the **Tools** menu and select **Record Macro – Record New Macro.**

Click the **Options** button on the dialog box.

Name the macro **Position_Database_Screen.**

Complete the description box.

Make sure that the **This Workbook** and the **Visual Basic** options are selected.

Click **OK.**

From now on your actions are being recorded!

7   Click the **Maximise** button on both the Excel application window and the ORDENTER document window.

Press down the **Ctrl** and the **Home** keys together – the cursor moves to cell **A1.**

Scroll down until row **56** appears at the top of the screen – the row containing the database titles.

Scroll across the worksheet until column **L** is the leftmost column; all the headings should be displayed now – see Unit 18 Figure 5.

Make any final adjustments to the position.

Click the **Stop Recorder** button now.

The fourth macro is recorded.

8   **Consolidation.**

Now use the Tools-Macro menu to run the four macros in the following order:

Set_Title_Screen – the title screen is set up.

Restore_Title_Screen – the normal Excel screen defaults are restored.

Position_Database_Screen – the database headings are positioned on screen.

Position_Title_Screen – the title box is positioned on the screen.

This sequence should give you an idea of the order in which the completed system will call the macros.

9   **Troubleshooting – stepping through a Macro.**

It is possible to execute a macro one step at a time; this is useful for testing and debugging.

Click the Sheet tab for the **ORDER SCREENS** sheet. It is displayed.

Open the **Tools** menu and select **Macro.**

Select the macro **Set_Title_Screen** from the list.

Click the **Step** button.

The Debug window appears at the bottom of the screen – the first line of the macro should be in a rectangular selection box – you may need to scroll it into view.

Drag the window and re-size it so that you can see the worksheet screen as well.

10 **Correcting a Macro.** (Information only) If one of your macros is not working properly there are various options:

a. You can edit the macro line – this can be very difficult for a complex macro unless you fully understand its syntax – better to either,

b. Delete the whole macro and start again (select the relevant macro lines on the macro sheet and use the Clear command) or,

c. Delete the lines of the macro from the incorrect line(s) to the end, then start recording again as follows:

Select the next blank line on the macro sheet

Open the **Tools** menu and select **Record Macro.**

Select the **Mark Position for Recording** option.

Select the worksheet ORDER SCREENS.

Open the **Tools** menu and select **Record Macro.**

Select the **Record at Mark** option.

Record the actions again.

Click the Stop Recorder button.

Activity 2 Creating a dialog box

We have designed our screens and four macros to control them.

The next step is to design a special 'custom' dialog box to allow the user to enter records into the orders database. It will use typical Excel features such as buttons, check boxes and drop down list.

Figure 1 shows the completed dialog box.

The dialog box will be controlled by a macro, created in the next activity.

1 **Opening a Dialog Sheet.** Open the **Insert** menu and select the **Macro** option.

Select **Dialog.**

A new dialog sheet is added to the workbook, named **Dialog1.** It contains a dialog box, blank except for two standard buttons and the Forms toolbar.

Maximise the sheet if necessary.

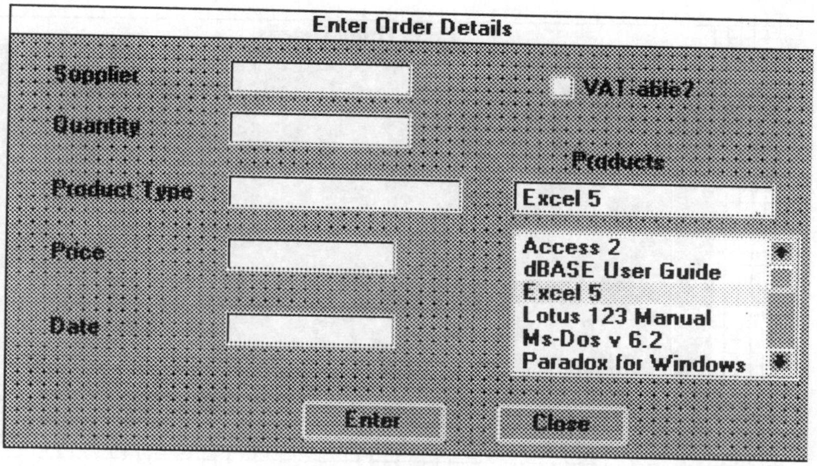

Enter Order Details

Supplier [   ]   VAT-able?

Quantity [   ]

Product Type [   ]   Products

[Excel 5   ]

Price [   ]   Access 2
                           dBASE User Guide
                           Excel 5
Date [   ]   Lotus 123 Manual
                           Ms-Dos v 6.2
                           Paradox for Windows

                    [Enter]   [Close]

Figure 1

Double click on the sheet tab for Dialog1 and re-name the sheet **ENTER ORDERS**

Click **OK.**

2   Click the edge of the dialog box – a selection border appears.

Move the screen pointer onto the bottom right-hand corner of the blank box and drag to enlarge it by about 30% – don't worry about exact sizes at this stage – all boxes and toolbars can be moved and re-sized by the usual 'dragging' method.

3   **Adding a Title.**

At the moment the default title of the dialog box is 'Dialog Caption'.

Drag the screen pointer along the title bar of the dialog box – it is selected.

Type the new title **Enter Order Details.**

Now drag the **OK** and the **Cancel** buttons to the bottom of the dialog box.

The dialog box should now look like Figure 2.

4   **Adding Labels**. Move the screen pointer onto the Forms toolbar and click the **Label** button (top left of toolbar)

Now move the pointer back onto the dialog box and drag to create a small label box. Use Figure 1 above as a rough guide, the size and position can be adjusted later.

Now click the label box and drag the pointer across the label to alter the default label to **Supplier.** You have created your first field label.

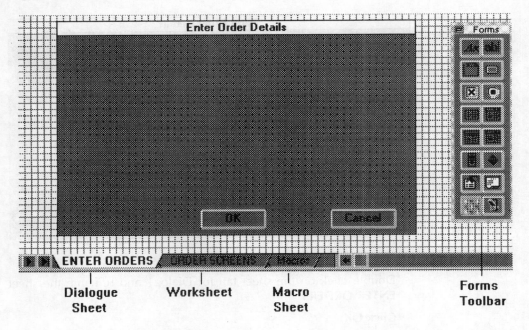

Dialogue Sheet   Worksheet   Macro Sheet   Forms Toolbar

Figure 2

5 Now repeat step 4 to create labels for:

    Quantity
    Product Type
    Price
    Date

Use Figure 1 as a rough guide. Again don't worry too much about their sizes and positions.

6 **Adding Edit Boxes.**

We need to add data entry boxes next to the labels so that the user can enter the order details.

Click on the **Edit Box** tool (top right of the Forms toolbar)

Move the pointer back onto the dialog box and drag to create an edit box next to the Supplier label – see Figure 3.

With the edit box still selected, move the screen pointer onto the Forms toolbar and click the **Control Properties** button (second from the bottom on the left of toolbar)

A dialog box appears, click the **Control** tab if necessary.

Text is the default option.

Click **OK.**

Alphanumeric text will now be accepted as input to the edit box. (a supplier's name could consist of all letters, eg 'Smith and Sons', or numbers and letters, eg 'A1 Trading')

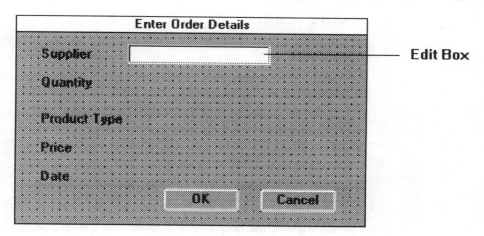

Edit Box

Figure 3

7   Now repeat step 6 to add edit boxes with the following control
     properties next to the other labels that you have created, refer to
     Figure 1 for guidance if necessary:

     Quantity   Integer (ie whole number)

     Product Type   Text

     Price   Number

     Date   Text

     Again don't worry too much about their sizes and positions.

8   **Correcting Mistakes.** If you wish to delete a box or text, simply
     click it to select it then press the Delete key.

9   **Adding a Check Box.**

     We need to enter a check box so that the user can enter whether
     VAT is due on an item. As most items are VAT-able an X will
     appear in the box by default, if the user deselects it then VAT is not
     payable.

     Click on the **Check Box** tool (third down on the left of the Forms
     toolbar)

     Move the pointer back onto the dialog box and drag to create a
     check box next to the Supplier box – see Figure 1 for guidance

     With the check box still selected, move the screen pointer onto the
     Forms toolbar and click the **Control Properties** button (second from
     the bottom on the left of toolbar)

     A dialog box appears, click the **Control** tab if necessary.

     Click the **Checked** option button.

     Click **OK.**

     Amend the label on the check box to **VAT-able?**

10   Adding a List Box.

The list box will contain items of stock that can be added to the database.

Click on the **Combination List Edit** tool (fifth down on the left of the Forms toolbar)

Move the pointer back onto the dialog box and drag to create a check box below the VAT-able box – see Figure 1 for guidance

A list edit box appears on screen. The scroll bars on the list box will allow you to find and select the stock item you want. The edit box is to add a new stock item.

11   Linking the List Box to the Product List.

With the list box only selected, move the screen pointer onto the Forms toolbar and click the **Control Properties** button.

Click the **Control** tab if necessary.

Select the **Input Range** box and type PRODUCT_LIST

This is the name of the cell range holding the list of products, cells U21-U32 on the ORDER SCREENS worksheet. (see Unit 19, Activity 1.9)

Click **OK.** When you return to the dialog box the list of products appears in the list box – enlarge it if necessary

The text box above the list box is linked to it – it may need enlarging too. Make sure that these two linked boxes do not become separated.

Use the **Label** button on the toolbar to create the heading **Product** over the text box. – see section 4 above if necessary.

12   Select the OK button and alter the label on it to Enter.

With the button still selected, move the screen pointer onto the Forms toolbar and click the **Control Properties** button.

Click the **Control** tab if necessary.

Make sure that the **Default** and **Dismiss** properties are set on.

Click **OK.**

13   Now select the Cancel button and alter its label to Close.

With the button still selected, move the screen pointer onto the Forms toolbar and click the **Control Properties** button.

Click the **Control** tab if necessary.

Make sure that the properties is set to **Cancel**

Click **OK.**

14   Now reposition all the elements in the completed screen to achieve a neat layout, using Figure 1 above as a guide. Figure 1 also gives an approximate guide to the lengths of the edit fields.

> **Hint:** First click the element to select it, then move the screen pointer onto the border to move it, or onto a selection handle to re-size it.

15 Finally select each element on the dialog box in turn and look in the Formula Bar at the top of the window.

You will see that Excel has assigned each type of object a number, the Enter button is Button2 etc. It is worth making a note of these numbers as you will be using them in the macro created in Unit 21.

16 Save the workbook.

Activity 3 Naming the cells in the database

We are going to create a macro that transfers the order details from the dialog box into the database held in the worksheet. The macro will also multiply price by quantity to calculate the total price of the order and apply VAT.

1 Open the **ORDER SCREENS** worksheet and scroll so that **L52** is the top left hand corner – see Figure 4.

We are going to name a number of cells that will hold the order details when they are first transferred into the worksheet.

	L	M	N	O	P	Q	R	S
52								
53								
54								
55								
56	Supplier	Product	Type	Quantity	Price	Date	VAT	Total
57								
58								

Figure 4

2 **Naming the database cells.**

Click cell **L52** then open the **Insert** menu and select the **Name** then the **Define** options.

Enter the name **SUPPLIER** and click **OK**. This cell name is easier to remember and can now be used in a macro instead of a cell reference.

3 Name the following cells in a similar way:

Give cell **M52** the name **PRODUCT**

Give cell **N52** the name **TYPE**

Give cell **O52** the name **QUANTITY**

Give cell **P52** the name **PRICE**

Give cell **Q52** the name **DATE**

Give cell **R52** the name **VAT**

Give cell **S52** the name **TOTAL**

4   Save and close the workbook.

Summary of commands

Note

Menu commands show the menu name first, followed by the command to choose from the menu, e.g. Edit-Clear means open the Edit menu and select the Clear command.

Insert-Macro-Dialog   Create custom dialog box

Insert-Name-Define   Name a selected object, eg cell(s)

Tools-Record Macro-Record New Macro   Record new macro

Controlling a dialog box

Skills to be learned	Activity
Macro – entering code	1

Previous skills needed to tackle this unit

Skill	*Covered in Unit*
Starting Excel	1
Basic mouse, menu and Windows operations	1

Important note

Units 19 to 24 form a unified development task – they all need to be completed in order for the purchase order application to work. Unlike previous units there is no point in doing any one unit in isolation from the others, they all build on each other.

Introduction

This unit continues the development of the purchase order application begun in Units 19 and 20. It shows you how to create a macro that will take the purchase order data from the dialog box created in the previous unit and store it in the worksheet.

You will need to key in the VB code for this macro, unlike previous macros it cannot be recorded.

Activity 1 Creating a macro to control the dialog box

We want to program the Enter button in the dialog box so that, whenever it is clicked, it will run a macro that takes the record held in the dialog box and adds it to the database. In Visual Basic this is called an *event handler* procedure – it handles or responds to the event of clicking a button.

This activity will introduce some programming concepts in Visual Basic. They will be introduced as we go along, so take the time to read the explanations rather than just copying the lines of program code.

First some general theory:

Objects. Visual basic is an object-oriented language, ie the program manipulates objects. Worksheets, windows, dialog boxes, buttons, menus and ranges of cells are all examples of objects. Objects can contain other objects, eg a worksheet contains cell ranges which contain values.

Some objects called **collection** objects contain sets of objects, eg a dialog box contains buttons and edit boxes. To identify an object you often need to identify its container as well, eg the dialog box that contains the edit box.

Properties. All objects have properties that determine how they look or how they work, eg a TextBox object has a Text property – the text it contains, a workbook can be active or not – the property *ActiveWorkbook*. Not all properties apply to all objects.

Methods are used to perform actions on objects. The object's properties determine what methods can be used with them, eg many objects can be opened, closed, copied or activated – worksheets, workbooks etc – but calculations can only be applied to certain types of numeric objects.

Syntax. To refer to the method you are applying to the object you use *Object.Method*
ie object name separated from method name with a full stop

1   Open the workbook ORDENTER.

Open the dialog sheet **ENTER ORDERS.**

Click the **Enter** button on the dialog box.

Move the pointer onto the Forms toolbar and click the **Edit Code** tool (on the right, second from the bottom)

A macro is opened with a code stub – the skeleton of a VB macro – you have to type the rest!

The first line – ' **Button2_Click Macro** is simply the macro name.

A single quotation mark at the start of any line means that it will be ignored by the program – it is a comment. It is there to document or explain the program. Space is given to add other comments.

You will recall that every element in a dialog box is given a number; the Enter button is Button2 – see Unit 20.

The final two lines:

Sub Button2_Click()

End Sub

mark the start and end of a subprocedure. The main statements (lines of code) in a program fit between the Sub and the End Sub statements.

2   Move the screen pointer to the start of the **End Sub** line and click to position the cursor.

Press the **Enter** key to create a blank line.

Position the cursor on the blank line and carefully type in the following VB statements:

The line indentations are for readability; use the Tab key.

```
' Declare variable to hold calculations
    Dim Vatrate
'Copy supplier name from dialog box to named cell in order sheet
    Sheets("ORDER SCREENS").Range("Supplier").Value = _
    DialogSheets("ENTER ORDERS").EditBoxes("9").Text
```

Hints: Blank lines can also be inserted for readability

You may enter the statements in upper or lower case.

Remember that the number of the edit boxes may be different in your dialog box – check this.

Notes on entering VB code

Press Enter after entering each line; it will automatically be checked and formatted for you. Any errors will be highlighted and an error message appear. Usually they are simple typing errors, ones to check especially are:

When you split a long statement over two lines you must add a space followed by an underscore (_) character to the end of the first line – miss the space or use the wrong character and it won't work.

Use the double quotes " " and round brackets ( ) as shown, eg, in ("ENTER ORDERS")

Don't include spaces around the full stops, eg, in ("SUPPLIER").Value

Help on VB Code. Locate the cursor on the word and press the F1 key. Help on that term is provided. You will find it provides examples of code as well.

Explanation of the VB statements

The two lines starting with a single ' character are explanatory comments and will be ignored by the program – they are for your guidance only.

The **Dim** statement (short for dimension) is used to declare variables before they are used in the program. Variables store values used in the program and have to be given names; in this case we are going to calculate the VAT payable and total order price so we need a variable to hold the VAT rate.

The **Range** statement continues over two lines. It identifies a cell range called SUPPLIER in the worksheet ORDER SCREENS and makes its value equal to edit box 9 on the dialog sheet ENTER ORDERS. This is an effective way of copying the supplier name from the dialog box into the worksheet. (you will recall that SUPPLIER is the name we gave to cell L52, and edit box 9 is a name Excel uses to identify the edit box holding the supplier name – see Unit 20, it may be different on your dialog box)

3   Testing Your First Line of Code.

The complete macro should look like this now:

```
' ENTER ORDERS_Button2_Click Macro
'
'
Sub Button2_Click()
' Declare variable to hold calculations
Dim Vatrate
    'Copy supplier name from dialog box to named cell in order sheet
    Sheets("ORDER SCREENS").Range("Supplier").Value = _
        DialogSheets("ENTER ORDERS").EditBoxes("9").Text
End Sub
```

Activate your dialog sheet ENTER ORDERS

Open the **Tools** menu and select the **Run Dialog** option.

The dialog box is displayed (notice that it has no dotted grid on it – these are displayed when you are designing the dialog box not when you are running it)

Click on the **Supplier** edit box to select it and enter any name.

Click the **Enter** button.

After a few seconds the dialog box closes, leaving the dialog design displayed.

Activate the worksheet ORDER SCREENS and check cell L52 – it should contain the data from the dialog box.

Troubleshooting. If nothing has happened, or you get an error message, don't worry.

Return to the module sheet MACROS containing the macro code and check:

❏   The spelling of the code.

❏   The code number of the Supplier Edit Box – see Unit 20.

❏   The names of the dialog sheet, the worksheet and the cell name.

4   Now enter the rest of the macro as shown below, *remember to check that the number of the object on your dialog box is the same as mine – see Unit 20.*

Hint: You may find it quicker to copy and paste the lines, and then modify them.

```
' ENTER ORDERS_Button2_Click Macro
'
'
```

```
Sub Button2_Click()
' Declare variable to hold calculations
Dim Vatrate
    'Copy supplier name from dialog box to named cell in order sheet
    Sheets("ORDER SCREENS").Range("Supplier").Value = _
        DialogSheets("ENTER ORDERS").EditBoxes("9").Text
    'Copy quantity from dialog box to named cell in order sheet
    Sheets("ORDER SCREENS").Range("Quantity").Value = _
        DialogSheets("ENTER ORDERS").EditBoxes("10").Text
    'Copy product type from dialog box to named cell in order sheet
    Sheets("ORDER SCREENS").Range("Type").Value = _
        DialogSheets("ENTER ORDERS").EditBoxes("11").Text
    'Copy product price from dialog box to named cell in order sheet
    Sheets("ORDER SCREENS").Range("Price").Value = _
        DialogSheets("ENTER ORDERS").EditBoxes("12").Text
    'Copy order date from dialog box to named cell in order sheet
    Sheets("ORDER SCREENS").Range("Date").Value = _
        DialogSheets("ENTER ORDERS").EditBoxes("13").Text
    'Copy product name from dialog box to named cell in order sheet
    Sheets("ORDER SCREENS").Range("Product").Value = _
        DialogSheets("ENTER ORDERS").EditBoxes("17").Text
End Sub
```

Now test that the dialog box is working correctly as before – see section 3 above. You will need to enter some test data in the edit boxes on the dialog box – use the mouse or the Tab key to select each data entry box – see section 7 to change the tab order.

Debug as before if necessary.

5   Checking and calculating the VAT.

If the check box is checked then we want to add the current rate – 17.5% – to the total value of the order and transfer this to the worksheet cells we have designated – see Unit 20.

The VAT calculation is simply quantity multiplied by item price multiplied by 0.175.

If no VAT is payable then VAT is set to 0

The VAT rate is held in a variable called Vatrate; this saves entering the rate for every order and makes it easy to amend if the VAT rate changes.

Insert a blank line before the **End Sub** line and insert the following VB statements:

```
'Calculate VAT @ 17.5% if VAT box is checked (xlOn)
    Vatrate = 0.175
    If DialogSheets("ENTER ORDERS").CheckBoxes("14").Value=xlOn _
    Then
        Sheets("ORDER SCREENS").Range("VAT").Value = Vatrate*_
        Range("QUANTITY").Value * Range("PRICE").Value
```

```
                    Else
                        Sheets("ORDER SCREENS").Range("VAT").Value = 0
                    End If
                'Calculate order total = (price * quantity) + VAT
                    Sheets("ORDER SCREENS").Range("TOTAL").Value = _
                        Range("QUANTITY").Value * Range("PRICE").Value _
                        + Range("VAT").Value
```

Hints: Make sure that **End Sub** finishes the Macro

The Excel constant for a check box being set on is 'xlOn' The 2 characters in the middle are lowercase 'l' and uppercase 'O' – don't use numbers or it won't work.

* is the multiplication sign.

6   Test the dialog box again with the check box on and off. Check that the VAT has been calculated and copied correctly to the worksheet cells **R52** and **S52**.

If it works then congratulate yourself – your first efforts at typing in VB commands can be fiddly error-prone and frustrating. It will get easier as you practice!

Troubleshooting. If nothing has happened, or you get an error message, don't worry.

Return to the module sheet containing the macro code and check:

The spelling of the code and the other characters – especially brackets, the double quotation marks, the full stops and the space and underscore used to join the parts of a line

The code number of the Edit Box – see Unit 20.

The names of the dialog sheet, the worksheet and the cell name.

7   **Changing the Tab Order. (Optional)**

If you were entering data into the dialog box using the Tab key you may have noticed that the edit boxes were not selected in any particular sequence.

First select each edit box in the preferred sequence and make a note of the edit box numbers.

Open the **Tools** menu and select the **Tab Order** option – a dialog box appears.

First select an edit box from the list then click the up or down arrow key to change its position.

When you are finished click **OK**.

8   Save and close the workbook.

Summary of commands

Note

Menu commands show the menu name first, followed by the command to choose from the menu, e.g. Edit-Clear means open the Edit menu and select the Clear command.

Tools-Run Dialog	Run a dialog box
Tools-Tab Order	Change order edit boxes selected

Further Macros

Skills to be learned	Activity
Conditions – introducing	2
Loops – introducing	2
Message box – creating	2

Previous skills needed to tackle this unit

Skill	Covered in Unit
Starting Excel	1
Basic mouse, menu and Windows operations	1

Important note

Units 19 to 24 form a unified development task – they all need to be completed in order for the purchase order application to work. Unlike previous units there is no point in doing any one unit in isolation from the others, they all build on each other.

Introduction

This unit continues the development of the purchase order application begun in Units 19 – 21. It introduces the programming concepts IF and DO and uses them to let the user either continue using the dialog box or to quit.

Activity 1   Adding the records to a database

The macro Button2_Click transfers the data from the dialog box to a cell range in the worksheet ORDER SCREENS. The next macro will transfer it from the cell range to a database held in the ORDER SCREENS worksheet.

This is a fairly simple macro and can be recorded. It involves:

    a.   defining a cell area as a database,

    b.   copying and pasting the cells into it and,

    c.   inserting a blank row into the database for the next record.

1   Open the workbook ORDENTER.

If necessary open the worksheet ORDER SCREENS and scroll so that cell **L52** is in the top left hand corner of the window. As you have been testing the dialog box in the previous unit, cells L52 to S52 will probably contain some test data, if not create some – see Figure 1.

	L	M	N	O	P	Q	R	S
49								
50								
51								
52	JM Software	Lotus 123 Manual	Textbook		5	15.95	25-Aug	13.96	93.71
53								
54								
55								
56	Supplier	Product	Type	Quantity	Price	Date	VAT	Total
57								

Figure 1

First we need to define certain cells as a database area. (see Unit 10 if necessary) We can then record a macro that adds records to it.

Select the 8 field names. (cells **L56** to **S56**), *plus* the 2 rows of 8 cells directly underneath.

You have now selected the cell range L56 to S58.

Open the **Insert** menu and select the **Name-Define** options.

A dialog box appears, enter the name **DATABASE** then click **OK**

2   Open the **Tools** menu and select the **Record Macro-Record New Macro** option.

A dialog box appears – click the **Options** button..

Name the macro **Add_Order** and complete the **Description** box, eg 'adds record to database'.

Make sure that the options **This Workbook** and **Visual Basic** are selected.

Click **OK**.

You are now recording.

3   Click the row designator number for row **57** – the whole row is selected.

Open the **Insert** menu and select **Rows** – a blank row is inserted.

Select the record in row 52 (cells **L52 – S52**)

Open the **Edit** menu and select Copy – the record is framed by a dotted box.

Click cell **L57.**

Open the **Edit** menu and select **Paste** – the record is copied to the database

Press the **Esc** key to remove the dotted box.

Click the Stop Recorder button.

4   Whenever this macro is run a blank row will be inserted in to the database area and the new record copied in from row 52 – see Figure 2.

Try this macro using the Tool-Macro command.

				Quantity	Price	Date	VAT	Total
49								
50								
51								
52	JM Software	Lotus 123 Manual	Textbook	5	15.95	25-Aug	13.96	93.71
53								
54								
55								
56	Supplier	Product	Type	Quantity	Price	Date	VAT	Total
57	JM Software	Lotus 123 Manual	Textbook	5	15.95	25-Aug	13.96	93.71
58								

Figure 2

5   **One Macro Sheet or Many? (Optional)** Open the **Tools** menu and select the **Macro** option.

Select **Add_Order** from the list of macros and click the **Edit** button.

You are taken to the correct place on the macro sheet to see the macro code.

Now check the name of the macro sheet – Excel may have placed this macro on a new module sheet or it may be added to the bottom of an existing sheet. As you can always locate the macro using the Tools menu it may not make any difference to you. However if you should wish to print off your macros you may want them all on the same sheet. (extra sheets also use up more main memory)

You can transfer macros to one sheet using Copy and Paste, then use the Edit-Delete Sheet to remove the unwanted sheet.

6   **Making Sure that the Worksheet is Active.**

The macro Add_Order will not run unless the worksheet ORDER SCREENS is active (ie on top).

To ensure that it always is active insert the following two lines (shown in bold) at the start of the macro after the first line:

```
Sub Add_Order()
    ' Open the worksheet ORDER SCREENS
    Worksheets("ORDER SCREENS").Activate
    Rows("57:57").Select
    Range("L57").Activate
    Selection.Insert Shift:=xlDown
    Range("L52:S52").Select
    Selection.Copy
    Range("L57").Select
    ActiveSheet.Paste
    Application.CutCopyMode = False
End Sub
```

7   Testing the Macro.

Open the dialog sheet ENTER ORDERS

At the moment the data from the first record is still displayed – we will fix this later.

Open the **Tools** menu and select the **Run Dialog** option.

Type in a new record over the existing record, using data of your own,

Click the **Enter** button to complete entering the record.

Open the **Tools** menu and select the **Macro** option.

Select **Add_Order** from the list of macros and click the **Run** button.

The new record should have been copied into the database.

Open the worksheet ORDER SCREENS to check this.

You may need to adjust the column width of some of the database columns to accommodate the field lengths

Activity 2   Macros that call macros

We now need a macro to combine the activities of using the dialog box and adding the record to the database. We will also create a procedure that gives the user the option to use the dialog box more than once. At the moment clicking the Enter button closes the dialog box, however the user may well wish to continue adding more records.

We will add this macro to the end of the Add_Order macro.

1   Open the **Tools** menu and select the **Macro** option.

Select **Add_Order** from the list of macros and click the **Edit** button.

2   Scroll to the end of the macro, insert a few blank lines *after* the **End Sub** line and type the following macro:

```
'
' Display_Dialog Macro
' Calls up dialog box, displays it until user finished, then adds
' record to database
Sub Display_Dialog()
    ' Set up variable to hold user response to message box
    Dim Continue
    ' Set up continuous loop until No button on message box clicked
    Do Until Continue = vbNo
        ' If Enter button on the dialog box is clicked
        If DialogSheets("ENTER ORDERS").Show _
        Then
            ' Open the worksheet ORDER SCREENS
            Worksheets("ORDER SCREENS").Activate
            ' Run the Add_Order macro to add record to database
            Application.Run Macro:="Add_Order"
    ' If Close button on Dialog box is clicked exit the Do loop
    ' and end macro
        Else
            Exit Do
        End If
    'Display a message box prompting user to add another order
    Continue = MsgBox(Prompt:="Enter Another Order?", _
    Buttons:=vbYesNo + vbInformation, _
    Title:="Enter Purchase Order")
        'If No button on message box exit the loop and end macro
        If Continue = vbNo _
        Then
            Exit Do
        End If
    Loop
    ' Return to the title screen
    Worksheets("ORDER SCREENS").Activate
    Application.Run Macro:="Set_Title_Screen"
End Sub
```

3   **Explanation of Macro.** If you are new to programming then read this explanation carefully, it introduces some fundamental programming concepts.

Conditions. A macro can be designed to offer the user a choice, in this case to continue or quit, using an *If* condition. The macro can then branch, ie take alternative actions, depending on user choice, using *Else*. Every If condition needs an *End If* to show where it ends.

Looping. We want the macro to keep running and start again if the user chooses to continue, ie to loop. A *Do Until...* statement marks the start of the loop and a *Loop* statement the end. The user leaves the loop *(Exit Do)* when the condition is no longer true. The whole macro is enclosed in this loop.

You should find that the comments in the macro explain each line fairly fully, some additional explanations and hints follow:

vbYes and vbNo are visual basic special constants generated by clicking a Yes or a No button. A variable Continue is set up to hold the response.

MsgBox creates a small message box with a title, message and Yes/No buttons.

An *If* condition tests for a *No* response to the message and ends the loop. If Yes is clicked then the macro returns to the start of the loop and re-displays the dialog box.

When the loop is terminated (either by the user clicking the Close button on the dialog box or clicking the No button on the message box) the macro **Set_Title_Screen** is called and displays the application start-up screen.

4   **Testing the Macro.**

When you have typed in the code open the **Tools** menu and select **Macro.** Select the macro **Display_Dialog** from the list and click the **Run** button.

If it runs do the following:

a.   Enter a new record in the dialog box and click **Enter**

b.   Check the record is being added to the database

c.   The message box should appear – click **Yes.**

d.   Repeat steps a and b, but this time for c click **No.**

e.   The title screen should appear – if so you will need to run the Restore_Title_Screen macro to restore the screen defaults.

5   **Debugging the Macro.**

If you get a mysterious-looking error message don't worry often the incorrect element is highlighted. Return to the macro and check the following:

Does every **If** have an **End If ?**

Check that Then is on the same line as If, or as I have done, joined to the previous line by an underscore _ preceded by a **space.**

Check that **If** and **End If** are on separate lines. (Excel VB can be very fussy about this and you may have to re-type them. If they are wrong Excel sometimes misleadingly identifies the Do loop as the error)

Check that you have spelt the commands, the worksheet and the macro names correctly.

6   Save and close the workbook.

Summary of commands

Note

Menu commands show the menu name first, followed by the command to choose from the menu, e.g. Edit-Clear means open the Edit menu and select the Clear command.

Insert-Name-Define	Name a selected object, eg cell(s)
Tools-Macro	Select a macro to run, edit, delete etc.
Tools-Record Macro-Record New Macro	
	Record new macro
Tools-Run Dialog	Run a dialog box

Creating a data form and a custom menu

Important note

Units 19 to 24 form a unified development task – they all need to be completed in order for the purchase order application to work. Unlike previous units there is no point in doing any one unit in isolation from the others, they all build on each other.

Introduction

This unit continues the development of the purchase order application begun in Units 19 – 22. It creates a data form so purchase order records can be edited or deleted and creates a custom menu that replaces the standard Excel menu bar.

Activity 1   Using a data form

Excel provides a standard form for you to add, delete, or edit records – see Unit 9, Activity 4. This will form one of the options in our application and be called by a macro Call_Data_Form.

1   Open the workbook ORDENTER.

Open the Tools menu and select the **Record Macro** then the **Record New Macro** option.

A dialog box appears – click the **Options** button.

Name the macro **Call_Data_Form** and complete the **Description** box, eg 'uses data form for editing'.

Make sure that the options **This Workbook** and **Visual Basic** are selected.

Click **OK.**

You are now recording.

2   Click on the sheet tab for ORDER SCREENS to activate it (even if already selected).

Open the Tools menu and select the **Macro** option.

Run the macro **Position_Database_Screen** – the database cells should now be displayed.

Click anywhere on the database, eg on one of the heading cells in row 56.

Open the **Data** menu and select **Form** – a data form is displayed.

Click the **Close** button on the form.

Open the **Tools** menu and select the **Macro** option again.

Run the macro **Set_Title_Screen.**

The title screen appears.

Click the Stop Recorder button.

3   **Testing the Macro.** Open the Tools menu and select the **Macro** option.

Run the macro **Restore_Title_Screen** to restore the screen defaults.

Now run the macro **Call_Data_Form.**

The data form is displayed, click the Close button.

The **Set_Title_Screen** macro will be called next.

Run the macro **Restore_Title_Screen** again.

4   **Hints:**

If your macro doesn't work, try deleting it (use the Tools-Macro menu) and re-recording the above steps.

If it still doesn't work check that the database is still defined – see Unit 22, Activity 1, Section 1.

If not, re-define it and try the macro again.

5   **Documenting the Macro.**

Open the **Tools** menu and select the **Macro** option.

Select the macro **Call_Data_Form** and click the **Edit** button.

Your macro should resemble the following, add the comments shown in bold.

```
' Call_Data_Form Macro
' Macro recorded 06/04/95 by j muir
' Calls up a data form for editing
' Sub Call_Data_Form()
    Sheets("ORDER SCREENS").Select
    ' Position screen to show database
    Application.Run
Macro:="ORDENTER.XLS!Position_Database_Screen"
    ' Select the database
    Range("N59").Select
    ' Call the data form
    ActiveSheet.ShowDataForm
    ' Return to title screen
    Application.Run Macro:="ORDENTER.XLS!Set_Title_Screen"
End Sub
```

Activity 2   Printing, saving and quitting macros

We will write two short macros – one to print the database and one to save and quit the workbook. Turn on the printer for this activity. (you can still carry out these activities without a printer)

1   **The Print Macro.**

Open the Tools menu and select the **Record Macro** then the **Record New Macro** option. A dialog box appears – click the **Options** button.

Name the macro **Print_Database** and complete the **Description** box, eg 'Prints database records'.

Make sure that the options **This Workbook** and **Visual Basic** are selected.

Click **OK**.

You are now recording.

2   Click on the sheet tab for ORDER SCREENS to activate it.

Open the **Tools** menu and select the **Macro** option.

Run the macro **Position_Database_Screen.**

The database cells should now be displayed, click cell L56 – the first heading in the database.

Open the **Edit** menu and select **Go To** – a dialog box appears.

Click the **Special** button – the 'Go To Special ' dialog box appears.

Click the **Current Region** button then **OK.**

The whole database area should now be selected.

3   Open the **File** menu and select **Print** – a dialog box appears.

Click the Selection button in the Print What section.

Click **OK.** Wait until the database has printed.

Open the **Tools** menu and select the **Macro** option.

Run the macro **Set_Title_Screen.**

The title screen appears.

Click the Stop Recorder button.

Run the macro **Restore_Title_Screen** to restore the screen defaults.

If the print-out is not to your satisfaction then you may need to adjust the page set up. If so delete and re-record the macro.

4   **Testing the Macro.**

Now run the **Display_Dialog** macro to add another record.

Run the **Print_Database** macro to test the print macro.

Make sure that the full database is printed, *including* the new record.

Run the macro Restore_Title_Screen to restore the screen defaults.

5   **The Save and Quit macro.**

The macro will save the whole workbook and then quit Excel.

Name the macro **Save_Quit** and start recording as before.

Save the workbook (File-Save) and then stop the recorder.

6   **Editing the Save_Quit Macro.**

Open the **Tools** menu and select **Macro.**

Select the **Save_Quit** macro from the list then click the Edit button.

To complete this macro we need to insert a Quit method before the End Sub in order to quit Excel.

Insert the line shown below in bold.

Your macro should now resemble the following.

```
' Save_Quit Macro
' Macro recorded 06/04/95 by j muir
'
Sub Save_Quit()
    ActiveWorkbook.Save
    Application.Quit
End Sub
```

7   Test the macro; it should save the workbook and then exit Excel.

8   Run Excel again and open the workbook ORDENTER.XLS.

Activity 3   Creating the custom menu

We have created macros to run all the major database operations – adding records, updating and searching, printing the database and exiting. We now need to design a custom menu that offers these options; it will resemble a standard Excel bar menu in appearance and operation. It will open automatically when the workbook is opened to replace the standard Excel menus.

1   Open the workbook ORDENTER and activate a module sheet. (any one)

Open the **Tools** menu and select **Menu Editor.**

2   A dialog box appears. It offers two lists of standard menus and menu items.

Click the top item in the **Menus** list **(&File)** to select it.

Now click the **Delete** button on the dialog box. Keep doing this until all the standard menus are deleted. The Dialog box should now look like Figure 1.

3   **Adding the Menu Title.**

With the Menus list still selected, click the **Insert** button on the dialog box. Type the title **&Purchase Orders** in the **Caption** box.

Click **Insert** again and the title is added to the Menus list

4   **Adding the Menu Items.**

Select **End of Menu** in the **Menu Items** box.

Click the Insert button and type **&Save and Exit** in the **Caption** box.

Now click the down arrow on the **Macro** box – a list of macros appears.

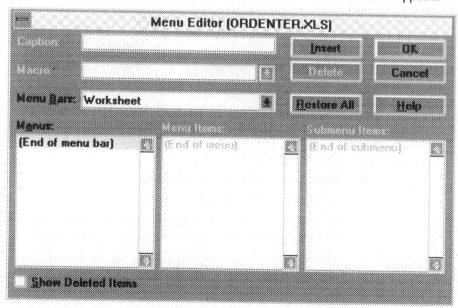

Figure 1

229

Select the macro **Save_Quit.**

Click **Insert** again and the item is added to the Menu Items list.

You have now added a menu option and its associated macro.

5   Now continue to add the following items and macros to the menu using Figure 2 as a guide: (the hyphen will create divider bars between certain menu options and has no associated macro) The menu items will display in the reverse order to that shown here.

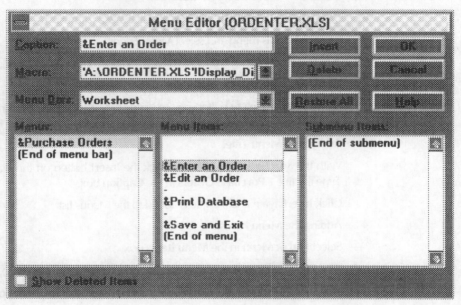

Figure 2

Menu Items	Macro
&Restore_Excel_Menus	Restore_Title_Screen
&Print Database	Print_Database
&Edit an Order	Call_Data_Form
&Enter an Order	Display Dialog

Finally click the **OK** button.

6   **Testing the Menu and the Macros.**

Activate the Worksheet ORDER SCREENS.

The Custom menu is displayed, when the menu is opened it should look like Figure 3. If not you will need to go back and edit it.

This menu can be run whenever the workbook ORDENTER is opened and ORDER SCREENS is the active sheet.

```
Purchase Orders
   Enter an Order
   Edit an Order

   Print Database
   Restore Excel Menus

   Save and Exit
```

Figure 3

7 Now test the menu options in turn, making a note of anything that does not work correctly:

a. **Enter an Order.** Take this option. The dialog box should appear.

Enter a new order and click the **Enter** button. Check that the record is added to the database.

The message box 'Enter Another Order'?' should be displayed now.

Click the **Yes** button. You should be returned to the dialog box.

This time click the **Close** button. You should be returned to the special title screen.

b. **Edit an Order.** Take this option. The data form should be displayed. Use the buttons and try editing a record then click the **Close** button. You should be returned to the special title screen.

c. **Print Database.** Make sure that the printer is turned on. (if you have no printer press the Cancel button when the print message box is displayed) Take this option and check that the new record is printed too. You should be returned to the special title screen.

d. Restore Excel Menus. Take this option. The default toolbars, gridlines etc are restored. Notice that the main menu bar is not. We will add this in the next unit.

e. Save and Exit. The workbook should be saved and closed and you should exit Excel. Start Excel again and re-open the workbook. Check that the new record was saved.

8 **Troubleshooting:** If any of the above operations don't work correctly make a full note of the problem. Don't worry – most applications don't work perfectly the first time!

Return to the menu editor and check that you have assigned the correct macros to each menu choice. Remember that you can test individual macros a step at a time using the Tools-Macro menu.

9 Save and close the workbook.

Summary of commands

Note

Menu commands show the menu name first, followed by the command to choose from the menu, e.g. Edit-Clear means open the Edit menu and select the Clear command.

Data-Form	Use a data form with a database
Tools-Macro	Select a macro to run, edit, delete etc.
Tools-Menu Editor	Build a custom menu
Tools-Record Macro-Record New Macro	Record new macro

Completing the application

Skills to be learned	Activity
Application – backing up	1
Dialog box– clearing fields	1
Main Menu Bar – restoring	2

Previous skills needed to tackle this unit

Skill	Covered in Unit
Starting Excel	1
Basic mouse, menu and Windows operations	1

Important note

Units 19 to 24 form a unified development task – they all need to be completed in order for the purchase order application to work. Unlike previous units there is no point in doing any one unit in isolation from the others, they all build on each other

Introduction

This unit completes the development of the purchase order application begun in Units 19 – 23. It tests the whole application and shows you how to make some final refinements to the dialog box and the custom menu.

Activity 1   Enhancing the application

By now the Purchase Order system is up and running, but there are still some rough edges:

a.   When the dialog box appears the previous record is still displayed.

b. The worksheet ORDER SCREENS needs to open automatically whenever the workbook is opened and display the title screen.

c. The Restore Excel menus option needs to restore the main menu bar as well.

d. The Excel screen 'jumps' as the macro commands are executed.

We will put these problems right in the remaining activities.

1 **Backing Up Your Application.**

Open the workbook ORDENTER.

Before you start tinkering with the workbook make a copy of it as a backup.

Open the workbook ORDENTER and select **Save As** from the **File** menu.

Save the workbook under the new name ORDBAK – make sure that the correct drive is selected before you click OK.

2 **Clearing the Custom Dialog Box.**

We need to clear out the contents of the custom dialog box so that it is blank when another order is added.

Let's recap on how the dialog box macro **Button2_Click** transfers data from the dialog box to the database cells in the worksheet.

a. The custom dialog box was designed using the Dialog Editor – see Unit 20 Activity 2.

b. A macro was written to display the dialog box – see Unit 21, Activity 1.

c. When this macro is run the user can enter a record – which is then stored in the worksheet.

d. An example of the VB code that transfers the supplier name from the edit box in the dialog box to a named cell in the worksheet ORDER SCREENS is:

```
Sheets("ORDER SCREENS").Range("Supplier").Value = _
DialogSheets("ENTER ORDERS").EditBoxes("9").Text
```

3 Open the **Tools menu** and select **Macro.** Choose the macro **Button2_Click** and click the **Edit** button. Locate the code shown above, insert a blank line and add the line shown in bold, so that the section of code now contains these lines:

```
'Copy supplier name from dialog box to named cell in order sheet
Sheets("ORDER SCREENS").Range("Supplier").Value = _
DialogSheets("ENTER ORDERS").EditBoxes("9").Text
DialogSheets("ENTER ORDERS").EditBoxes("9").Text = " "
```

4 Now open the **Tools menu** and select **Macro.** Choose the macro **Display_Dialog** and click the **Run** button.

Now enter a new record in the dialog box and press the **Enter button.**

When the message box 'Enter Another Order'?' is displayed click the **Yes** button.

When you are returned to the dialog box check that the Supplier field is blank.

This time click the **Close** button. You should be returned to the special title screen. Restore the Excel menus and open the MACROS worksheet again.

5   **Consolidation.** You can now blank out all the edit boxes in the same way.

Edit the **Button2_Click** macro and add the extra lines.

Hint: The amended version the code for this and the other macros used in this application are shown at the end of this unit. Remember that the serial numbers of the edit boxes may vary from yours – see Unit 20.

6   **Make the amendments and then test the macro as follows:**

a.   Run the **Display_Dialog** macro.

b.   Add a new record and press the **Enter** button. The message box 'Enter Another Order'?' should be displayed now.

Click the **Yes** button. You should be returned to the dialog box.

Check that the dialog box is cleared and click the **Close** button.

You will be returned to the special title screen.

c.   Take the Restore Excel Menus option.

7   **Troubleshooting**: When you are entering the new record you may get an error message caused by an error with an edit box in the dialog box. This may be caused by Excel no longer treating the edit box as part of the dialog box. If this happens do the following:

a.   Close the dialog box and activate the dialog sheet ENTER ORDERS.

b.   Click the edit box that is causing the problem to select it and press the **Delete** key.

c.   Create a new edit box to replace it – use the Edit Box button, top right on the Forms tool bar. (See Unit 20)

d.   Note the reference number of the edit box (Unit 20)

e.   Edit the **Button2_Click** macro again, amending the edit box number, eg

EditBoxes("9") to EditBoxes("12")

f.   Test the macro again.

Activity 2   Restoring the Excel menu bar

To improve the application still further the **Restore Excel Menus** option needs to restore the main menu bar. To do this we must add a final command to the **Restore_Title_Screen** macro.

1 Open the **Tools** menu and choose the **Macro** option.

Select the **Restore_Title_Screen** macro from the list and click the **Edit** button.

Add this final line to the macro *before* the End Sub command.

    ActiveMenuBar.Reset

2 Now test the option as follows:

Activate the ORDER SCREENS worksheet

Select the **Restore Excel Menus option** – the main menu bar is restored; if not check your macro again.

Activity 3   Making a macro run automatically

We will create a special macro named Auto_Open that will automatically run when the workbook ORDENTER is opened. We will use it to call the macro Set_Title_Screen and display the custom menu. This will have the effect of automatically setting up the title screen when the workbook is opened. The macro can be typed into any module sheet of the workbook

1 Open a module sheet, scroll to the end, and enter this macro:

```
'
' Auto_Open Macro
' Runs the title screen macro when the workbook is opened
'
Sub Auto_Open()
        Sheets("Order Screens").Select
        Application.Run Macro:="ORDENTER.XLS!Set_Title_Screen"
End Sub
```

2 Test the macro by closing, saving, then opening the workbook.

The title screen and the custom menu should automatically be displayed.

Activity 4   Turning off screen updating

Once you have the whole application working correctly you can hide from the user what is happening 'behind the scenes'. In several macros there is an appreciable delay while the screen is being updated; if you turn off updating until the end of the macro then it will work more quickly and smoothly. The command is

Application.ScreenUpdating = False to turn off screen updating, and **Application.ScreenUpdating = True** to turn it on again. If you consult the list of macros at the end of this unit you will see it applied to the macro Set_Title_Screen. Insert these two commands and test the macro. If it works successfully then apply it to the macros Restore_Title_Screen and Display_Dialog.

Summary of commands

Note

Menu commands show the menu name first, followed by the command to choose from the menu, e.g. Edit-Clear means open the Edit menu and select the Clear command.

Tools-Macro   Select a macro to run, edit, delete etc.

Listing of Macros used in the purchase order application

Note. All the macros developed in units 19 – 24 appear below and can be used to check against your application. Remember that some details are bound to differ slightly, eg the reference numbers used for the elements of the dialog box.

```
' Set_Title_Screen Macro
' Macro recorded 25/03/95 by j muir
'
'
Sub Set_Title_Screen()
    Application.ScreenUpdating = False
    Sheets("ORDER SCREENS").Select
    Application.WindowState = xlMaximized
    ActiveWindow.WindowState = xlMaximized
    With ActiveWindow
        .DisplayGridlines = False
        .DisplayHeadings = False
        .DisplayHorizontalScrollBar = False
        .DisplayVerticalScrollBar = False
        .DisplayWorkbookTabs = False
    End With
    With Application
        .DisplayFormulaBar = False
        .DisplayStatusBar = False
    End With
    Toolbars(1).Visible = False
    Toolbars(2).Visible = False
    With Application
        .ShowToolTips = True
        .LargeButtons = False
        .ColorButtons = True
    End With
```

```
            Range("B3").Select
            Application.ScreenUpdating = True
    End Sub
' Restore_Title_Screen Macro
' Macro recorded 25/03/95 by j muir
'
'

Sub Restore_Title_Screen()
    With ActiveWindow
        .DisplayGridlines = True
        .DisplayHeadings = True
        .DisplayHorizontalScrollBar = True
        .DisplayVerticalScrollBar = True
        .DisplayWorkbookTabs = True
    End With
    With Application
        .DisplayFormulaBar = True
        .DisplayStatusBar = True
    End With
    Toolbars(1).Visible = True
    Toolbars(2).Visible = True
    With Application
        .ShowToolTips = True
        .LargeButtons = False
        .ColorButtons = True
    End With
    ActiveMenuBar.Reset
End Sub

' ENTER ORDERS_Button2_Click Macro
'

Sub Button2_Click()
' Declare variable to hold calculations
Dim Vatrate
    ' Copy supplier name from dialog box to named cell in order sheet
    Sheets("ORDER SCREENS").Range("Supplier").Value = _
        DialogSheets("ENTER ORDERS").EditBoxes("19").Text
        DialogSheets("ENTER ORDERS").EditBoxes("19").Text = " "
    'Copy quantity from dialog box to named cell in order sheet
    Sheets("ORDER SCREENS").Range("Quantity").Value = _
        DialogSheets("ENTER ORDERS").EditBoxes("10").Text
        DialogSheets("ENTER ORDERS").EditBoxes("10").Text = " "
    'Copy product type from dialog box to named cell in order sheet
    Sheets("ORDER SCREENS").Range("Type").Value = _
        DialogSheets("ENTER ORDERS").EditBoxes("23").Text
        DialogSheets("ENTER ORDERS").EditBoxes("23").Text = " "
    'Copy product price from dialog box to named cell in order sheet
    Sheets("ORDER SCREENS").Range("Price").Value = _
```

```
        DialogSheets("ENTER ORDERS").EditBoxes("25").Text
        DialogSheets("ENTER ORDERS").EditBoxes("25").Text = " "
    'Copy order date from dialog box to named cell in order sheet
    Sheets("ORDER SCREENS").Range("Date").Value = _
        DialogSheets("ENTER ORDERS").EditBoxes("13").Text
        DialogSheets("ENTER ORDERS").EditBoxes("13").Text = " "
    'Copy product name from dialog box to named cell in order sheet
    Sheets("ORDER SCREENS").Range("Product").Value = _
        DialogSheets("ENTER ORDERS").EditBoxes("17").Text
        DialogSheets("ENTER ORDERS").EditBoxes("17").Text = " "
    'Calculate VAT @ 17.5% if VAT box is checked (xlOn)
    Vatrate = 0.175
    If DialogSheets("ENTER ORDERS").CheckBoxes("14").Value = xlOn
_
    Then
        Sheets("ORDER SCREENS").Range("VAT").Value = Vatrate * _
        Range("QUANTITY").Value * Range("PRICE").Value
    Else
        Sheets("ORDER SCREENS").Range("VAT").Value = 0
    End If
    'Calculate order total = (price * quantity) + VAT
        Sheets("ORDER SCREENS").Range("TOTAL").Value = _
            Range("QUANTITY").Value * Range("PRICE").Value _
            + Range("VAT").Value
End Sub

' Position_Database_Screen Macro
' Macro recorded 05/04/95 by j muir
' Positions database column headings
'
Sub Position_Database_Screen()
    Application.WindowState = xlMinimized
    'Application.WindowState = xlNormal
    'Application.WindowState = xlMaximized
    Range("A1").Select
    ActiveWindow.SmallScroll Down:=55
    ActiveWindow.SmallScroll ToRight:=11
    Application.WindowState = xlNormal
End Sub
'

' Add_Order Macro
' Macro recorded 05/04/95 by j muir
' Adds record to database
'
Sub Add_Order()
    ' Open the worksheet ORDER SCREENS
    Worksheets("ORDER SCREENS").Activate
    Rows("57:57").Select
```

```
                  Range("L57").Activate
                  Selection.Insert Shift:=xlDown
                  Range("L52:S52").Select
                  Selection.Copy
                  Range("L57").Select
                  ActiveSheet.Paste
                  Application.CutCopyMode = False
End Sub
```

' Display_Dialog Macro
' Calls up dialog box, displays it until user finished, then adds
' record to database
```
Sub Display_Dialog()
' Set up variable to hold user response to message box
Dim Continue
' Set up continuous loop until No button on message box clicked
Do Until Continue = vbNo
      ' If Enter button on the dialog box is clicked
      If DialogSheets("ENTER ORDERS").Show _
      Then
          ' Open the worksheet ORDER SCREENS
          Worksheets("ORDER SCREENS").Activate
          'Run the Add_Order macro to add record to database
          Application.Run Macro:="Add_Order"
      'If Close button on Dialog box is clicked exit the Do loop
      ' and end macro
      Else
          Exit Do
      End If
'Display a message box prompting user to add another order
Continue = MsgBox(Prompt:="Enter Another Order?", _
Buttons:=vbYesNo + vbInformation, _
Title:="Enter Purchase Order")
      'If No button on message box exit the loop and end macro
      If Continue = vbNo _
      Then
          Exit Do
      End If
Loop
'Return to the title screen
Worksheets("ORDER SCREENS").Activate
Application.Run Macro:="Set_Title_Screen"
End Sub
```

' Call_Data_Form Macro
' Macro recorded 06/04/95 by j muir
' Calls up a data form for editing
'
```
Sub Call_Data_Form()
```

```
        Sheets("ORDER SCREENS").Select
        Application.Run
Macro:="ORDENTER.XLS!Position_Database_Screen"
        Range("N59").Select
        ActiveSheet.ShowDataForm
        Application.Run Macro:="ORDENTER.XLS!Set_Title_Screen"
    End Sub

' Print_Database Macro
' Macro recorded 06/04/95 by j muir
' prints database records
'
'
    Sub Print_Database()
        Sheets("ORDER SCREENS").Select
        Application.Run
Macro:="ORDENTER.XLS!Position_Database_Screen"
        Range("M59").Select
        Selection.CurrentRegion.Select
        Selection.PrintOut Copies:=1
        Application.Run Macro:="ORDENTER.XLS!Set_Title_Screen"
    End Sub

' Save_Quit Macro
' Macro recorded 06/04/95 by j muir
    Sub Save_Quit()
        ActiveWorkbook.Save
        Application.Quit
    End Sub

'Auto_Open Macro
'
' Runs the title screen macro when the workbook is opened
'
    Sub Auto_Open()
        Sheets("Order Screens").Select
        Application.Run Macro:="ORDENTER.XLS!Set_Title_Screen"
    End Sub
```

Appendices

Solutions to selected consolidation activities

Appendix 1

A	G	H	I	J	K
INCOME	**Week 6**	**Week 7**	**Week 8**	**Week 9**	**Week 10**
Opening Bals.	£495.00	£365.00	£235.00	£105.00	-£25.00
Grant					
Bank Loan					
Parents					
Total Income	£495.00	£365.00	£235.00	£105.00	-£25.00
EXPENDITURE					
Accommodation	£60.00	£60.00	£60.00	£60.00	£60.00
Food and Travel	£35.00	£35.00	£35.00	£35.00	£35.00
Books	£15.00	£15.00	£15.00	£15.00	£15.00
Other	£20.00	£20.00	£20.00	£20.00	£20.00
Total Expenditure	£130.00	£130.00	£130.00	£130.00	£130.00
CLOSING BALS.	**£365.00**	**£235.00**	**£105.00**	**-£25.00**	**-£155.00**

Appendix 2

	A	E	F	G	H	I	J	K
1		S - TERM 1						
2								
3	INCOME	Week 4	Week 5	Week 6	Week 7	Week 8	Week 9	Week 10
4	Part Time Job				£20.00	£20.00	£20.00	£20.00
5	Parents					£30.00		
6	Total Income	£750.00	£615.00	£480.00	£385.00	£320.00	£225.00	£130.00
7								
8	EXPENDITURE							
9	Accommodation	£65.00	£65.00	£65.00	£65.00	£65.00	£65.00	£65.00
10	Food and Travel	£35.00	£35.00	£30.00	£30.00	£30.00	£30.00	£30.00
11	Books	£15.00	£15.00	£0.00	£0.00	£0.00	£0.00	£0.00
12	Other	£20.00	£20.00	£20.00	£20.00	£20.00	£20.00	£30.00
13	Total Expenditure	£135.00	£135.00	£115.00	£115.00	£115.00	£115.00	£125.00
14								
15	CLOSING BALS.	£615.00	£480.00	£365.00	£270.00	£205.00	£110.00	£5.00

Appendix 3

	A	B	C	D	E	F
1		Insurance Sales - First Quarter				
2						
3		Motor	Life	Property	Total	
4	Jan	1465	1243	2456	5164	
5	Feb	1345	1456	1987	4788	
6	Mar	1132	2310	1598	5040	
7						
8	Quarterly Average	1314	1670	2014	4997	
9	Quarterly Total	3942	5009	6041	14992	
10	% of Total	26.29%	33.41%	40.29%		
11						
12		This worksheet shows a sales analysis of				
13		the of the three major insurance categories				
14						

Appendix 4

	A	B	C	D	E
1	**Order No.**	**Order Date**	**Co.Ref**	**Co. Name**	**Value**
2	14005	11-Mar	965	Tilley Transport	1678.00
3	14003	11-Mar	1289	Marsden Products	4456.00
4	14009	12-Mar	1289	Marsden Products	1652.54
5	14007	09-Mar	1453	Wilson Garages	2654.00
6	14000	10-Mar	1453	Wilson Garages	3200.00
7	14002	11-Mar	1453	Wilson Garages	98.76
8	14008	12-Mar	2245	Goldfield Stables	123.85
9	14006	10-Mar	2375	Patel Kitchens	55.54
10	14001	08-Mar	2413	Patel Industries	1466.00
11	14004	10-Mar	2413	Patel Industries	567.00

Appendix 5

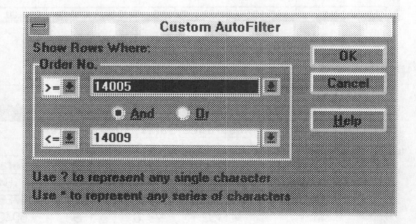

Appendix 6

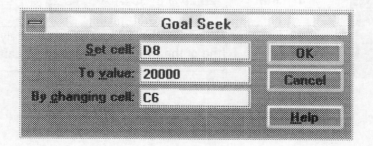

Appendix 7

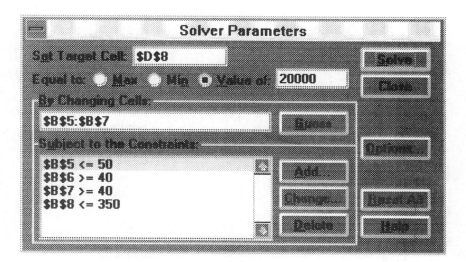

Index